On
Irish
Themes

James T. Farrell *(Photo by Elden Cave)*

On Irish Themes

by

James T. Farrell

Edited with
an Introduction
by
Dennis Flynn

Foreword by
William V. Shannon

University of Pennsylvania Press
Philadelphia
1982

The following materials are from the James T. Farrell Collection, University of Pennsylvania Library, and are used with permission of Cleo Paturis and Edgar M. Branch, Executors.

Box 2-"The Work of Frank O'Connor" (n.d.);
Box 7-"Observations on the First Period of the Irish Renaissance" (n.d.);
Box 61-"Notes on Irish Literature" (n.d.);
Box 739-Letters and diary notes: to Felix Kolodziej, 30 July 1938; to Meyer Schapiro, 30 July 1938; to Jim Henle, 31 July 1938; to Meyer Schapiro, 6 August 1938; diary note, 6 August 1938; diary note, 8 August 1938; diary note, 9 August 1938; diary note, 10 August 1938; to Jim Henle, 14 August 1938; to Felix Kolodziej, 24 August 1938; diary note, 27 August 1938; and to Leon Trotsky, 11 December 1938.
Box 29-"Notes on James Joyce and Ibsen" (n.d.);
Box 69-Letter and diary notes: to James O'Donovan, 1 February 1939; diary note, 15 February 1939; and diary note, 3 June 1939;
Box 84-"On an American Writer's First Visit to London" (n.d.);
Box 200-"Our Own Weren't All Handy Andys" (n.d.);
Box 233-"The Spirit of Irish History" (n.d.);
Box 500-"Freedom in Ireland" (n.d.);
Box 619-"James Joyce" (n.d.);
Box 645-"James Joyce Essay—4 starts" (n.d.);
Box 664-"The World Is Today: William Butler Yeats" (n.d.);
Box 738-Letters and diary notes: diary note, 2 June 1938; to Al _____, 26 June 1938; and to Jim Henle, 6 July 1938;
Box 739-Letters and diary notes: to Jim Henle, 28 July 1938; to George Novack, 28 July 1938; to Jim Henle, 30 July 1938; to Felix Kolodziej, 31 July 1938; to Jim Henle, 4 August 1938; to Ferdinand Lundberg, 6 August 1938; to Jim Henle, 6 August 1938; diary note, 7 August 1938; to Jim Henle, 11 August 1938; diary note, 12 August 1938; to Hortense Alden, 14 August 1938; to Hortense Alden, 16 August 1938; diary note, 18 August 1938; to Jack Farrell, 20 August 1938; diary note, 20 August 1938; diary note, 21 August 1938; diary note, 22 August 1938; diary note, 23 August 1938; to Alfred Rosmer, 25 August 1938; and to Jim Larkin, 8 September 1938;
Box 840-Letters: to Brian Moore, 12 July 1979; to Harry Levin, 13 July 1979; and
Box 858-"The Irish-Americans" (n.d.).

Sources of Farrell's published writings:

A World I Never Made. Copyright © 1936 by James T. Farrell; copyright © renewed 1963 by James T. Farrell.
James Joyce: Two Decades of Criticism, edited by Seon Givens. Farrell's essay "Joyce's *A Portrait of the Artist as a Young Man*" copyright 1945 by James T. Farrell; copyright renewed 1972 by James T. Farrell. "Postscript on *Stephen Hero*" copyright 1954 by James T. Farrell.
Reflections at Fifty and Other Essays. Copyright © 1954 by James T. Farrell; copyright © renewed 1982 by Dorothy Farrell.
A Note on Literary Criticism. Copyright © 1936 by James T. Farrell; copyright © renewed 1963 by James T. Farrell.
When Boyhood Dreams Come True. Copyright © 1946 by James T. Farrell; copyright © renewed 1973 by James T. Farrell.

Library of Congress Cataloging in Publication Data
Farrell, James T. (James Thomas), 1904-1979.
 On Irish themes.
 Includes bibliographical references and index.
 1. English fiction—Irish authors—History and criticism—Addresses, essays, lectures.
2. Ireland in literature—Addresses, essays, lectures. 3. Ireland—Addresses, essays, lectures. I. Flynn, Dennis.
II. Title.
PR8797.F37   1982   823'.009'9415   82-60301
ISBN 0-8122-7860-7

Printed in the United States of America

To the memory of
Julia Daly
and
Delia Flynn

Contents

Contents

Foreword

It is with a piercing sense of loss, both personal and intellectual, that I commend to the public these Irish essays by James T. Farrell. He died three years ago this month while I was overseas serving as the United States Ambassador to Ireland.

Jim Farrell and I had been friends for twenty-nine years, our friendship growing deeper and closer as I grew older. It began in 1950 when I was a very young author and my first book, *The Truman Merry-Go-Round*, written in collaboration with Robert S. Allen, had just been published by Vanguard Press, a small publishing house. Vanguard's most famous author was Farrell. I asked the head of the firm, James Henle, a Kentuckian with courtly manners and an ironic sense of humor, if he would introduce me. A quick phone call and I was on my way to the Yorkville apartment where Jim then lived with his wife, Hortense, and their son, Kevin.

I wanted to meet him because he was the author of *Studs Lonigan* and the Danny O'Neill novels, all of which I had read and admired. As I was to write many years later in my book *The American Irish*, "Few college-educated Irish Catholics reach manhood without making [Studs Lonigan's] acquaintance twice, once in life and once in the pages of Farrell's novel. It is a book—Joyce's *Portrait of the Artist as a Young Man* is another—that has become part of a young Irishman's coming of age."

Farrell's analysis of Joyce's achievement is the subject of two of the best essays in this collection. Elsewhere, he expresses regret that he twice passed up opportunities in Paris to meet Joyce because, in part, he feared seeming to be a literary disciple of the older man. This is a common and understandable fear among young writers trying to define the true nature of their own talent. No such hesitancy blocked my own relationship with Farrell, because, although I am interested in literature, my own writing ambitions were centered in history and political journalism rather than in fiction.

I soon discovered that in addition to the novels and short stories for which he was famous, Farrell had also written some illuminating essays on literary and historical themes. Moreover, although these volumes of nonfiction form a relatively slight portion of his published output of more than fifty volumes, he was capable—if he had so chosen—of writing major works of historical and political analysis.

I have never known another person so widely and diversely read. He had read all of the best American writers from the early masters, such as Hawthorne and Melville, to his own contemporaries. He had read all of Marx, Engels, Trotsky, and Lenin as well as many lesser writers in the Marxist tradition. He was at home in European literature from Shaw and Ibsen to Mann and Kafka and the great Russian writers. He was fond of French literature, being particularly devoted to Balzac and Proust. He was equally at home with European history and had mastered the historical literature of the French Revolution and the Napoleonic period. He was deeply interested in philosophy; he treasured his friendship with John Dewey and was conversant with the writings of Dewey, Mead, Peirce, and William James. India and Israel were other interests of his; he wrote for magazines in India and wrote a book about Israel, *It Has Come to Pass*.

I mention the catholicity and variety of Jim's interests because those qualities are also evident in these Irish essays. He writes about Irish literature with the insights of a widely read critic who is also himself a novelist and short-story writer. He writes about Irish history and nationalism from the perspective of a man who read about and pondered European history as well as nationalist movements around the world. He writes about James Connolly, the great Socialist and nationalist leader of 1916, from the vantage point of one who had once shared Connolly's Catholicism, his socialism, and his belief in revolution. Finally, he brings to his memoir of Jim Larkin, the hero of the Irish labor movement, his own life experience as the son and grandson of workingmen and his own keen novelist's eye for the realistic details of an extraordinary human being. From his description, for example, one can see Larkin down on his hands and knees searching through the dusty shelves of his sister's house looking for Connolly's papers.

From his earliest days in New York, Jim had been first suspicious and then overtly hostile to Stalinism and the repressive government of the Soviet Union. But this did not divert him from his hopeful faith that what would later be called "socialism with a human face" could be constructed on the basis of the writings of Marx and Engels. He came to know Leon Trotsky in exile in Mexico and admired him for his courage, integrity, and intellectual brilliance.

By the time I met Jim in 1950, his interest in the various dissident Marxist movements, such as Trotskyism, had begun to wane. By the 1960s when a whole new group of young people was developing faith in "the revolution" as an event that would transform the human condition, Jim had lost his revolutionary faith. He now saw human history not with his earlier confidence in the Marxian analysis but as a problematic and open-ended enterprise.

Jim observes in these essays that Irish atheists usually wind up in the arms of the Church. Although Jim did not return to the Catholic Church, his attitude toward it softened significantly compared to the acerbic remarks contained in his letters and diaries in 1938. In his last years, almost nothing pleased him as much as meeting or receiving a letter from a priest or a nun who admired his work, particularly one based in Chicago. The Church as a human institution had changed and so had Jim.

Much that is in this volume is new to me except for the essays on Joyce. When he and I met and talked from time to time in Washington and New York, our conversations were usually about American politics and contemporary world affairs. I was a Washington newspaperman, and he was eager to hear my news and gossip. When we spoke of other matters, they were usually discussions of history, of great crises such as the French Revolution and the American Civil War, and of historical personalities such as Robespierre, Napoleon, Lincoln, and Woodrow Wilson. These themes reflected my own intellectual interests. What he gained from me in the latest Washington gossip, he repaid in effect with his knowledge and insight and illuminating speculation about history. Much as I had read, he seemed always to have read even more, and our conversations often ended with him lending me books from his personal library.

When Jim stayed with me in Dublin in 1978 for a few days, he commented several times on how much Ireland had changed for the better in forty years, how much more prosperous the people looked, how much cleaner and better fed the Dublin children were. They were happy days for him. He enjoyed meeting again old literary acquaintances, such as Sean O'Faolain, and making new ones, such as Benedict Kiely, and attending a play at the Abbey.

I said at the outset that I miss him both personally and intellectually. I miss him as one might any friend, for the sound of his voice, the warmth of his smile, the friendliness of his personality. I miss him intellectually not only because it is no longer possible to draw upon the riches of his extraordinarily well-stocked mind, but also because he could help me make sense of my four years in Ireland if he were here. He and I did not often talk about Ireland, perhaps because we took our Irishness for granted and also partly because I was not aware until reading this book of how extensively he had written on Irish themes.

Jim liked the Irish people and was proud of being Irish. But toward the Irish as toward himself, he could not help but turn his unsparing honesty and his passion to know more and understand more.

For those who did not have the pleasure of knowing James T. Farrell in person, this volume is a gallant substitute. It conveys the acute analytical power of his mind, his curiosity and openness and eagerness to learn, his good humor, and his generosity of spirit. He was a man worth knowing, and he has left us a book of essays worth reading, about a people he knew and studied and loved.

August 1982   WILLIAM V. SHANNON

Acknowledgments

Publication of *On Irish Themes* brings to reality a project Farrell first conceived in the 1940s and later discussed with me in 1976. Until his death in 1979, I benefited from his advice and criticism. Since then, Cleo Paturis and Edgar M. Branch have generously encouraged me, as has Charles Fanning. I am grateful to all these friends for their understanding and support, though I know the book succeeds or fails only if my selections and quotations from Farrell's archives tend to bring his work more clearly and fully before the reading public. I hope the book will help keep fresh the recognition Farrell has always had from *his* readers and help provide others with an opportunity to *become* his readers, so that a day of general recognition—long overdue and strangely so—may soon arrive. To that end I have devoted my efforts.

The book would have taken much longer to complete had I not received a fellowship from the National Endowment for the Humanities. I owe similar gratitude to Bentley College for a faculty development grant and for the expertise and efficiency of its Solomon R. Baker Library, office services, media services, and xerox room. I wish also to acknowledge the help I received from the University of Pennsylvania's Van Pelt Library, where Farrell's archives are held, and from the Harvard University Libraries. Finally, the readers' criticisms and the technical assistance of the staff at the University of Pennsylvania Press have been indispensable to me. To all these organizations and to their individual members who have worked with me, I owe a debt I can never fully repay.

My father introduced me to Farrell's writings when I was in high school. He was not a man with much schooling, but he recognized in Farrell a great author writing about, among other things, the reality of Irish immigrant experience in America. That reality was known to my father primarily through his mother, my grandmother, whose name with the name of Farrell's own grandmother graces the dedication page of this book.

DENNIS FLYNN

xiii

Introduction

I

During a creative span of over fifty years, James T. Farrell wrote many essays on Irish literature and history, discrete pieces occasionally overlapping, constituting a sort of mosaic rather than a unified presentation of his thought on Irish matters. These Irish essays are not a replacement for the two lengthy manuscripts on the concept of the nation in Irish writing that were lost (along with many of his annotated copies of Irish books) when in 1946 a flash fire erupted out of faulty wiring in the wall of his New York apartment. For years after this fire, Farrell tried to get a publisher's assignment to stay in Ireland long enough to redo work once done and write a series of articles or possibly a book something like his book about Israel, *It Has Come to Pass* (published by Theodore Herzl Press in 1958). But for Ireland no such opportunity arose, and we are left with sundry essays on Irish writing and history. Most of those published through the 1950s are collected here, along with a selection of letters and diary notes as well as two other unpublished items.[1] Among Farrell's papers left at the University of Pennsylvania, much more about Ireland—another two decades of largely unpublished articles, correspondence, and diary notes—remains to be edited and printed. The present introduction anticipates that work and draws on some of the unpublished material.

Farrell's Irish writings are integral to the body of his work, arguing that literature ought not to be used as a mere instrument in the service of nation or ideology, yet assuming, with John Dewey, that art is a social product created not purely for expression's sake but for the evaluation of life. As an artist, Farrell looked beyond nationalism and policy to the pursuit of truth and the dignity of individual experience. With these aesthetic values, he stood against the criticism or condemnation of art and artists by zealous nationalists as well as other political and religious ideologues. He opposed the tendency to label the first writers of the

---

1. Publication histories of texts collected here are given in footnotes to the texts. A complete list of Farrell's nonfiction publications on Irish matters is supplied in the Appendix.

so-called Irish Renaissance—Russell, Yeats, Synge, and others—as strictly "Anglo-Irish," Protestant, or in essential disharmony with the national or social aspirations of Ireland. Despite what he regarded as their political or theoretical weaknesses, Farrell observed that early writers of the Irish Renaissance had contributed to the literature of Ireland much that was true and real. On the other hand, Farrell also defended James Joyce against the ideological strictures of Marxists and others. Like some of his acquaintances among Republicans who had fought in vain to secure a socialist Ireland, Farrell admired Joyce above all other Irish writers, even though Joyce had in effect turned his back on the Irish national movement.

Farrell's relation to Joyce—one of great ambiguity as well as of great intensity—is crucial to our understanding of his attitudes toward Irish literature and history. Joyce's realism about the nation was of course the main object of Farrell's admiration, a realism more fundamental than the stunning pyrotechnics Joyce delighted to perform with the English language. As Farrell explains it, the focus of Joyce's work was on the reality of individual Irish character and on the real problems of Ireland, however compressed and refracted through the peculiar mind and experience of Stephen Dedalus or other unlikely Dubliners. In *A Portrait of the Artist as a Young Man* and in *Ulysses,* the historical experience of Ireland suffuses Joyce's ironic presentation of Stephen's *fin de siècle* sensibility, a bitter pose in relation to Ireland's continued subjugation under the rule of nineteenth-century British parliamentary majorities. In another sense, Stephen's pose mocks the efforts of the Irish Renaissance to find escape from the iron rule of England in fanciful Gaelic myths, games, and language.

Joyce was the first writer to introduce the city as a central motif in Irish literature. He presents Dublin as an English artifact, a paralyzing threat to Stephen's soul as an artist. For Stephen, to engage the life of Dublin under English domination, even in opposition or rebellion, is as if to gaze at a Gorgon of social and political frustration. Yet Stephen's greatest suffering is, as Farrell points out, not political or social but religious. Roman Catholicism, strangely entwined in the social order and in the national movement, is the strongest ideology in Ireland, and Stephen struggles to accept or reject it. His struggle, eventuating in that traumatic scene with his mother of which in *A Portrait* we learn only indirectly, unfits Stephen entirely for the spiritual enthusiasms of the Irish Renaissance, so that nothing in Ireland—not the English oppressor, not the Catholic Church, not the Gaelicism of literary men and women —can hold him in the nightmare all Ireland's history has become. He must awaken, break out.

Stephen prepares his exodus by forging as a weapon an aesthetic theory grounded in the Thomist intellectual tradition of continental culture. With it he rebels against his insular world of oppression and answers his vocation as poet/priest; but, as Farrell shows in his discussions of *A Portrait* and *Stephen Hero,* at the root of this development in fiction lay Joyce's scorn of illusion about Ireland and the nation, a realism related to his early enthusiasm for Ibsen. In "Joyce and Ibsen" we have Farrell's most suggestive contribution to Joyce studies (and one of the best of his many fine essays in literary criticism). Ibsen was a second, spiritual father for Joyce, who could not fervently look up to or admire his natural father. As Joyce appeared to reject his mother with the Church, so was his father in some sense included in the rejection of Ireland Joyce's expatriation implied. Ultimately he became, like Ibsen, a citizen of Europe, in voluntary exile, a condition and a relationship most pointedly expressed in his play *Exiles.*

Farrell's handling of this play shows a remarkable sympathy for both Joyce's development as an artist and his personal relationship to Ibsen. Farrell is precise in describing these, and gradually in his discussion of the play itself he outlines the limits of Joyce's dependence on Ibsen. It is not simply the psychological structure of the drama, its time sequence, and "retrospective analysis" that derive from Ibsen's example. There are also the themes of guilt and truth which haunt the hero of *Exiles* as they do Ibsen's heroes and heroines. Farrell draws particular attention to the relation between *Exiles* and *When We Dead Awaken.*

Ibsen's hero, Rubek, is a sculptor who creates a statue of a woman and, in his concentration on the ends of art, drains out of their relationship all his love and inspiration. His guilt before her leads to a tragic end. Joyce's Richard Rowan is also a kind of artist, but he stands aloof from both art and life in an effort to avoid guilt and find a freedom with respect to his wife, whom he has tried to craft in life as Rubek carved his model in stone. The relationship of Richard and Bertha Rowan seemed to Farrell to bring out features of modern marriage transcending the boundaries of parochial Ireland. Farrell was particularly impressed by the coldness and hardness of heart of Richard Rowan, whose almost vindictive self-concern amounts to an effort to control his own destiny by controlling others. Seeking to avoid guilt in the domination of his wife, he simply limits and minimizes his emotional commitments in their marriage; his guiding purpose seems, in Farrell's words, "not to be more guilty than is absolutely necessary."[2]

---

2. "Notes on James Joyce and Ibsen" (n.d.) [29]. Bracketed numbers in these footnotes locate unpublished manuscripts—essays, letters, or diary notes—in numbered boxes

Farrell's analyses of Joyce reflect many concerns of his own fiction: the relationships of sons to fathers and mothers, of husbands to wives, and of artists to lovers. One thinks in these connections especially of such characters as Danny O'Neill, Studs Lonigan, Bernard Clare, Bill Martin, and Eddie Ryan. Farrell appreciated that Joyce was the most influential on other writers of all twentieth-century writers, but he also distanced himself from Joyce in various ways. Except for *Gas-House McGinty* and the last volumes of the *Studs Lonigan* trilogy, Farrell's novels show little of Joyce's histrionic verbal virtuosity, and even these books are constructed deliberately on a philosophical foundation in Dewey and George Herbert Mead, quite different from Joyce's fundamental outlook. Farrell's selective enthusiasm for Joyce was highest while he himself fought, somewhat bitterly, to break chains and escape paralysis as an artist. But in later years he saw Joyce from varying perspectives.

A gauge of this variation is his repeated comparison of Joyce and Proust. Early in his career he favored Joyce's "rigorousness, restraint, and stern dignity," as opposed to Proust's "narrowness of range" and "repetitive succession of agonies of heart."[3] Later he wrote that, though Joyce was a great genius, his work no longer seemed as stimulating. He came to reconsider his earlier estimate: "Among writers of the twentieth century, the one whom I love the most is Marcel Proust."[4] He spoke of a certain "coolness" about Joyce's work, especially *Finnegans Wake,* in which, Farrell asserted, Joyce was compounding a language all his own, with a good deal of "stunt stuff."

> It is a kind of rejection of all our art, and all our standards, methods and conceptions of art at the present. But then, I swing with a remark of Dewey's in *Art as Experience.* Dewey says that the only demand you can make of an artist is that his product be communicable in some sense to someone.[5]

Farrell suspected that Joyce's work in *Finnegans Wake* was "a signal of a man of genius with colossal egotism" and that the book came to the point of not meeting Dewey's single demand. Yet in his lectures to students of Joyce's *A Portrait* during the last decade of his life, he re-

at the University of Pennsylvania's Farrell collection. See Neda M. Westlake, "The James T. Farrell Collection at the University of Pennsylvania," *American Book Collector* 11 (Summer 1961): 21–23.

    3. "Rescued at Last," *Scribner's Magazine* 95 (February 1934): 16, 19; reprinted in this volume as "A Note on *Ulysses.*"

    4. "James Joyce" (1965) [619].

    5. Farrell to Meyer Schapiro, 6 August 1938 [739]; published in this volume, pp. 169–73.

marked that, though Joyce had seemed "a squeezed lemon to me," he had reread the book with amazement: "At the beginning of my life as a writer I was overwhelmed by James Joyce. I find at the end of my life as a writer he overwhelms me again."[6]

II

Like Joyce, Farrell inherited from his mother, and especially from her surrogate, his grandmother, the ability to be hard; and, like Joyce's, his father was in many ways a defeated and pathetic figure with limited ability to serve as an example for his aspirations. But in his early development as a writer, Farrell was unlike Joyce in that, as he said, "I've never been anyone's disciple."[7] And though he hurt his family in his struggle to write, he never exhibited toward them Joyce's characteristic coldness and defensive irony, or his utter rejection of his home for the sake of art. Farrell's loyalty to family is an obvious element in portrayals of his parents and especially of his immigrant grandparents in the autobiographical novels and short stories. They are not figures of ridicule or anger. Through them Farrell had imbibed an at-first unconscious sense of Ireland and Irish life that made him feel at home with Irishness:

> Those who were my ancestors were Irish. They are my people. I am of them and from them. All the memorials of my father in our family are a couple of pictures, love and pride in him, the feeling that the grave he has in Potter's Field is the proudest grave there is, and his union card.[8]

His father's and grandfather's hard lot as teamsters was an underlying element in Farrell's sense of the Irish as a people subject to economic exploitation and social injustice.

As early as his days in high school, he was made aware of this

---

6. Excerpt from my transcription of Farrell's taped lecture on Joyce at Glassboro State College of New Jersey, 26 September 1973.

7. Dennis Flynn and Jack Salzman, "An Interview with James T. Farrell," *Twentieth Century Literature* 22 (1976): 4. For Farrell's life and early development as a writer, I have relied mainly on Edgar M. Branch, *James T. Farrell* (New York: Twayne, 1971), and "American Writer in the Twenties: James T. Farrell and the University of Chicago," *American Book Collector* 11 (Summer 1961): 25–32.

8. "Our Own Weren't All Handy Andys" (n.d.) [200]. On the other hand, while in Ireland, Farrell wrote ironically, "Many people may call me Irish, but if I am Irish, I must be a really Irish foreigner. But so much for being moody" (Farrell to Hortense Alden, 16 August 1938 [739]).

injustice by a Carmelite priest, his teacher, Father Albert Dolan, who aroused the young Farrell's indignation with stories of the Black and Tan war and the hunger strike of Terence MacSwiney.[9] Later, in 1927, having quit the University of Chicago (giving up a scholarship) to become a writer, he heard a lecture in New York by Ernest Boyd, author of *Ireland's Literary Renaissance,* an experience that stimulated Farrell to study and learn as much as he could about Ireland. In 1930 he began to draft an application for a research grant "to make a thorough study of modern Irish literature, analyzing and interpreting it in terms of its ideological bases and social setting."[10] This application illustrates the seriousness and deliberation of Farrell's career from its inception, qualities that steadily deepened and enriched his achievement. A fundamental part of his program to develop as a writer was this carefully conceived critical project to understand and explain the social and ideological matrix of a modern national literature.

He spent 1931–32 in Paris, but during the year he did not seek out Joyce. He was working to complete his trilogy and another novel, *Gas-House McGinty,* both of which included much that was clearly influenced by Joyce. Yet Farrell worked on alone, also pursuing his Irish studies project. This reading continued for several years back in New York, even though his grant proposal was treated negatively. At this time, Farrell had to support the writing of his fiction mainly by reviewing Irish and other books for various magazines. His early reviews are represented in the present volume by two pieces done for *The New Republic,* in which Farrell gave early recognition to Frank O'Connor and Sean O'Faolain as the leading Irish writers of fiction after Joyce. Malcolm Cowley, then literary editor of *The New Republic,* gave Farrell a review copy of O'Connor's *The Saint and Mary Kate* in 1932. At the time, O'Connor was not widely read in this country; his collection of stories, *Guests of the Nation* (1931), had received some favorable review, but to Farrell he was still unknown. Farrell was steadily impressed as he read O'Connor's novel, and he successfully urged Cowley to give the book more than the usual unsigned review note. He read *Guests of the Nation* also, and he was even more impressed. The title story struck him as one of the finest stories in the English language.

Sean O'Faolain was another writer then beginning to be known in

---

9. "I wrote an indignant essay, and it was almost printed in the Chicago Catholic diocese weekly, *The New World,* but this was not original, and most of the material came from what Father Dolan told us in class" ("Freedom in Ireland" [n.d.] [500]).

10. "Notes for G[uggenheim] Outline," in "Notes on Irish Literature" (n.d.) [61], published in this volume.

America. Farrell reviewed his second novel, *Bird Alone,* for *The New Republic* in 1936. He compared O'Connor and O'Faolain in this review, before learning that the two were friends and had been fellow protégés of Daniel Corkery and fellow Republicans during the Irish Civil War. It is interesting that though O'Faolain's early work seemed relatively flawed to Farrell, in later essays on the two writers Farrell's estimate of O'Connor did not keep pace with his growing respect and enthusiasm for O'Faolain's work.

After ten years as a writer, Farrell himself had finally published a best-seller (*A World I Never Made* sold over 5,000 copies in 1936, Farrell's best sale by far of his then eight published books), and he followed it up with a sequel, *No Star Is Lost* (1938). In these novels occurs his earliest extended treatment of an Irish-born character: Mary O'Flaherty, the grandmother of Danny O'Neill. She is a feisty, unpredictable harridan who makes her family toe the mark, but Farrell conveys also a wisdom and a dignity in the illiterate old woman who has suffered the trauma of immigration. In her grandson's eyes she becomes part of the image of suffering Ireland, an image Danny carries through his development in successive novels toward his destiny as an artist.

Farrell finished correcting proof for *No Star Is Lost* at dawn on the very morning he was to sail again from New York to Europe, a journey that would climax with his first visit to Ireland. But first he went to England, and on the way, when the boat put in briefly at Cobh, he armed himself with a blackthorn walking stick. Years later he told the story, with some regret, of the "comedy of misunderstandings, buffooneries, insults, and false identities" that was his first trip to London:

> I had suddenly rediscovered my Irish ancestry, and I flaunted it, fighting the battles which had already been fought, and flaunting myself, like a comic Gael, who had invaded the lair of the Ancient Saxon and would best with him tongue and blackthorn stick.[11]

Armed with his "Irish gun," Farrell prowled the London streets at night, feeling safe in the strange city and noting that the English seemed afraid of him in personal encounters. His attitude at the time is conveyed by his observation that the Irish

> know the British too damn well, and see through them. But the Irish don't see through themselves. However, Mr. Gladstone and such men of greatness bear some of the responsibility for the present state of barbarism in Eire.[12]

---

11. "On an American Writer's First Visit to London" (n.d.) [84].
12. Farrell to Jim Henle, 6 July 1938 [738].

From London he traveled to Paris, where once again he failed to look up Joyce, despite his plan to go next to Ireland and despite again being in the same vicinity for six weeks. Nevertheless, he did discuss Joyce with Sylvia Beach, and he agreed half-jokingly with her that Joyce must be shunning the English language in *Finnegans Wake* partly because he was Irish. He was fascinated to learn that Joyce "follows life in Dublin from Paris with a sort of microscopic intensity, asking about landmarks, buildings, if they changed, even reading the death notices in the Dublin papers."[13] And yet Joyce had rejected Ireland. From Paris, Farrell himself felt the prospect of going to Ireland at first rather depressing. But as the time drew nearer he began to look forward to it more. For one thing, he planned to do important work there, including research toward someday writing a novel on the Irish immigrant in America. He decided to spend at least a month in Ireland, and this month provided a background in experience for most of his subsequent writing on Irish matters.

III

Farrell's first full day in Ireland was 27 July 1938. He was not surprised to find in Dubliners "an unfortunate race in a backward country." There was about the city an obvious drabness in contrast to Paris or London; poverty was almost as deep as he had seen in Mexico; men standing around talking and staring in the streets all day; children begging for coppers; dirty, pregnant women; and "kids and kids and kids."[14] This first impression of Irish poverty was the overwhelming experience of his whole stay in Ireland and gave the inspiration for his

---

13. Farrell to Meyer Schapiro, 6 August 1938 [739]; see below, p. 170. Farrell's failure to seek a meeting with Joyce, despite his real fascination with the older writer, had been a puzzle he discussed in Ireland, as we learn in a letter to Hortense Alden (14 August 1938) [739]. Cf. from later years an unfinished essay on Joyce which breaks off abruptly: "It is and always will be a matter of regret that I never—"; "James Joyce Essay—4 starts" (n.d.) [645]. And also Farrell's letter to Brian Moore (12 July 1979) [840], written only seven weeks before his death: "I wish that I had looked up Joyce when I was in Paris in 1931–32, or 1938. But I didn't." At the time of this writing, Farrell had just completed a careful reading of Richard Ellman's biography of Joyce (*James Joyce* [New York: Oxford University Press, 1959]). On the following day (13 July 1979) he wrote to Harry Levin: "I had always regretted that I had never looked up Joyce, partly out of shyness, and partly not to waste his time, with the further partial motivation that I didn't want to give the impression that I was a younger writer going to him for aid, help, praise, or in discipleship —although I admired him tremendously, and had been much influenced by his writing —more so than by that of Dreiser. Had I known him, I doubt that I could truly have liked the man" [840].

14. Farrell to Jim Henle, 28 July 1938 [739].

story "A Summer Morning in Dublin in 1938," the unvarnished account of his visit to some slum tenements in the company of a young doctor on 24 August, just three days before his return trip to New York.

He had remarked on the poverty of Dubliners during his first week in Ireland, but he could find no one at first who would discuss it seriously.

> Irishmen of course deny it. It is a matter of pride. O'Faolain says that the Irish have money but that the standard of living is low. Then the next minute someone else tells you that the Irish live up to and over their means. It is all funny.[15]

The contagious, ironical amusement of the Irish at themselves was a keynote of Farrell's letters to friends during the first part of his visit. But with this he seems to have contracted a recurrence of the mood that had seized him in London, and again he experienced somewhat of a comedy of misunderstandings. Sean O'Faolain was one of several Irish writers Farrell had looked up immediately on his arrival in Dublin. O'Faolain had reviewed the British edition of *Studs Lonigan* unfavorably, and at their first meeting Farrell regretted having "taken the aggressive a bit"; he feared they had not gotten along well. O'Faolain and others had shown him an easy, spontaneous, and informal hospitality, but in spite of their surface warmth he had found them in some ways baffling. This was an experience he would encounter repeatedly in Ireland. People were easy to talk to, much easier than the English or the French. And yet to "gain objective facts" was like pulling teeth. Farrell was dumbfounded by what he felt was O'Faolain's general anglophilia, and particularly by his remark that he enjoyed going to London for a good meal. "London! Merciful Mother of God!" Farrell quipped that O'Faolain was a good bet to receive "a King's medal when he reaches a few more years." And on the whole he adjudged O'Faolain "a bit soft . . . a literary man with a literary mind only."[16]

A second writer who invited Farrell over for tea on the spot was Peader O'Donnell. O'Donnell's was not a literary mind only; he had been, during the Civil War and after, one of the Irish Republican Army's chief propagandists and agitators, until his leftist leanings got him expelled from the IRA in 1934. Farrell had read and praised O'Donnell's novel about Aran, *The Way It Is with Them,* but his problem on meeting O'Donnell was that the man sounded like a Stalinist. When Farrell mentioned that, to judge from what he had learned in France and

---

15. Ibid., 30 July 1938 [739].
16. Ibid.

England, World War II was inevitable, O'Donnell flabbergasted him by calling him an old pessimist, advising him to attend international writers' conferences and do something for peace. In spite of this, Farrell found him quite charming.

> O'Donnell insisted on calling me O'Farrell and telling me that the O'Donnells have driven the O'Farrells out of Donegal; so I said that is why I never trust an O'Donnell and am disillusioned in the presence of an O'Donnell.[17]

Another Dublin literatus Farrell met was Oliver St. John Gogarty, Joyce's Buck Mulligan, who also promptly invited the American to tea and showed great kindness, lending books and an umbrella when it had begun to rain as Farrell was leaving. But Gogarty had spent their visit inveighing against "that Jew de Valera," who he thought was ruining the country, driving it into the state England was in, that is, "pretty red." Farrell thought Gogarty "close to a fascist."[18] Apparently little or nothing was said about Joyce.

Unable to get straight answers from Dubliners, Farrell supplied some of his own. The proximate cause of the poverty he saw was the high cost of relatively inferior goods—itself a result of the tariff barriers by which the de Valera government had in recent years been encouraging Irish competition with British production. These tariffs, Farrell saw, were part of the government's effort, deprived of the six northern counties, to stimulate home industry (especially in rural areas where no unions had been organized), but they also led to an economic war with England that had been ruinous for consumers. The ideals of the revolutionary decade around World War I had been lost, Farrell thought, in a kind of Thermidor of the Irish middle class.

Such developments of course had a long history, and for Farrell the meaning of Ireland's situation was symbolized in a legend he heard about Ross Castle at Killarney, the last castle taken by Cromwell's troops in the seventeenth century. The Irish under their O'Donoghue chief had held out against a better equipped and mounted English force by fighting on the boggy terrain surrounding the castle. But the English made use of an old prophecy to defeat the O'Donoghue, a prophecy that the castle would never be taken by land. The water approaches to the castle were too shallow to let in men-of-war, but the English built flat-bottomed boats in Dingle Bay and sailed up in these. "One cannon was fired, and the O'Donoghue, thinking that the prophecy had been

---

17. Farrell to George Novack, 28 July 1938 [739].
18. Farrell to Jim Henle, 28 July 1938 [739].

fulfilled, surrendered."[19] The legend symbolized for Farrell the historic defeat of the Irish nation and in general the superiority of a modern nation over one less advanced. Ireland seemed defeated in many ways, never having developed machine industry or a large middle class during the period when other European nations had been not colonies but colonizers. Thwarted and kept in poverty, many of the Irish had been forced or drained from the country, while others went to jail or died for treason against a British Crown. Along with defeat of Irish national aspirations had grown a feeling for martyrdom, a psychology of defeat.

In the same way, Irish national fortunes in the twentieth century had received another terrible blow in 1916, when the Irish labor movement, led by James Connolly and the Irish Citizen Army, spearheaded the uprising against the British that went largely unsupported and was drowned in blood and cannon fire during Easter Week. The defeat of the Easter Rebellion had meant the defeat of the working class, and the fortunes of the nation had been, according to Farrell, "tied to the tail of Sinn Fein,"[20] an essentially bourgeois political party.

> When Connolly was executed, no one carried on his social ideas here. Today, they might canonize Connolly as a saint, but there is a complete wall of silence surrounding his social ideas, and the tradition in Ireland out of which he derives—that of Fintan Lalor and Michael Davitt.[21]

Farrell came to Ireland already inclined to what he thought of as the Connolly tradition in Irish politics; on one occasion, when he was inquiring after a copy of James Fintan Lalor's *Faith of a Felon*, he was jestingly accused of being a Bolshevik by "an old Sinn Feiner who had become a judge."[22] The Irish revolution, Farrell thought, had devolved into a bourgeois state with a labor movement sunk in apathy, a middle class attentive to profit, and a church "preaching the glories of Heaven, the joy of martyrdom, and the virtue of poverty and suffering."[23]

Farrell directed irony at various facets of Irish life during the first weeks of his stay, at none more than at the Church. "I note that there are 200 Catholic churches in Dublin. Enough said."[24] But it was not enough. Appalled and fascinated by the religiosity of Dubliners, Farrell was reminded of his family in Chicago during his early years. He was shocked on his first Sunday morning in Dublin to find that everything

---

19. Ibid., 4 August 1938 [739].
20. Farrell to Hortense Alden, 14 August 1938 [739].
21. Farrell to Alfred Rosmer, 25 August 1938 [739].
22. Excerpt from my transcription of Farrell's taped lecture on Joyce at Glassboro State College of New Jersey, 16 September 1973.
23. Farrell to Alfred Rosmer, 25 August 1938 [739].
24. Farrell to Jim Henle, 28 July 1938 [739].

was closed, "like a coffin," except the churches, and that outside the Pro-Cathedral over two hundred people had queued up, unable to fit inside. He noted the slum children with their parents, all dressed up looking strangers to their Sunday best; and then after Mass,

> they come home from the churches in droves. The streets are quiet, but they do not wear rubber heels. You hear the steady echo of footbeats on the stones, and it comes as a surprise in the quiet atmosphere.[25]

He went on to observe that the Church in Ireland had become part of the national movement against British Protestant ascendancy. In other countries, such as France and Russia, the Church had stood against national revolutions and had been dispossessed as a consequence. But the fight for Irish political freedom had been at the same time a fight for freedom of worship, and though the Church had often played both sides against the middle in revolutionary struggles, the Catholicity of the Irish people had been confirmed in the Irish effort to maintain the integrity of their own societal life.

Another Irish institution Farrell scrutinized was the newspapers, in which he found little but local news of the thefts of cows, political corruption, bribing of juries, and other connivance, as well as feature stories to the glory of Erin, such as the one headlined: "Irish Kings Among Boxers." It seemed to Farrell that what with newspapers and pubs there was a superfluity in Ireland.

> Who cares over here what happens beyond these lovely shores? And as for what happens here, well it is known in a pub that a cow has been stolen even before that cow is stolen. If something is unknown about a Dooblin man, he and/or his friends just go into a pub, have a pint of Guinness, and tell all and sundry what that unknown something is. You see, newspapers are not really needed. Everybody knows what happens without newspapers.[26]

The pubs were closed on Sundays until two-thirty, but when open they were the scene of much comedy in Dublin. Farrell mentioned in a pub that he had been in Paris recently and one old Irishman soon was whispering

> about the buggering of little boys and the raping of eight-year-old girls, and the awfulness of the Folies Bergeres. He had wonderful gestures, sweeping ones which an actor could acquire only after years of practice.[27]

Someone else in a pub told Farrell that the Irish were descended from the Egyptians; a young medical student insisted that according to Catho-

---

25. Ibid., 31 July 1938 [739]; published in this volume, pp. 165–69.
26. Farrell to Felix Kolodziej, 31 July 1938 [739].
27. Farrell to Jim Henle, 31 July 1938 [739]; see below, p. 166.

lic theology a baby could be aborted in order to save the life of the child; and he encountered one argument straight out of an O'Casey play, in which two old "harps" wrangled over Anglo-Irish relations with a relentlessly monotonous yet somehow appropriate disregard for each other's platitudes.

Although Farrell was struck initially by the spontaneous hospitality of Dubliners, later this warmth and absence of formality seemed perhaps hollow and not enough to compensate for a sense that the intellectual life of the city was parochial, that backbiting and scandal were popular sports, "more popular than thinking."[28] The content of newspapers seemed reflected in the conversation of Dublin intellectuals, certainly a cut above the arguments in pubs, but essentially the talk of small-town cliques. He found it difficult to talk to anyone about much except Ireland and gossip. The experience contributed to a general sense of the Irish mentality that was reinforced by other perceptions. Confronted with the "Irishman's scorn for time, his feeling that the American is the victim of a timepiece," Farrell retorted that lack of a sense of the importance of time was one of the most egregious examples of Irish backwardness, so that buses and trains were extremely unreliable and literally cost one hours of frustration and disappointment.[29] The food in Ireland was also uncivilized, Farrell thought. "What they do with food is something that resides among the mysteries."[30] In general he found that the pace and tone of Irish life "retains something of a Victorian character."[31] The Irish seemed "deficient in certain sensory capacities," with little sense of how to make color a value in life: gardens, clothing, wall coverings, etc., all seemed "dull and dreary." Irish culture had not produced great painters. The city of Dublin remained "an eyesore" with public statues "beyond imagining."[32] He objected also to the driving of livestock through Dublin streets, and yet he marveled that withal the Irish—friendly, likeable, charming—seemed to persist with a tranquil pride in their own way of life.

He found the commitment to revival of Gaelic the most remarkably preposterous example of this public pride. The language had become a shibboleth in the national movement for independence, and since the establishment of the Free State an attempt to spread Gaelic had been made an adamant policy of each government, whatever the party. Compulsory in the schools and for civil servants, the language

---

28. Ibid., 11 August 1938 [739].
29. Ibid., 30 July 1938 [739].
30. Farrell to Meyer Schapiro, 30 July 1938 [739]; published in this volume, pp. 162–65.
31. Ibid., 6 August 1938 [739]; see below p. 172.
32. Ibid., 30 July 1938 [739]; see below, p. 163.

was nevertheless obviously impossible to sub'stitute for English and had to be translated on each public sign. It could never be used outside the country, and yet great expense of labor and capital was being wasted on this quixotic project. Farrell actually found intelligent Dubliners maintaining that all Irishmen would be speaking Gaelic instead of English before the end of the century; others, however, ridiculed this notion.

> O'Faolain says . . . that even if it is learned in schools from teachers who don't know it themselves, one can't read the Gaelic folklore. Another writer, Dennis Johnston, says that anyway there is no literature at all of worth in Gaelic except some dirty poems that are on the index. So there you are. The business seems fantastic.[33]

Akin to the Gaelic obsession, Farrell thought, was the tenor of criticism in Irish literary circles. He objected particularly to what seemed a crippling prejudice on the part of the Irish intellectual against discussion of literature in a context of social references.

> No truly critical movement of much force, insight, and erudition has ever developed in Ireland along with the literary renaissance, and the formal discussions of Irish literature tend to be a bit too anecdotal, muddled, and over-simplified. An interest in the social origins, backgrounds, and influences in Irish literature, for instance, has never grown here.[34]

Instead, mixed in promiscuously with literary discussions he found "religious crackpottery" and the Gaelic revival.

IV

On the whole, then, Farrell's initial impressions of Ireland were mixed. After a few days, he traveled west hastily on a tour touching Galway, Inishmore of the Aran Islands, Killarney, and Cork, before returning to Dublin for the opening of a two-week festival of the Abbey Players. From Cork he wrote of his bemusement by some blarney from a member of the Dail, Frank MacDermott, who had told him that in Ireland "nothing of the hand of man is much interesting. What is interesting has been made by the hand of God." Farrell wryly acknowledged the truth of this, but he had seen and heard enough also that he could

---

33. Farrell to Ferdinand Lundberg, 6 August 1938 [739].
34. Farrell to Jim Henle, 11 August 1938 [739].

penetrate these ironies. "I don't, incidentally, think that the Irish are really such a happy-go-lucky race, and all that. To me, they are a bit dour."[35] In the west he had been duly struck by the natural beauty of the countryside, especially the coast and the lakes of Killarney, and he had made some brief notes on the Aran Islanders and their stark way of life. He had planned also to visit Athlone and Mullingar, where his grandparents had come from, but with the poor bus and train service there was not time.

Back in Dublin by 5 August, Farrell attended the Abbey Theatre's production of Frank O'Connor's play *The Invincibles,* the second Abbey play he had seen. (On his first night in Dublin he had been to Dennis Johnston's *The Moon in the Yellow River.*) He thought O'Connor's play perhaps the finest Irish play since O'Casey's *The Plough and the Stars.* It presents the aftermath of the notorious murder in Phoenix Park of two high officials of the British administration in 1882. The assassins were mainly Dublin working-class men whose desperate deed for Ireland was universally condemned. In the play, some of them are shown as they awaited execution in Kilmainham jail, and Farrell was particularly impressed by the way O'Connor (with his collaborator, Hugh Hunt) had built into the plot structure and the quite vivid characterizations of the assassins an analysis of revolutionary political techniques, bringing out "the inadequacy and ineffectiveness of terrorism as a political weapon." Also, Farrell was surprised at the Dublin censorship situation; a play such as this attacking the Church could not have been produced in New York: "The Archbishop and Al Smith, not to mention the Fire Department and Mrs. Murphy, would all be up in arms." In later conversation he learned the explanation: Certain Sinn Fein politicians had been Abbey fans since their student days, and they shielded the Abbey from the rigorous censorship applied to books and movies in Ireland. Moreover, as Sean O'Faolain told him, a playwright in Ireland can get away with very extreme attacks on either the Church or the nation, providing that he always attacks one in the name of the other. Farrell was delighted with the behavior of the audience during *The Invincibles,* wildly protesting and applauding political speeches in the play, clapping lustily for Ireland, laughing loudly and (to Farrell) inexplicably at certain junctures, and venting disgust when Ireland or the Church was bitterly denounced by one of the terrorists. And then there was "one gent whose voice pierced the darkness: 'Onward the Invincibles!' "[36] Sean O'Faolain was later critical of O'Connor for his sympathy with the terrorists in

---

35. Ibid., 4 August 1938 [739].
36. Ibid., 6 August 1938 [739].

this play, saying that it played to the mob. Farrell, however, continued to feel that *The Invincibles* was one of the finest tragic plays in the Abbey repertory.

The Abbey Festival opened the next night with a formal reception at the Municipal Gallery of Modern Art. Present were the elite of Dublin, including politicians, journalists, and writers. Farrell had little chance to talk seriously with anyone: "Everybody at these gatherings is on good behavior." (He himself had skipped the tails or tuxedo worn by most of the men.) But among those he did meet were Ernest Blythe, onetime Minister of Finance in the Cosgrave government and later to become Managing Director of the Abbey; and Brinsley Macnamara, author of *The Valley of the Squinting Windows* (1918), which Farrell had read before 1932. He took a look through the art gallery but found nothing to praise; he was especially put off by a large canvas of Sir James Lavery's, *"The Blessing of the Colors,* in which an IRA soldier kneels and a bishop in full regalia blesses a large Irish flag."[37]

On Sunday, 7 August, Farrell returned to what had impressed him most about Dublin:

> Took a walk in slums by the Liffey. Sometimes the dirt and filth in Ireland seem overpowering. Many of the children were dirty, almost filthy. There were two tots in a buggy who were especially so, almost turning one's stomach as one got a passing look at them.[38]

He was immersing himself in "the wrong and the suffering, the shame and the degradation," of which he had read earlier in the writings of James Connolly.

The Abbey Festival proper opened on Monday with the first in a series of lectures by authors and critics accompanying productions of classic Abbey plays.[39] On the first night, Farrell saw Yeats' one-act *Kathleen ni Houlihan* ("a few odds and ends to make a situation, and then the entry of Kathleen"), with Eileen Crowe in the title role; then afterward Synge's *The Playboy of the Western World,* which he loved, with Ria Mooney as Pegeen Mike and Arthur Shields as Christy Mahon. The next morning, Farrell met Frank O'Connor, who had just returned from England to deliver the festival lecture on Synge. Farrell had formed definite opinions about *The Playboy,* and they differed from those of

---

37. Diary note, 7 August 1938 [739].
38. Diary note, 8 August 1938 [739]; published in this volume, pp. 174–76.
39. The festival program and texts of all the lectures were published in an edition by Lennox Robinson, *The Irish Theatre: Lectures Delivered During the Abbey Theatre Festival Held in Dublin in August 1938* (London: Macmillan, 1939).

O'Connor and his teacher Daniel Corkery, author of *Synge and Anglo-Irish Literature*. O'Connor put the play in the context of the Irish Renaissance as a rejection of Irish middle-class values and a return to the purity of the Irish folk, akin to the work of Yeats and Lady Gregory with Celtic folk myths and religion. To Farrell this seemed partly true but "all muddled up." After the lecture, he got together with O'Connor and O'Faolain, and he pointed out that an important element of the character Christy Mahon is a growth in self-consciousness that "is not a simple folk self-consciousness" but a kind of psychological development occurring in the world only after the emergence of a middle class. Such a psychology can be found in "the bones of the time in which Synge wrote, and Synge had some of these bones." Moreover, the interest of Yeats, Lady Gregory, and Synge in the peasantry ought itself to be seen, Farrell thought, in a wider European context, not simply as an Irish phenomenon. O'Connor answered with an attack on "naturalism" in literature and argued that to the extent Synge allowed it he destroyed the purity of his central myth. Farrell could not make sense of this, but he liked O'Connor anyway: "O'Connor impressed me as having more character than the other writers whom I have met here. He is a thin fellow, with greying hair, a thin face, great charm, and an easy manner."[40] O'Connor invited Farrell to visit the next week at his home in Wexford.

Later on, the evening of 9 August, Farrell saw Synge's *The Well of the Saints*, "a wonderful experience," with Cyril Cusack as Martin Doul.

> It is a fable, a fable which becomes the *raison d'être* for the revelation of a most mordant irony. The play is one of the bitterest and most beautiful of modern plays. The manner in which the characters lash one another with their tongues, the nature of Martin Doul's vision and language after his sight is restored, these are wonderful insight and fantasy combined, and they become occasions for Synge's truly mordant irony.

Later that night *Riders to the Sea* was played, "Synge's finest play, wonderful in its quietness and simplicity," a climax spoiled, Farrell thought, by the inadequacy of Eileen Crowe.[41]

On 10 August, Farrell saw the world premiere of Yeats' *Purgatory*, which became the *cause célèbre* of the festival next morning when a Jesuit priest from Boston raised a question about the play's meaning during a lecture by F. R. Higgins. Higgins did not know what to say, and

---

40. Diary note, 9 August 1938 [739]; published in this volume, pp. 176–78.
41. Diary note, 10 August 1938 [739]; published in this volume, pp. 178–79.

Lennox Robinson interceded with the opinion that only Yeats (who was not present) could answer. The exchange became front-page news in the Dublin papers, and Yeats was interviewed. Farrell thought this "downright insulting":

> to have a pother on what it means, and to have had those who pretended to like it say nothing and being publicly unable to say anything at all of what it means, and then to have the newspaper reporters coming along and asking Mr. Yeats what, after all, it really did mean? In this instance, the Catholic priest did make some sense.[42]

Farrell himself did not record any reaction to *Purgatory*.

It may have been on one of these occasions that Farrell ran into Yeats. As he told the story years later, he had met the great poet in the men's room at the Abbey, and Yeats, whom Farrell admired above all twentieth-century poets, acknowledged his self-introduction with "a simple, tired courtesy."[43] It must also have been during these days that, outside the Abbey, Farrell encountered Maud Gonne MacBride, who seemed to him still beautiful in her seventies, but with a beauty different from that which Yeats, "the poet of pure sensibilities," had celebrated in youth.[44]

During the balance of the week, Farrell saw Yeats' *On Baile's Strand* ("Yeats is not a dramatist") and Shaw's *The Shewing Up of Blanco Posnet* ("in the best Shavian manner"), but he was beginning to feel overexposed to the Abbey, and one night he went to see some common vaudeville instead.[45] He spent some time reading, finishing O'Faolain's biography of Constance Markiewicz in two days and, at the same time, Peader O'Donnell's second novel about Aran, *The Islanders.* He faulted O'Faolain's narration of the struggle for independence and the Civil War because he thought it did not penetrate events to their basis in class relationships. O'Donnell's novel he thought comparable to Synge, and he called it "a fine minor work, much beyond O'Faolain." He bought and started copies of O'Donnell's *The Knife* and Corkery's book on Synge, which seemed "hog wash."[46]

The following Tuesday, 16 August, came the visit to O'Connor, whose conversation Farrell found "decidedly assertive, and asserting a lot that makes no sense to me." Among O'Connor's assertions were that

---

42. Farrell to Hortense Alden, 14 August 1938 [739].
43. "The World Is Today: William Butler Yeats" (n.d.) [664].
44. "The Spirit of Irish History" (n.d.) [233].
45. Diary note, 12 August 1938 [739].
46. Farrell to Hortense Alden, 14 August 1938 [739].

the writer must brood within himself and avoid becoming "external-ized," that too great an interest in social questions will externalize a writer, and that "all long novels can be written in a shorter and more concentrated form." O'Connor talked again against realism in literature, which puzzled Farrell, who thought O'Connor's own writing superior to O'Faolain's precisely because of a strong realistic vein. They also differed about religion:

> He argues that God gives us personality, and gives some men the magic that makes them great and strong personalities. So I said, it was more likely that a particular neural organization in their organism had more to do with it than God. And that further, if God fit his pattern, God was just playing the game that the Dublin politicians were, and that made God a peculiar kind of a God.[47]

But Farrell was impressed by O'Connor's learning, his knowledge of Russian literature in the original language, and his intelligent insights into Irish politics and history.

During the last two weeks of his stay in Ireland, Farrell was sick. His diary on 18 August records symptoms that were to recur before his operation for stomach ulcers fifteen years later: "principally a pain in my stomach, located directly in the region of the solar plexus, but now and then spreading outward."[48] He had been unable to sleep for two nights and found his energy and curiosity dampened. On the morning of 19 August, fearing serious illness, he called up a doctor, Dr. Robert Collis, who came to his hotel room and diagnosed the problem as indigestion. Farrell had already begun refraining from alcoholic drinks and some of the "charms of Irish cooking," but the doctor prescribed further limits on his diet and also invited him to dinner at his own house.

This treatment improved the situation slightly, but Farrell found he had to change his plans. He had intended "a round or two of the public houses in the slums here—the O'Casey world," but, unable to drink beer, he knew this would be awkward. And he had planned another attempt before he left to visit Westmeath, the county of his grandpar-ents, but the state of his stomach discouraged that.[49] His illness got him to counting the days before his return to New York. Reflecting on his whole experience of Ireland thus far, he was dissatisfied.

> I am still puzzling to get more of a sense of the "rhythm," the pattern of mind of the Irishman. Irishmen often remain as puzzles to me. There is a

---

47. Ibid., 16 August 1938 [739].
48. Diary note, 18 August 1938 [739].
49. Farrell to Jack Farrell, 20 August 1938 [739].

strange way in which they react, a certain deviousness of mentality, I often suspect.[50]

Venturing again to the Abbey Festival, Farrell finally heard a lecture he enjoyed, as Dennis Johnston spoke with candor about the pressures brought to bear on the Abbey Theatre by politicians and theologians. He saw another performance by Eileen Crowe, in Teresa Devery's *Katie Roche* ("completely unimportant as a play but with charm and interest for two acts"), and on the last night of the Festival, *Shadow and Substance* by Paul Vincent Carroll, whom Farrell had met in New York and thought "extremely clever." At a party winding up the festival, Farrell met actor Arthur Shields and R. M. Fox, who later published a biography of James Connolly.[51]

V

On Sunday morning, 21 August, Farrell went to see a Gaelic football match at Croke Park; on his way out after the match, he was approached by a man with a maimed right hand. As they talked together the man grew more confidential. He introduced himself as a former editor of a defunct journal called *Ireland Today*. He said his name was Jim O'Donovan, and Farrell invited him to lunch. Over lunch, "shy and hesitant," O'Donovan explained that he had been in jail as an IRA man and had even gone on a hunger strike while in jail. But, he said, he had dropped out of the IRA in 1925 or 1926. Farrell seems to have been very cautious and to have questioned O'Donovan tactfully but closely. O'Donovan told him that he was "nationalist still, and Catholic," and he said he wanted Farrell to meet some other IRA men at his home the following night. He mentioned "Moss" Twomey and some others—Cullen and Sheehy were names Farrell recalled while writing in his diary afterward. Farrell sought to know more about the politics of these men. He elicited the information that Sheehy had supported the Loyalist side in the Spanish Civil War, for which, O'Donovan said, he had actually been "forced off of *Ireland Today*." But—and this Farrell was disappointed to conclude—Sheehy's politics were apparently "popular front."[52] In all his time in Ireland thus far he had not found a single radical who seemed able to distinguish the reactionary nature of Stalinism.

---

50. Diary note, 20 August 1938 [739].
51. Ibid., 21 August 1938 [739].
52. Ibid., 22 August 1938 [739].

Farrell was taken to O'Donovan's home in the Shankill district of south Dublin on the night of 22 August. There he met Maurice Twomey, Sean Dowling, and Andy "Cullen," as Farrell recalled the name (this was actually Andy Cooney, former Chief of Staff of the IRA). Sheehy (probably John Joe Sheehy) did not appear after all. The five men talked about literature, politics, and recent Irish history very late into the night. The old IRA men explained that they did not want Farrell to get the impression the Abbey crowd was Ireland. They told him that the only Irish writer they liked at all was James Joyce, even though Joyce had repudiated everything they stood for. They saw in Joyce a man of lower-middle-class origins like themselves, whose feelings and responses to all sorts of things were like theirs. In this sense he was their writer. Farrell was again keenly interested in the politics of these soldiers. He found them, like many Irishmen he had met, curiously insular and eccentric in their political attitudes, with good words for Mussolini as well as for Stalin, paradoxically favoring totalitarianisms of the right and the left. The solution to this puzzle appeared to lie in Twomey's statement that the main thing was "to fight British imperialism at home and never mind about the other imperialisms." On the whole they seemed relatively uninterested in general political discussion, and only warmed up in reminiscing about the IRA in the early 1920s. Stories were told about Michael Collins, Cathal Brugha, and other figures of the revolutionary period. It was suggested that one mistake the IRA had made was that "they hadn't bumped off a few archbishops." Another was the failure to recruit soldiers returning to Ireland from service in the British Army after the establishment of the Free State; instead the Free State Army got these men. In his diary entry the following day, Farrell noted: "O'Donovan is very quiet and shy, but probably the most intelligent of the lot." He had learned that O'Donovan's hand was maimed in an explosion as he manufactured grenades during the Civil War. While he thought less of the talk of Dowling and Cooney, Twomey seemed "heavy mentally, but plodding, and he thinks, regardless of what one judges the content to be."[53]

Seamus "Jim" O'Donovan was a remarkable man. Educated as a chemist he had risen to prominence in the IRA in November 1920 when he was chosen Director of Chemicals at an army convention that resolved to carry the Black and Tan war onto English soil. For this purpose he had organized workshops and training programs in the manufacture and use of explosives. Then, when these efforts were undercut by a split

---

53. Ibid., 23 August 1938 [739].

in the IRA at the time of the truce with England, O'Donovan had opposed the treaty by which the Irish Free State was created and, in effect, the partition of Ireland was affirmed. During one rancorous army meeting of "Treatyites" and "anti-Treatyites," O'Donovan with quiet fury had told Michael Collins that he was a traitor because of his actions in support of the treaty. O'Donovan fought against the new Free State in the Civil War that followed, continuing as Director of Chemicals in the dissident wing of the IRA after his release from jail in July 1924. By 1938 he had made a new career for himself and was a member of the Electricity Supply Board, a quasi-government agency in Dublin. He had married the sister of Kevin Barry, a famous martyr of the Black and Tan period.

Maurice Twomey was another remarkable man who had first served briefly as IRA Chief of Staff in Cooney's absence during 1926, and later was appointed Cooney's successor in the fall of 1927. He held this position during eight and a half very difficult years, while some of the goals of the IRA were being co-opted by the Free State politicians of de Valera's party, Fianna Fail, and while the military capability of the IRA continued to be insufficient for the realization of its main goal: establishment of a republic in all thirty-two counties. Twomey's role in these years was the grueling one of maintaining the army as a military organization even though outlawed and underground, resisting the strong temptation to relax into chiefly political splinters. He did this rather well until he was arrested and imprisoned in the spring of 1936. He had been released just a few months before the meeting with Farrell and was at the time reluctantly serving out a six-month tour as Adjutant-General for the sake of the army's continuity. In 1938 a complete shake-up in the IRA leadership had brought to the top a group of men whose plans and policies Twomey was too old or too prudent to support with much enthusiasm.[54]

O'Donovan, however, had been approached by the new leadership and persuaded to assist in taking up his old project of sabotaging England. At the very time of the meeting with Farrell, O'Donovan must already have been deeply involved in plans for the training of men and the manufacture of explosives for use in his so-called "S-plan." This

---

54. Scattered information about O'Donovan and Twomey has been culled from J. Bowyer Bell, *The Secret Army* (London: Sphere Books, 1972); Timothy P. Coogan, *The I.R.A.* (New York: Praeger, 1970); C. Desmond Greaves, *Liam Mellows and the Irish Revolution* (London: Lawrence & Wishart, 1971); and Ernie O'Malley, *The Singing Flame* (Dublin: Anvil Books, 1978).

plan, which O'Donovan and the others evidently concealed from Farrell, was nevertheless probably uppermost in all their minds on that night. Had they mentioned the subject, Farrell would certainly have disapproved of the whole thing. After seeing O'Connor's *The Invincibles* he had written:

> Terrorism has often been a political weapon in the Irish national revolutionary movement. And often, of course, the Irish terrorists have been like their Russian terrorist brethren. The Russian terrorists would sometimes have the bomb for the Czar in their hands, and it would go off and blow them up, and the Irish terrorists similarly destroyed themselves.[55]

O'Donovan's "S-plan," or rather a much less sophisticated version of it, was actually implemented beginning in January 1939, horrifying and dismaying the governments of both England and Ireland. The campaign was a disastrous failure, accelerating the decline of the IRA as a coherent organization during the early 1940s. Even without knowing of the "S-plan," Farrell himself concluded after his experience with the IRA men that they were "licked," and as far as he could see, their organization was heading down a road of reaction near to fascism.[56] They seemed ignorant of the fact that Ireland was no longer a victim merely of England but also of larger economic and political forces. Irish nationalism correspondingly had become not a progressive but a reactionary movement.

But this encounter with the IRA had put Farrell in touch for the first time with something central to his interest in Ireland. For one thing, just as he was about to leave Ireland, he felt he was piercing the walls of silence and penetrating the puzzle of Irish character.

> Ireland, it must be remembered, is a difficult country for one to gain objective facts in. Sometimes, to get objective facts is like pulling teeth, and the teeth do not come out easily. The outside world of course has many curious notions concerning the Celt in these green sections of God's famous globe. One of them is that the Irishman is such a sentimental creature. There is much less sentimentality in him than people think. Often, the Irishman is hard, and often he is very vindictive.[57]

---

55. Farrell to Jim Henle, 6 August 1938 [739].

56. Farrell to Alfred Rosmer, 25 August 1938 [739]. After he had returned to America, Farrell read in newspapers about the IRA bombing campaign, but he never seems to have connected it with O'Donovan. In his letter to O'Donovan on 1 February 1939 [69] he makes no reference to the bombings. In other references early in 1939, Farrell expresses his initial view that provocateurs, not the IRA, were responsible and later that the bombings by the IRA were stupid (diary notes [15 February and 3 June 1939] [69]).

57. Farrell to Felix Kolodziej, 24 August 1938 [739]; published in this volume, pp. 181–83.

Something else Farrell began to sense for the first time was a tangible link to the revolutionary period leading up to the Easter Rebellion. At least through the time of Twomey's administration, the IRA had been the nearest thing to a continuing force upholding the radical ideal of a socialist republic. That force was now virtually spent, but in talking with these soldiers far into the night, Farrell had almost glimpsed for the first time the Dublin of revolutionary days, "death slinking up and down the streets, violence ready to burst out anywhere, and nerves at the trigger edge," and yet a city with a revolutionary spirit deriving from the French Revolution, with people up all night in the streets, ready at a signal to strike for freedom.[58]

VI

The two figures who had most personified this spirit for Farrell were James Connolly and Jim Larkin. Both men were of working-class origins and had risen to voice the social and economic discontent of their class. They were very different men—Larkin impulsive, direct, a great orator; Connolly more controlled and deliberate—but they seemed complementary. To Farrell their distinctive quality was the ability to fuse with the spirit of the Irish national movement the idea that independence must be joined to fundamental social change addressing the root causes of injustice in Ireland. Connolly especially impressed Farrell as a fine thinker, whose theoretical soundness on social questions had been based on direct experience and a hard-won grasp of economic realities unattained by many more leisured students. He admired Connolly's courage, consistency, and thoroughness in theory and in the application of theory to political action. Disagreeing with those who had criticized Connolly for leading the labor movement into the Easter Rebellion, Farrell defended Connolly against Sean O'Casey's charge that he had died not for socialism but for nationalism. The logic of Connolly's actions, Farrell thought, was that, with the onset of the world war, forces outside the sphere of Irish revolutionary conflict threatened to engulf the labor movement in reactionary waves of nationalist enthusiasm. Unless labor acted, and in fact led the way to resistance against involvement in the war, conscription and repression of the movement would soon shatter all chance for socialism in Ireland. Only by spear-

---

58. Farrell to Hortense Alden, 14 August 1938 [739].

heading the Irish national movement in rebellion against the British could labor give some direction to events, and the fight for independence became a priority in this sense. Connolly died, not betraying or abandoning socialism but averting the complete submergence of the Irish labor movement in violent years of warfare against Britain's enemy.

In 1938 the one man in Ireland Farrell connected with Connolly's radical spirit was Jim Larkin. He had brought Connolly to Dublin and had led the transport workers in the great strike of 1913, when the Irish labor movement had been in the vanguard of European labor militancy.[59] Farrell met Larkin at the headquarters of his union—The Workers' Union of Ireland—late on the morning of 24 August, after Dr. Collis had taken him along on a round of visits to his patients in the slums. Farrell's first impression of Larkin's great physical size is described in his essay on Larkin, along with the events of their next two days together. Larkin took Farrell to see the slums again and to see slum clearance projects he had fought for; they went out to Howth, where Larkin lived and where the Irish Volunteers had landed guns in 1914; they went to a hospital and a slaughterhouse, both organized by Larkin's union; they went to see the surreptitious memorial to the Invincibles, scratched continually and anonymously in the grass of Phoenix Park—and everywhere they went Larkin talked garrulously, disconnectedly, with flashes of the eloquence of his days of glory. As they rode in Larkin's car through the slum streets, "seeing the poor in their filth, standing in front of the filthy buildings in which they were forced to live like animals," suddenly Larkin would utter his strong denunciation, evoking the Jim Larkin of the past, "at whose words the poor of Dublin came out into the streets in thousands, and flung themselves against the might of Britain and the Irish bourgeoisie."[60]

As striking as Farrell's sense of Larkin's historic stature, even in decline, is the compassion he shows for Larkin's weakness and bitterness, that "characteristic defiant defeat that runs through so much of Irish history." Larkin had served briefly as a member of the Dail, but in several elections he had not been successful, even though running in a working-class district of north Dublin. Farrell could see that he felt betrayed. Larkin was bitter also about the fate of the labor movement in the Easter Rebellion, which had broken out while he was out of the

---

59. On Larkin, see Emmett Larkin, *James Larkin, Irish Labour Leader, 1876–1947* (Cambridge, Mass.: M.I.T. Press, 1965).

60. Farrell to Leon Trotsky, 11 December 1938 [739]; published in this volume, pp. 184–90.

country, powerless to influence events. He told Farrell that when he had left in 1914 to raise funds in America, he had warned Connolly not to involve the Irish Citizen Army with the Irish Volunteers, the armed force of the bourgeois national movement. Larkin had not himself been able to return to Ireland until 1924, when Connolly had long been dead, and in the intervening years no one had been able to rebuild the shattered morale of the defeated Irish working class. "Larkin was a great and courageous agitator, but not a leader of a defeated army." Unable to use his old tactics of direct action on the wave of a rising and militant movement, he had been politically isolated and finally embittered. Nevertheless, Farrell saw that Larkin remained "the only figure of commanding proportions in the Irish labor movement," a movement otherwise reduced to bureaucratic trimmers and (in Larkin's colorful phrase) "twisters."[61]

Meeting Jim Larkin, a giant of a man physically and historically, was the high point of Farrell's visit to Ireland. Here he came as close as he possibly could to the tradition of James Connolly. And where other Irishmen had puzzled him, he was able to understand Larkin with little difficulty. For instance, he was not put off, was in fact appreciative of Larkin's irony in calling him a "Trotskyist" and in warning his own son that Farrell's "psychological" novels might "endanger your immortal soul." Farrell saw that Larkin could have been his guide to much in Ireland that he had not understood, or had comprehended only with difficulty; and he regretted not having met with Larkin sooner. One feels that, in Larkin, Farrell may have sympathized with characteristics of his own father. Certainly great physical size and staunch union loyalty were shared traits; apart from these were the two men's strong Catholicism and family pride. Larkin introduced Farrell to his family and treated him with more than ordinary hospitality. His offer to give Farrell some of Connolly's papers, as well as his personally cooking the eggs prescribed for Farrell's diet during their two whirlwind days—these things suggest a fatherly attitude toward the younger man. He gave Farrell copies of three plays from the old Abbey repertoire, including *The Labour Leader* by Daniel Corkery, whose hero, he told Farrell, had been modeled on himself. Reciprocating shortly after his return to New York, Farrell sent Larkin a copy of *No Star Is Lost.*[62]

After his return, Farrell first set to work on his story "A Summer Morning in Dublin," and during the following years of World War II he began to use all he had seen and heard in Ireland and to put to-

61. Ibid.
62. Farrell to Jim Larkin, 8 September 1938 [739].

gether his essays on the nation in Irish literature. When drafts of these essays were lost in the fire in 1946, he tried to "salvage" some of what he could remember of his work. Larkin's death in 1947 occasioned *in memoriam* Farrell's personal and anecdotal article recounting their visit together, and R. M. Fox's biography of Connolly was a stimulus to produce five Connolly articles—a good introduction to Connolly's life and thought, including extensive quotations. In these pieces, the story as well as the articles written for *New International* (a publication of the Trotskyist Socialist Workers' Party), Farrell expressed some of the political concerns that were currents running through much of his work during these years.

VII

Farrell's visit to Ireland had come at the climax of his career as a writer, if we measure that career by its public success. He had fought his way free of a great deal of the "legacy of fear" he ascribed to his descent from immigrant Irish Catholics in Chicago.[63] Crossing Washington Park, he had used the University of Chicago as a ladder or stepping-stone to a new life in the world of art and literature. His quitting college to be a writer in 1927 was nothing less than what Edgar M. Branch has called "an act of faith."[64] Eleven years later he was an internationally published author, and his return to ancestral Ireland was a symbolic justification of that act of faith in himself. But more than this it was, as was everything for Farrell, an experience to write about in order to learn more not only of its meaning but also of his own nature. As such, Farrell's visit to Ireland, and the studies and writings that anticipated or flowed from it, constitute a highly significant episode of his biography, and moreover provide us with a moment at which we can try to characterize his achievement.

Farrell's critical attitudes toward Irish writers and Irish culture are indicative of the moral seriousness and idealism underlying his development as an artist. He grew sharply disappointed, for example, over the failure of Irish criticism to meet the challenge of Irish poets and novelists in the twentieth century. What was needed, he thought, was a

---

63. "A Legacy of Fear" was a working title for Farrell's *The Face of Time;* see "How *The Face of Time* Was Written," in *Reflections at Fifty and Other Essays* (New York: Vanguard Press, 1954), p. 40.

64. "James T. Farrell and the University of Chicago," p. 26.

criticism directed toward the same truths animating the finest writers of the Irish Renaissance and their successors. But Irish critics, even some who were themselves fine artists, seemed unable to free their critical thinking from dogmatisms and sloth. Nationalism and various ideologies were clogging minds that ought to have pierced through to critical truths. Above all, Farrell sought to clarify the criticism of Irish literature by grounding it in those categories he had found in the American philosophers Dewey and Mead:

> The function of art, of literature, in any society is therefore the evaluation of personal experience. It aims to express the wants, hopes, ideals, sufferings, feelings of people. It concerns itself with the meaning of life; it interprets and constructs meanings. It tells why a people lived, why they affirmed or denied their experience on this planet.[65]

The critic must recognize that literature, in evaluating and explaining experience, cannot be held in check, directed, or manipulated for the ends of policy. In this respect literature has an inevitable kinship with life itself: "It is characteristic of life that it constantly tends to overflow the intellectual categories which are set up as the basis for apprehending, organizing, understanding, controlling, and changing it."[66] So literature and its traditions must be dealt with by criticism in the context of social life as it has been lived; the critic cannot substitute some more facile rationale for a canon of true judgment.

A good example of how Farrell applied these ideas to the work of Irish writers can be seen in his powerful and balanced critique of Frank O'Connor. One of O'Connor's earliest stories, "Guests of the Nation," showed that he was an artist of uncommon talent and perception. The "Nation" of the title is a value in Irish life that comes to expression in the narrator's feeling, voiced early in the story, that "disunion between brothers seemed to me an awful crime." This feeling for the brotherhood of Irishmen as a nation comes into tragic conflict with the narrator's experience of two British prisoners whom he must put to death, for the sake of the "Nation," although he has come to know them too as brothers of a sort. O'Connor's story is able to focus and dramatize in the content of the characters' consciousness real elements and antinomies in twentieth-century Irish experience. In his play *The Invincibles,* O'Connor again portrayed the idea of the Nation at work in Irish life, and he added here a concept of equal import for Ireland—the Church.

---

65. "Notes for G[uggenheim] Outline," in "Notes on Irish Literature" (n.d.) [61]; see below, p. 38.

66. *A Note on Literary Criticism* (New York: Vanguard Press, 1936), pp. 95–96; reprinted in this volume as "On Some Marxist Critics of Joyce."

Irish terrorists are imbued with Nation and Church as causes worth dying for, but in their final days before execution by the British it becomes clear to the Invincibles that their Church and Nation have abandoned them as common criminals. Again O'Connor is able to show how key values of Irish life are revealed under tragic circumstances to involve unresolved contradictions that are causes of human suffering. Farrell's criticism of O'Connor goes to the heart of his strength as a realist in portraying the experience of the Irish. Painfully, Farrell goes on to argue that O'Connor, having exposed some of the basic problems and polarities of Irish life, has not been able like Joyce to "create his own artistic structure out of these antinomies."[67] O'Connor's later work to Farrell seems in the nature of compromise, falling back on a spurious resolution in local color and Irish charm, a comedy of great skill but little artistic aspiration.

This quality of O'Connor's later work was something Farrell also had identified as a real feature of Irish life in general. The superficial self-denigration of the Irish, a humorous evasion or defensiveness, Farrell interpreted forthrightly as "deviousness," albeit charming. Along with this he was aware of a hardness beneath the surface sentimentality of the Irish. These characteristics had traditionally expressed themselves, Farrell thought, in the disastrous political life of the Irish nation. His own experience of Ireland inspired and deepened his commitments to social justice and to a socialist organization of economic institutions. He went to Ireland already aligned with that tradition of Irish social thought represented by such men as Lalor and Connolly. In his letter to Leon Trotsky, written a few months after he returned to America, he expressed a pessimism about the political future of Ireland:

> There is a lot of talk about Ireland, and little is done about Ireland, and a characteristic attitude is sure and what is the bother. Ireland is no longer merely a victim of England, but of world economy now. Irish nationalism correspondingly has altered from being a progressive movement to a reactionary movement. Fascism could easily triumph in Ireland were fascism vitally necessary to the new rulers of Holy Ireland.[68]

Since the advent of Mussolini in the 1920s, many had dreaded the coming of another world war, and the threat of war was on Farrell's mind more than any other fact of political life in 1938. On his way through London from Paris, he had fallen in with two Irish lads in a Piccadilly pub, one of whom "said he would like the war to come

---

67. "The Work of Frank O'Connor" (n.d.) [2]; published in this volume.
68. Farrell to Leon Trotsky, 11 December 1938 [739]; see below, p. 188.

because it would mean some 'excoitement.' "[69] He and his friend were looking for work, having come to England because of Irish poverty and the influence of the Church. Farrell could find no trace of radicalism in either of them, and this sort of experience was reinforced by what he found when he arrived in Ireland. Particularly irksome to him was the role of the Church. He told Trotsky,

> The Church tells the Irish that they are going to live forever and be happier in Heaven, and this engenders patience. There is a mystic fascination with death in Ireland. In all the homes of the poor, the walls are lined with holy pictures, those of the Sacred Heart predominating. The poor live in utter patience.[70]

On the other hand, the Church was a buffer against what Farrell clearly regarded as the worst of all social evils:

> Stalinism is very weak in Ireland, practically inconsequential. It amounts to a few pensionaries. Ireland does not need Stalinism. It has Rome. Rome handles these problems with the necessary efficiency. Rome confuses the struggles, poses the false questions, sidetracks protests as Stalinism now does in advanced countries.[71]

But this was scant satisfaction.

Farrell's wonder at the phenomenon of Irish Catholicism was deepened by his recognition that *"religion is never a separate question, divorced from all of the political questions and struggles of a period."*[72] Nowhere was this truth impressed on him more than in relation to Jim Larkin and James Connolly, socialist revolutionaries who were also strong Catholics. In their minds socialism and Catholicism did not seem contradictory; Connolly in fact linked them explicitly in opposition to a matched pair, capitalism and Protestantism. In "A Portrait of James Connolly," Farrell contends that this constellation in Connolly's thought depends on the link between ideas of community and of the dignity of the individual, both of which were rooted in Catholic tradition as well as in the political ideals springing out of the French Revolution. Their linkage was objectified in Connolly's strong commitment to a political democracy that would protect the community and enhance individual freedom in an Ireland free from the domination of British Protestant capital. While at the same time sharply criticizing Catholicism's moral record (he quotes Lea's *History of the Inquisition*), Farrell thus respected the

---

69. Diary note, 2 June 1938 [738].
70. Farrell to Leon Trotsky, 11 December 1938 [739]; see below, p. 188.
71. Ibid.; see below, p. 189.
72. "Portrait of James Connolly—IV: The Politics of Connolly's Catholicism," *New International* 14 (1948): 80; reprinted in this volume as "A Portrait of James Connolly."

religious beliefs of Larkin and Connolly. Addressing a Trotskyist, and presumably an atheist, readership in *New International,* he wrote with understanding about Larkin that "Jim was a Catholic, and he was proud that Ireland had a Christian civilization. The world needed (he said) a Christian civilization, based on the sanctity of the family. He spoke with pride of his own family life."[73] Farrell's discussions of Connolly and Larkin show that despite his own anti-Catholic stance since the late 1920s, vigorously pronounced in some of his letters from Dublin to radical friends, he did not despise anyone's faith. As in his fiction, he was able imaginatively to respect the faith of others though he had given up his own.

This brings us to what may be the central question in discussing any episode in Farrell's life—its bearing on the development of his own fiction. Farrell went to Ireland with the express "idea of someday writing a novel on the Irish immigrant in America."[74] Already he had drawn the figure of Mary O'Flaherty in two novels of the O'Neill/O'Flaherty pentalogy, later completed in 1952 with *The Face of Time* (earliest of the five-book series in its chronological setting), in which the main character is old Tom O'Flaherty, modeled on Farrell's immigrant grandfather. Tom's painful death of intestinal cancer near the end of the book crowns his experience of fear, toil, and bewilderment at the new life he had "come out to" in America; his nostalgia and reveries about the Old Country are the book's most poignant theme. Farrell's visit to Ireland and his study of Irish literature before and after that visit were fundamental to the conception of this work, which lies at the heart of his development as an artist.

In his essay "How *The Face of Time* Was Written," Farrell comments that in composing this work "I was not merely looking back, but was discovering what lay back behind the whirling, speeding motors of time, back at some of the roots of my life, and of our own common life."[75] He goes on to recall the example of Proust, "to me the greatest writer of the twentieth century," and to speak of "two basic motifs of my work . . . time and death."[76] These considerations apply as well to the entire pentalogy completed in *The Face of Time,* and also to Farrell's entire output in fiction. In another sense, the O'Neill/O'Flaherty novels can be seen as the keystone or foundation of Farrell's development as an artist. It

---

73. "Jim Larkin: Irish Revolutionist. Fighter for Freedom and Socialism," *New International* 13 (1947): 88; reprinted in this volume as "Lest We Forget: Jim Larkin, Irish Labor Leader."

74. Farrell to Al ——, 26 June 1938 [738].

75. "How *The Face of Time* Was Written," p. 39.

76. Ibid., p. 40.

was his purpose to "write so that life may speak for itself,"[77] to put into fiction various thoughts and feelings—such as those of Irish immigrants —that many have shared but that had never been thought worthy of inclusion in serious literature. He was consequently a most experimental and innovative writer. This experimental, innovative quality is his hallmark, rooted in his experience of first-, second-, and third-generation immigrants in America. His visit to Ireland helped him to describe these people's lives, mostly lives of mere aspiration and largely unrealized fantasies; of material success coming in time to seem emptier for a few; and of self-awareness for fewer still. In sloughing off the constricting though poignant and jealous traces of the old ethnic Nation (itself entrapped and isolated in a dominant culture), Farrell's characters suffer and achieve what most of the human race must face in the coming generations.

In this connection, one sees that Farrell's interest in Ireland as a descendant of immigrants, his responses to Irish life, and also his sense of himself as an artist all center at this moment in his career on that complex and ambiguous relation to Joyce to which he often recurred. Some features of this relation have already been observed: Farrell's failure to visit Joyce or establish any direct contact even when that would have been logical and convenient; his subsequent regret over this omission; his ambivalence while inclining to value alternatively either Joyce or Proust as artistic models; and his initial diffidence about *Finnegans Wake* as a work of art while acknowledging its genius. Farrell observed once that to read Joyce intelligently "would take about fifteen years," and he admittedly read Joyce continuously after 1927.[78] But Farrell's philosophical orientation, for one thing, caused him to regard some elements of Joyce's work with skepticism and perhaps a certain disapproval of what he called a "coolness." Part of this was the place of Thomism and of Catholicism in general in Joyce's art. For Farrell, Joyce remained a Catholic artist despite his apparent rejection of Catholic religion. Joyce's image of the artist, as presented in the thinking of Stephen Dedalus, is of the artist as a priest. In Farrell's view, while he shared with Joyce the "common experience" of having felt an early vocation to the Catholic priesthood, he himself had completely reoriented his world view on the rational bedrock of pragmatism, while Joyce remained imaginatively dominated by Catholic categories.

There was nothing crude or self-congratulatory about this attitude on Farrell's part. But the level view he took of Joyce and Stephen

---

77. Ibid., p. 41.
78. "An Interview with James T. Farrell," *Thought* 8 (23 June 1956): 13–14.

Dedalus separated idiosyncratic elements of religious feeling, cultural parody, and aestheticism from what Farrell regarded as the essential presentation of common features of Irish experience after the collapse of the Parnellite movement in Joyce's youth. Stephen Dedalus was not representative of Irish character in general, except as his responses to Church and Nation implied participation in the national division and demoralization that had been part of Ireland's recent history. From this point of view, Farrell evaluated Joyce's early attraction to Ibsen's cosmopolitanism, and here we can see another ambivalence in relation to Joyce. Though Farrell had not contacted Joyce, Joyce *had* written to Ibsen; and, as Farrell shows, he had done so rather tactlessly in his callow and confused enthusiasm: "In March, 1901, on the occasion of Ibsen's seventy-third birthday, Joyce addressed a letter of felicitation to him. It is admiring, youthful, and self-conscious; and it approaches the presumptuous and even the unconsciously cruel."[79] Holding this view of Joyce's relation to Ibsen, Farrell avoided discipleship in spite of Joyce's influence on his work. Asserting that "I've never been anyone's disciple," he had avoided personal contact with Joyce.

VIII

Farrell's interest in Ireland continued unabated throughout his life. After his return from Ireland, in *Father and Son, My Days of Anger,* and *The Face of Time* he gave further treatment to his immigrant characters, the grandparents of Danny O'Neill. And his nonfiction Irish writings continued until his death. This is not the place for extended discussion of these copious unpublished writings of later years, but they include essays on Synge and Constance Markiewicz; reminiscences at the deaths of Irish writers and public figures he had known or read; and several interesting comparisons of Ireland and India as nations that struggled for freedom from British colonial domination. These comparisons illustrate Farrell's tendency to view the whole complex of Irish national experience from an international viewpoint as something of an object lesson for victims of industrial capitalism, especially colonial nations. In this context should be understood his requirement, in an unfinished essay on recent interest in Irish studies, that the focus of such studies be not personal roots merely but the "establishment of correlations,

---

79. "Joyce and Ibsen," in *Reflections at Fifty,* p. 67; reprinted in this volume.

connections, causes and effects, influences and mutual influences between Ireland and America, Ireland and the world, and Irish-Americans
and their immigrant forebears."[80] It was as part of this program that
Farrell carried on his lifelong study of Ireland and its culture.

In 1974 he was finally able to see Athlone and Mullingar, County
Westmeath, where his grandparents had grown up before their emigration. He wrote that, like other Americans abroad, he traveled seeking
to understand the present through contact with a past. With this in
mind he went to see "the steeple of Athlone," atop a nineteenth-century
cathedral that his grandmother had often recalled.

> I went to see the tower at midnight. It pointed towards a moonlit sky,
> through which thousands of bright shiny stars had been carelessly flung
> like jewels tossed on an enormous rug. The tower seemed to belong to the
> sky. I looked at it. It had been one of the wonders of my grandmother's
> girlhood. It was a visible and tangible memorial of that lost past which I
> had been looking for. And I had found it.[81]

The incident is an emblem of Farrell's work in Irish studies. A descendant of Irish immigrants, he strove to understand and chronicle in literature some of the past correlations and connections that helped account
for his experience. In this he faced a task of universal interest for current
generations. For wherever we live and whoever our forebears, we are all
in a sense children of immigrants in a modern world we never made.

---

80. "The Irish-Americans" (n.d.) [858].
81. "Finding My Irish Past Along Shannon's Shores," *Family Weekly*, 2 May 1976, p.
11.

On Irish Themes
by
James T. Farrell

Ireland as distinct from her people is nothing to me; and the man who is bubbling over with love and enthusiasm for "Ireland" and can yet pass unmoved through our streets and witness all the wrong and the suffering, the shame and the degradation brought upon the people of Ireland—aye, brought by Irishmen upon Irish men and women—without burning to end it, is in my opinion a fraud and a liar in his heart, no matter how he loves that combination of chemical elements he is pleased to call "Ireland."

—JAMES CONNOLLY

It is my divine mission to preach subversion and discontent to the working classes.

—JIM LARKIN

From
A World I Never Made [1]

He went out to the kitchen.

"Mother?" he said, askingly.

"Yes, Son!"

"Mother, tell me something about Ireland."

"I'm not Irish. I'm English. My name was Fox before I married your grandfather."

"But I'm Irish, ain't I? My friend, Father Hunt, told me, 'Daniel you're a fine young Irishman!' "

"Oh, Son, Ireland is a poor country. They are so poor in the old country that it would make your hair stand up on end on the top of your little head."

"You mean that the people in Ireland are poor like my Mama and Papa and they don't have electric lights and radiators?"

"The people go hungry. The English and the landlords, ah, but they're swell people. They have all the money, and they go riding through the fields with their dogs on the hunt for the fox," she said, then she put the dishes away, filled her clay pipe and began to smoke.

"Your Mama and Papa, are they poor in Ireland, too, like my Papa and Mama?"

"They are in Heaven with your grandfather and your Aunt Louise, may their souls rest in peace. And sure, I'll be going there soon myself with me old bones."

"No! No, Mother! I don't want you to go away from me," Danny said with overseriousness.

"Grandson, you're not an O'Neill or an O'Flaherty, you're a Fox," she said, looking at him lovingly.

"Mother, do they have automobiles in Ireland?" he asked as she sat watching him by the enamel-topped table.

---

1. *A World I Never Made* (New York: Vanguard Press, 1936) was the earliest of Farrell's five novels about the O'Neill/O'Flaherty family and in particular about Danny O'Neill, an autobiographical character, who lives with his grandmother more as a son than as a grandson. Excerpted here are pp. 51–53.

"We saw nary an automobile in Ireland."

"Why don't they have automobiles in Ireland?"

"Sure, they'd run behind the bushes and think it was the work of the Devil if they saw an automobile in the town of Athlone or at the Mullingar Fair."

"And did you go to school to the Sisters in Ireland when you were a little girl, like I'm doing now?"

"Sister, my sister, she was a scholar and went to school. I ran the fields and fed the pigs. I can see my mother sending me to school. If I asked her to do that, she would have skinned the hide right off of my backside."

"Gee!"

"And they have mean men in Ireland. Mean landlords. Me mother's landlord, Mr. Longacre, he was so mean that he would make you eat dirt off a shovel. And when the poor people had nothing to pay the landlords, they were put off the land, and they became tinkers, or they came out to America."

"Is that why John Boyle came to America and is a motorman?"

"His mother was a little girl in the old country. They had nothing to eat but potatoes. I ran the brush with her, barefooted."

His grandmother went to the ice box, and returned with a bottle of beer. She sat by the table, drinking.

"Mother, when I am a man I'm going to get some fairies and I'm going to go with them and fix those landlords in Ireland who are so mean," Danny said.

"Ah, the landlords would shave you without soap."

"I think the fairies that Aunty Margaret reads me about would do something to those mean landlords," Danny said.

"They're the hand of the Devil. Father McCarthy in the old country always said the fairies were a queer people and they were in league with the Devil himself."

"They are nice to boys and girls in the book. Did Aunty Margaret ever read you about the three spinning fairies?"

"Ah, I'll never be seein' the old country again," she said; she drained her glass of beer, poured the remainder of her bottle into the empty glass.

Danny went to the sink, filled a glass of water, sat at the opposite end of the table, watched his grandmother, and imitated her as she drank the rest of the beer. Looking at her closely, he saw a tear slide down her creased cheek.

"Mother, why are you crying?" he asked.

Notes for G[uggenheim] Outline[1]

[Two Drafts]

I

My project is to study modern Irish literature as the outgrowth of Irish life and culture. My investigation will be conducted on the basis of certain assumptions concerning literature, which I accept as hypotheses. Literature is not a mere private expression, it is a social product. The primary concern of a work of art is value, values that might be sensational, intellectual, or a combination of both. The artist attempts to evaluate human experience and in so doing he uses what he will from his social heritage. His very interpretation of natural phenomena is distinctly dictated by the social past of his milieu, by the evaluations and interpretations of his predecessors. Even though expression be his conscious driving force, yet he deals in values already socialized. Investigation of literature therefore must not be purely aesthetic, must not be made in terms of an art-for-art's-sake convention. The function of art, of literature, in any society is therefore the evaluation of personal experience. It aims to express the wants, hopes, ideals, sufferings, feelings of a people. It concerns itself with the meaning of life; it interprets and constructs meanings. It tells why a people lived, why they affirmed or denied their experience on this planet.

My study of Irish literature then will be pursued with the aim of understanding, interpreting, analyzing, and criticizing Irish writing in relationship to Irish life. It will require a knowledge of the ideological and social past and present of Ireland. It will analyze the motives and themes used by Irish writers not merely as situations provided for the application of literary skill, but as imaginative representations of the life and efforts of the Irish people. The Irish ideology dependent on three principal sources—(a) the bardic past with its heroic attitude, (b) the medieval synthesis, (c) cultural and political nationalism—will be traced through the writings of modern Irish life, and that ideology will be criticized wherever it is a defective and yet a real factor in determining

---

1. Printed from unpublished "Notes on Irish literature" (n.d.) [61].

motives and ends of action at the present time. My standard will be relative, not absolute. I shall not be primarily concerned with final or international estimates of the men I study. Rather I shall be interested in their work as a refraction of their times and country.

I propose mainly to deal with the newer Irish writers. The work of Yeats, AE, Synge, and others of the earlier period of the Irish Literary Renaissance has already been interpreted, and much cannot be added.

II

My project is to make a thorough study of modern Irish literature, analyzing and interpreting it in terms of its ideological bases and social setting. A study of the ideology involves (a) a consideration of the pagan past viewed by Ferguson, O'Grady and others and exploited as a source of inspiration by the older men of letters who were responsible for the first efflorescence of the Renaissance: Yeats, Russell, Todhunter, Synge, and their contemporaries; (b) a consideration of the medieval synthesis which blotted out pagan Ireland, and gave the country a Christian, Romish ideology; (c) nationalism, which gave the coloring to Irish politics, a decidedly more important phenomenon in nineteenth-century Ireland than the literary and dramatic arts. A study of the Irish social setting will expand from this ideology and will include the economic life of the country, and the social institutions which go to the generation of the collective life of the Irish people. This study will be related specifically to the literature produced in the country. The manner of relation will be principally through the consideration of values, of the technique of constructing, and the manner of affirming, as well as the context of values in Irish life, and will analyze the bases of literary products. It will indicate how the literature has gone through stages—Anglicization, pagan romanticism, and nationalism, to realism—with implications of social criticism, and will indicate how and where any Irish writers are becoming socially constructive in their works.

Observations on the First Period of the Irish Renaissance[1]

Dedicated to the memory of Ernest Boyd [2]

Nationalism—the concept of the nation—permeates all Irish thinking: it pervades Irish writing. However, one cannot interpret nationalism in Irish writing as though it were a hardened and unchanging conception. The concept of the nation, the precise character of nationalism in Irish writing, has gone through various changes in the course of the last hundred years.

In Ireland, disputes concerning propaganda and literature have been focused in terms of the national movement. In the politics of the national movement, there have been two tendencies, one which put the political question of national sovereignty first, and the other which stressed the social question. Figures representing these tendencies in the early twentieth century were Arthur Griffith, the leader who played the key role in founding Sinn Fein, and James Connolly, the national martyr and social revolutionary. The difference here can be suggested in the question Which comes first, the national or the social question?

A difference somewhat parallel can be seen when we touch on the question of literature and propaganda. Do the political interests of the national movement, narrowly conceived, come before the interests of a literature created in pursuit of an image of truth? Can literature be judged in terms of a fixed national aim so that it is turned into a political handmaiden?

Discussing these questions years ago in his book *Principles of Freedom*,

---

1. Reprinted from "The Irish Cultural Renaissance of the Last Century," *Irish Writing* 25 (1953): 50–53. The title here, as well as the dedication, are printed from a revised typescript carbon of the essay (n.d.) [7]. The essay has been reprinted in *James T. Farrell: Literary Essays, 1954–1974*, ed. Jack Alan Robbins (Port Washington: Kennikat Press, 1976), pp. 58–62.

2. Farrell's Note: In this analysis, I am indebted to the late Ernest Boyd for his book *Ireland's Literary Renaissance*, although my interpretations vary from his. His writings on Irish literature, and a lecture of his on Irish writing which I heard in 1927, were a main stimulus to my interest in Irish writing. This will explain why I take the liberty of dedicating this piece to his memory.

the late Terence MacSwiney, an Irish martyr, declared: "It is because we need the truth that we object to the propagandist playwright."[3] It is this idea of an image of the truth which is denied by those who crudely apply political measuring rods to literature.

And it often happens that both sides in a political struggle—especially, perhaps, when this struggle breaks out in war and violence—will see literature in the same terms. Thus, in an investigation conducted by the British Government after the Easter Rising, a British official claimed, in his testimony, that the Rebellion might have been averted if the Abbey Theatre in Dublin might have had a longer period in which to influence the Irish people. This official saw literature and art in the same terms as did those whom Terence MacSwiney answered in the brief sentence listed above. He merely wanted literature to pour water rather than fire on the spirits of the Irish.

These remarks suggest the relevance of showing permutations in the concept of nationalism and of the nation as we find these in Irish writings. Here, however, there is only space for a few broad illustrations.

The democratic Young Irelanders of 1848 got their ideas from the Great French Revolution. To them, the freedom of Ireland, the creation of a sovereign Irish nation, meant creation of a political condition that would enable Irishmen to realize their dignity and individuality as human beings.

Men like John Mitchel, or the eloquent James Fintan Lalor who came after Mitchel and the other Young Irelanders, were fighting rebels. They opposed O'Connellism and Daniel O'Connell. John Mitchel and Thomas Davis were cultivated men. They represented a high level of taste and culture in the Ireland of their time. Davis, a ballad singer, critic and essayist, along with his contemporary, the poet, James Clarence Mangan, are two of the fathers of modern Irish culture.

Instead of holding to a narrow political conception of culture, men such as Mitchel, Davis and Mangan had a broader democratic one. Culture was, to them, an instrument which would help the Irish to gain a greater sense of their dignity and individuality as Irishmen.

D. J. O'Donoghue, editor of Davis' essays, wrote concerning Thomas Davis: "In a few words, he sought to impress upon Irishmen the fact that they had much to be proud of in their history and character, and he saw that the surest way to induce a nation to rise to higher things

---

3. Terence MacSwiney, *Principles of Freedom* (Dublin: The Talbot Press, 1921), p. 150. On Farrell's early interest in MacSwiney, see Introduction, above, p. 6.

was to imbue them with the idea that they had accomplished much."[4]

John Mitchel in an introduction to Mangan's essays declared that "fresh, manly, vigorous national songs and ballads must by no means be neglected" as one of the ways to be used in rousing the Irish national spirit.[5] It must be stressed that these men were fighting rebels. To them, struggle meant the discovery of the road to manhood.

It is my opinion that the Irish cultural Renaissance is intimately bound up with resurgence of the Irish national spirit, the beginnings of Sinn Fein, the development of the modern Irish labor movement under the leadership of James Connolly and Jim Larkin, and the entire Irish movement in the post-Parnell period.

Following the defeat of Parnell, and the decline of his Irish party until it became a kind of political arena for Eloquent Dempseys,[6] new orientations were gradually sought out. Politically, the new orientations were developed into so-called Connollyism and Larkinism.

There are no simple causes to be discovered and cited in an attempt to explain the Irish Renaissance. It grew out of a condition in the country. At the same time, it was influenced from without by tendencies from England and the European continent. *Fin de siècle* aesthetics and reflections of French symbolism were brought to Ireland by Yeats and Synge.

The plays of Synge were organized on terms which fit into the aesthetic conceptions of men like Pater. Pater also influenced Joyce. George Moore carried into the Renaissance ideas of French naturalism.

Standish O'Grady, usually called the Father of the Renaissance, dealt artistically with the ancient Irish past. He presented the figures of the Irish legends on the Homeric level. A legendary Irish past offered the men of the Renaissance one of their sources of material. They went to the peasantry for speech and language and found among them—especially the peasantry of the west of Ireland—a basis for a language for poetry and for poetic drama. There were pagan elements in the Renaissance. In Yeats' poetry, for instance, definite pagan threads can be observed.

A number of these early figures of the Renaissance were Protestant. They were Anglo-Irish. To this day they and their successors have been criticized on the ground that they were not Irish and did not reflect the

---

4. Thomas Davis, *Essays Literary and Historical,* ed. D. J. O'Donoghue (Dundalk: W. Tempest, 1914), p. ix.

5. Actually quoted from Mitchel's introduction to the poems of Davis; see *The Poems of Thomas Davis,* ed. John Mitchel (New York: Haverty, 1854), p. iii.

6. William Boyle's play *The Eloquent Dempsey* dealt satirically with political demagoguery and was produced at the Abbey Theatre in 1906.

Irish spirit. In terms of the strict idea of nationalism which limits Irishmen to Catholics who do not have Anglican antecedents—at least back to the time of Cromwell—this criticism is justified.

But besides being narrow and parochial, it is unhistorical. The Anglo-Irish had all been in Ireland for a long time when the Celtic Renaissance was born. Their influences had become a part of the evolution of Irish history. The movement of these men of the early Renaissance can be interpreted as an effort on their part culturally to enter more fully into the life of Ireland. This is one of the features of the nationalism of the Renaissance.

This national cultural revival, based on the legendary past and on the language of the more economically and socially backward sections of the people, differs from the cultural ideas of the Young Irelanders of 1848. The latter conceived of the Irish as a people.

The characters of the early Irish drama are not a people, but a folk. Formally, the ideas and most of the work produced in the first period of the Renaissance were not political. Politics then didn't enter into this movement in the way that politics entered into the cultural ideas of the Young Irelanders.

If we consider Yeats' poetic drama, *Kathleen ni Houlihan,* we can, perhaps, note this difference more concretely. It is commonly known that when this play was first produced, there were riots. It aroused national resentment.

The lines spoken by simple characters in this poignantly poetic work, and the touching relation of these characters to Kathleen, their symbolic Mother Ireland, brings out the dignity and humanity in Irish peasants. The emphasis in the play is on martyrdom. In effect, *Kathleen ni Houlihan* calls on her Irish sons to go out and die for Ireland. And, also, we see here that the humanized image of Ireland, created in poetic symbol, is that of an old woman, a sad old woman.

The play most certainly does not fit the cultural prescriptions of Mitchel and Davis. We see this more strongly if we keep in mind the fact that the most popular image of England is John Bull. Along with *Kathleen ni Houlihan,* the other images created in this period include legendary and pseudo-Homeric figures. Here is a permutation in the Irish national conception as this is mirrored in literature.

At a later date, Padraic Pearse, who was to be executed as a leader of the Easter Rebellion, wrote a play manifestly under the influence of the first period of the Renaissance. *The Singer* attempts to dramatize the same kind of a mood as does *Kathleen ni Houlihan.*

The figure of Kathleen is a symbol of a whole nation. The emphasis on martyrdom is generalized by Kathleen. When this emphasis is made in a figure less representative, the generalized mood does not grow out of the play. But the heroic martyrdom of Pearse should be a caution against those inclined to denounce these two plays on purely political grounds.

The creations of this period of the Renaissance—and most notably those of Yeats and Synge—are significant in another way. This work should not be measured by formal conceptions of nationalism, if one seeks a sense of its importance in Irish culture.

Before the Renaissance, Irish culture was thin. Genuine work was largely overshadowed by the meretricious. The stage Irishman was often presented as the image of an Irish man.

Synge, Yeats, Lady Gregory and their contemporaries helped bring a note of reality into Irish writing. Their characters have a dignity and a naturalness of their own. Their language bespeaks this dignity. They are real, not false. The reality in all Irish writing which followed them is in their debt. They introduced an image of truth into modern Irish writing.

Joyce's
A Portrait of the Artist as a Young Man

with a Postscript on
Stephen Hero[1]

"This race and this country and this life produced me," declares Stephen Dedalus—artistic image of James Joyce himself—in *A Portrait of the Artist as a Young Man*. The *Portrait* is the story of how Stephen was produced, how he rejected that which produced him, how he discovered that his destiny was to become a lonely one of artistic creation. It is well to look into "this life" out of which Stephen came, to discuss some aspects of the social and national background of this novel. In Ireland a major premise of any discussion of her culture and of her literature is an understanding of Irish nationalism. And it is at least arguable that Joyce was a kind of inverted nationalist.

Ireland, when James Joyce was a boy, experienced a profound political defeat, the fall of Parnell. In that, once again, she was set back in her long struggle to attain nationhood. The aftermath was marked by a deeply felt and pervasive bitterness, often expressed in feelings of personal betrayal. And the *Portrait* reflects these moods. The brilliantly written scene, early in the novel, of the Dedalus family pitilessly quarreling at the Christmas dinner table is a highly concentrated representation of the magnitude of Parnell's fall in Ireland, suggesting how it cut through families with a knifelike sharpness. The family argument is personal, and its passionate anger seems to be in inverse proportion to the political impotence of those who are hurling insults at one another.

Whenever Stephen, as a youth, discusses politics, his tone is one of resentment. He identifies himself with the courageous men who have striven for, and been martyred in serving, the cause of Ireland; he feels that they have been let down by their own followers, by those whom

---

1. Reprinted from *James Joyce: Two Decades of Criticism*, ed. Seon Givens (New York: Vanguard Press, 1948), pp. 175–97. Without the "postscript," the substance of this essay had appeared in Farrell's *The League of Frightened Philistines and Other Papers* (New York: Vanguard Press, 1945), pp. 45–59, and earlier in even more abbreviated form in two parts in the *New York Times Book Review*, as "Joyce and His First Self-Portrait" (31 December 1944, pp. 6, 16) and "Joyce and the Tradition of the European Novel" (21 January 1945, pp. 4, 18).

they were trying to free. Stephen's reaction is not a singular one for the Ireland of his time. (In fact, it is even paralleled in the present period, for, just as Stephen blames the Irish people for Ireland's defeats, so do many contemporary radical intellectuals blame the workers for the defeats of socialism.) The Irish people have betrayed the future of Stephen Dedalus. This is the real sense of his bitterness. Even the monuments and memorials to Ireland's honorable heroes, Tone and Emmet, are tawdry, part of a tawdry Dublin present which Stephen resents.

Ireland's national aspirations generalized real, deep-seated needs. These had been choked up in the nineteenth century by a whole series of defeats, from the time of Emmet and Tone to that of Parnell. When such wide needs are thus thwarted, frustrated, they are revealed in a molecular way, a sense of multiple personal betrayal, a despair and disgust with politics, and a general feeling of embittered dissatisfaction and rejection. And, when such a social phenomenon is expressed in art, it usually is in terms of how it is immediately felt rather than in terms of its social rationale. This is how Stephen felt about the Irish political defeats, directly, and with painful immediacy.

The post-Parnell period was one of groping for new orientation. Irish nationalism found this politically in Sinn Fein and culturally in the so-called Irish literary renaissance, the Gaelic-language movement, and the Gaelic-sports movement.

In a diary note (quoted in Herbert Gorman's valuable informative biography *James Joyce*), Joyce once described Ireland as "an afterthought of Europe." This remark is to be interpreted as relating principally to Ireland's cultural backwardness. During the nineteenth century, Ireland, a backward country, suffering from continuous economic crises, lived through a succession of miseries. Famine, emigration, defeat—these were her lot. Irish culture was meager; it was also debased by much that was counterfeit, for instance, the literature of the stage Irishman. What culture there was had been nourished by the liberating influences of the great French Revolution and found its best expression in such patriots as Thomas Davis and James Clarence Mangan, as well as in the novelist William Carleton. Ireland's experiences gave her thin culture a tincture of sadness, at times a romantic sadness; an instance of this is Mangan's "Dark Rosaleen." In the first half of the nineteenth century, a disunified Germany created a German philosophy which, with Hegel, achieved a kind of spiritual unity in culture as a sublimation of the real need for the unity which was not attained on the plane of history. The sudden growth of this thin Irish culture in the post-Parnell period can be explained as a similar kind of cultural compensation.

There is a note of foreignness, of alienness, in the first stage of the

Irish literary renaissance. Nationalists often call it an Anglicized culture; what I think they really mean is that it did not adequately express Irish needs of the time. The progenitors of this movement were very talented people, and one of them, Yeats, was destined to become probably the greatest poet of his age writing in the English language. But they went to Irish materials as if from without. Sensitive to a disorientation that was pervasively felt at the time, needing sources of inspiration fresher than those of English literature and of the *"fin de siècle,"* when Victorian culture fell apart, they more or less discovered Ireland.

But what did they discover? This stage of the so-called renaissance produced the poetic drama. It found thematic material in the legends of Ireland's free and pre-Saxonized past. A fresh and poetic language was sought in the speech of the poorest, the most backward, section of Irish peasantry. Standish O'Grady, frequently referred to as the father of this movement, attempted to re-establish the old legends on a Homeric level. It seems as if all these writers were seeking to create images of great figures of their past in order to compensate (though perhaps not consciously) for their lack of leaders in the present, so that, with Parnell gone, they could still derive some cultural subsistence, some sense of pride and inspiration, from the image of Fergus and other heroes of the legends.[2] Thwarted on the historical plane, Ireland set up as a counter to England an idea of her own culture. Through culture, she would show that she was a nation. When Yeats wrote a play like *Kathleen ni Houlihan* with political implications, it is interesting to note that Kathleen ni Houlihan (Ireland, and a rather weak cultural image to set against that of John Bull) asks her sons not to live, fight, win, and build for her, but rather to go out and die for her, as if Ireland had been lacking in names to inscribe on her martyrology.

The emphasis of this stage of the movement was on the past. Where

---

2. FARRELL'S NOTE: Generally speaking, national cultural movements tend to create a sense of pride in a nation, in a national culture. There can be no doubt that this is involved in the Irish cultural renaissance. However, it has other aspects, too. For Ireland it has its clear-cut romantic emphasis. There is, therefore, something of romantic substitution to be seen in this movement. The idea of the nation and of a national Irish culture is clearer, more political, a more conscious idea, in the minds of earlier Irish writers—that is, Thomas Davis and John Mitchel. D. J. O'Donoghue, editor of Davis' essays, said of Davis: "In a few words he sought to impress upon Irishmen the fact that they had much to be proud of in their history and their character, and he saw that the surest way to induce a nation to rise to higher things was to imbue them with the idea that they had already accomplished much" [see above, n. 4, p. 42]. And John Mitchel said that Davis wrote "from a calm, deliberate conviction that among other agencies for arousing national spirit, fresh, manly, vigorous national songs and ballads must by no means be neglected . . ." [see above, n. 5, p. 42]. There is clearly a difference in the ideas of cultural nationalism in the case of Davis and Mitchel, on the one hand, and in the Yeats of *Kathleen ni Houlihan* on the other.

could Joyce fit into it? What could it teach him, a young genius who was so acutely sensitive to all the life of the moment? In the *Portrait,* the world presses on Stephen. His own thoughts are melancholy. His proud spirit cannot tolerate the painful burden of reality. He must rise above it. All this burden is not directly represented in the novel; some of it is reflected in memory and in conversation. No clear and full picture of Stephen's relationship with his mother is described. Through conversation, we learn that he has had a distressing quarrel with her, in which he told her that he has lost his faith. In addition, Stephen loses his respect for his father; he begins to develop that feeling of being fatherless which is so important a part of his character in *Ulysses.* But here Joyce does not develop these relationships in directly written scenes. Much is not touched upon—for instance, what of the relationship between Stephen's father and mother?

The *Portrait* contains only a most highly concentrated sense of the home, school, streets, and city which press so sharply upon Stephen's spirit. He is acutely sensitive to all that happens around him; he breathes in something of every wind that blows in Ireland. Joyce at this time felt more, saw more, brooded more than he allows Stephen to reveal to us. Stephen, as boy and youth, tramps the streets of Dublin. Sometimes in his walks he trembles with fears of damnation. Again, his mind is filled with lurid visions of sin, written of in purple passages suggestive of Pater's prose; but very often he searches, looks, listens. In these walks how much of Dublin must have attracted him, how much must have repelled him! How much the streets of Dublin must have told him of life, of men, of himself! How much of Ireland's real, historic past must have been poured through his senses, into the pulsing life of the present! Why is Stephen so melancholy? Obviously because he carries within him such a burden of the life of his country, his city, his race, his own family.

What Stephen sees is Irish history in the present, in terms of what has happened to Ireland and to Irishmen as a result of her defeats. But Stephen does not dwell on a tragic past in moods of regret. Rather, he is bitter because of the condition of the Ireland he knows, the Ireland inherited from a tragic historic past. During the period when he was still at work on *A Portrait of the Artist as a Young Man,* Joyce, in a letter, described Dublin as a "center of paralysis." It should be realized that it was Joyce who introduced the city realistically into modern Irish writing. The city—Dublin—is the focus of Ireland in his work and in his life. We see that this is the case with Stephen, the genius son of a declassed family. Stephen lives, grows up, in a Dublin that is a center of paralysis. Is he to have a future in such a center? Is he to prevent himself from suffering paralysis, spiritual paralysis? Stephen's painful burden of reality can be interpreted as a reality that derives from the history of Ireland's defeats and is focused, concretized, in the very quality of the men of Dublin. Stephen describes his own father to a friend as "a medical student, an oarsman, a tenor, an amateur actor, a shouting politician, a small landlord, a small investor, a drinker, a good fellow, a storyteller, somebody's secretary, something in a distillery, a tax gatherer, a bankrupt, and at present a praiser of his own past." Just as Stephen says he has been produced by "this race and this country and this life," so can the same be said of his father. It is in this way, and in the image of his own father, that we can realize how Stephen carries a sense of Ireland's history in his own consciousness. And at the same time he feels that he is a foreigner in Dublin, a foreigner in the sense that he is even forced to speak a language not his own. Just before his discussion of aesthetics with the Jesuit dean of studies, Stephen realizes that "the Ireland of Tone and of Parnell seemed to have receded in space." Stephen, living in the Ireland after their failure, thinks, while talking to the dean: "I cannot speak or write these words without unrest of spirit. His language [the dean's], so familiar and so foreign, will always be for me an acquired speech. I have not made or accepted its words. My voice holds them at bay. My soul frets in the shadow of his language." Stephen's thoughts are highly suggestive, highly important, for an interpretation of this novel. When Joyce walked the streets of Dublin as a youth, one can be sure that he constantly sensed the presence of the English in the major city of Ireland. One can speculate on how many little incidents, words, gestures, angers, glances of suspicion he must have grasped on the wing, all deepening a sense of the life of Dublin as a painful burden. The failure of the Irish to follow men like Tone and Parnell meant that he, Stephen, must fret in speaking a language not his own. Again, it is revealed how Irish history presses on Stephen as something concrete, immediate, as a condition of life that affects him, threatens him with paralysis of soul. Such being the case, it should be clear why Joyce could find no inspiration in a cultural renaissance that found so much of theme and subject in a legendary Irish past. A real Irish present was far, far too disturbing. Herein, I think, is the interpretation we should place on a remark Stephen utters in his own defense: "I am not responsible for the past." Nevertheless, to repeat, he has seen the consequences of that past all about him in the present.

And if this is the case, then Joyce was not going to be able to find literary inspiration where the leading literary men of the time found it. He did not have to discover Ireland. He carried too much of it already in his own being.

Moreover, Joyce was born and educated a Catholic. He was trained by Jesuits at the university which Cardinal Newman had helped to found. He admired Newman and was influenced by his writings. Behind the lucid prose Joyce saw revealed a man who had arrived at his conviction through spiritual agonies. Stephen is shedding convictions which Newman came to accept, but he, too, is going through spiritual agony in so doing.[3]

From his considerable reading in the literature of the church, the boy gained not only a sense of the past but also a sense of an ordered inner world and of a systematized *other* world. Eternity has filled his imagination. Still in his teens, he is shriveled by fierce fires as he sits in the chapel listening to the Jesuit retreat master describe with rigid logic the physical and spiritual agonies awaiting the damned in Hell. (This is one of the most magnificent passages in all of Joyce's work.) After hearing such sermons Stephen becomes almost physically ill. In fact, this is the period when he suffers most intensely. And his greatest sufferings are not imposed by the Dublin reality which disturbs him so much but by images of an Inferno as terrifying as that of Dante. He quivers and cowers before the vision of another world which must make that of the Irish legends seem the palest of mists. His spiritual struggle is one involving acceptance or rejection of this ordered other world.

He comes to reject it. But his struggle leaves Stephen with a deepened sense of melancholy. He has gained a penetrating sense of the depths of experience. In *Ulysses* Stephen will say that all history is a nightmare. Stephen has known what walking nightmares can be like. He is forging such a temperament that he will never be able to find interest, inspiration, scarcely even curiosity in the ghosts that Yeats sought in castles or in those spirits with whom A.E. tried to converse. His whole life, his education, his conception of an inner life, all must lead him to find literary materials different from those that could be shaped by his immediate predecessors. Inasmuch as he is to be a writer, the literary world should presumably be the one aspect of Dublin life where Joyce might find communion of spirit. But this analysis should

---

3. FARRELL'S NOTE: When the convert John Henry Newman, later to be cardinal, journeyed to Dublin to deliver his lecture "On the Scope and Nature of a University Education," he could little have dreamed that the most gifted student ever to be graduated from the university he was helping to found would be the author of *Ulysses* and *Finnegans Wake*.

show how he was gravitating toward a break with this literary world, as with all else in Dublin. The developing young artist is one who will be able to feel creatively free only if he directs his eyes toward the future and if he seeks a loveliness not yet born rather than one born centuries ago in Celtic Ireland.

Stephen is the homeless genius. He needs to expand, to feel free. He needs an arena adequate for his talents. He sees no future for himself unless he rebels, rejects. And beyond this Dublin, with its misery, its poverty, its Georgian houses, its sleek patricians, its English rulers, are the cities of the world. Beyond this Ireland, poor and culturally deprived, is the culture of the world. He has felt himself from early boyhood to be different and marked for a special destiny. He cannot and will not participate in politics; he cannot follow the literary men who are making a stir in Dublin. Where can he find a career open for his talents? His feeling of need for expansion and freedom is acute. Are not feelings such as these the kind that were generalized in Ireland's national aspirations? The problems he faces, the needs he feels with the vision of genius, others have felt, and they have fled. Before him Ireland has had millions of her wild-geese sons and daughters. Stephen knows all this. He knows how some have died of starvation; he knows how Tone and Emmet died; and he knows how many have died spiritually.

In terms of all these conditions Stephen's soul is being born. Wherever he turns he sees "nets flung at it to hold it back from flight." But he will be free. The homeless Irishman in Ireland, the homeless genius in the world, he will fly off like Icarus, onward and upward. Proudly rebellious, he has proclaimed: "I will not serve." Instead of the vocation he could not find as a priest, he will find it in service as a "priest of the eternal imagination." Creating without fetters, he will "forge in the smithy of my soul the uncreated conscience of my race." One of Ireland's most brilliant wild geese has found the wings with which he can fly away.

In the section above I discussed James Joyce's *A Portrait of the Artist as a Young Man* in relation to my interpretation of some aspects of its Irish setting and historical background. While I consider it important to see the novel placed in this setting, I think it must also be remembered that it belongs not only in modern Irish literature but also in the tradition of the European novel. The *Portrait* presents, in the character of Stephen, an image of the artist. The story depicts the growth of the artist from early childhood to the time in his young manhood when he realizes that his destiny is to be one of dedication to art. In many parts of the narrative the very style in which it is written has direct bearing on the theme. Stephen, feeling so fettered in his native land, sees in art his avenue of escape to freedom.

Joyce's conception of art is *"fin de siècle."* The influence of Pater on Joyce has often been remarked; Pater's view of aesthetics is certainly akin to the attitude toward art which Stephen adopts. In fact, Pater's novel *Marius the Epicurean* seems to be directly related to the *Portrait.* Marius, like Stephen, is being groomed for a life of dedication to an aesthetic ideal. Today, when one rereads the *Portrait,* its purple passages seem functional to the content. The prose of *Dubliners,* written before the *Portrait,* is more naturalistic, fresher, simpler; Joyce seems consciously to have adapted his style to his subject matter.

Herbert Gorman, in his biography *James Joyce,* quotes passages from Joyce's early critical writings. From these, and most especially from his essay on Mangan, it is clear that the young Joyce clothed his ideas on literature in a language strongly resembling that of Pater. He also used many images, concepts, and words traditionally considered poetic. When Stephen sees birds in flight, they are described as circling "about a temple of air." When Stephen composes a villanelle, he thinks of the words he has used as "liquid letters of speech. . . ." Poetic words are used consciously and continually. Stephen is, as Joyce was always to be, a word poet, interested in the sounds of words as much as in their meanings.

His language suggests some of Stephen's tastes as much as do any overt remarks concerning literary likes and dislikes. Stephen is something of a dandified aesthete of the age. We perceive this even in some of the languorous phrases that reveal his feelings. But at the same time this languor is altered by his genius, his temperament, his burden of pain, his reactions to the problems he faces. He rebels with an anger, a determination, a capacity for resentment that show him to be a more forceful, a stronger, character than, for example, Pater's Marius.

While rebellious in spirit, Stephen is strongly respectful of traditions. He does not set out to break with the best traditions of European culture; on the contrary, he finds the premises for his aesthetic ideas in the writings of Aristotle and Aquinas. As I pointed out above, Stephen strongly resents the thinness of Irish culture. He wants a rich culture, a great tradition. When he is set to fly off, he is going to rise not merely from the physical earth of Ireland but also from the cultural earth of western Europe.

His conversations, his reflections, indicate that he has already read copiously and that he has learned to assimilate and to use what he has read and to form his own judgments. Using premises from Aristotle and Aquinas, Stephen argues that art effects a purgation in the human consciousness. It cleanses it of all desire, all loathing, all hatred, all "kinetic" emotions. When one is so cleansed one is elevated and experiences an "ideal pity and terror," an emotional stasis. The *Portrait* itself is organized on the basis of Stephen's aesthetic theory by his successive rejections of a vocation, of family, religion, race, nation. Stephen himself discovers his destiny through a series of spiritual purgations which prepare him to come to art in a spirit of priestly dedication; in fact, he compares the artist to the priest.

Joyce's realism here is a realism of the mind, of the consciousness. Stephen's life is described in a highly concentrated and selective manner, deriving from this point of view. His own mind serves as the frame of reference for the story. Many events of his life are revealed to the reader only after they have been assimilated into Stephen's consciousness and he has stamped his own evaluation upon them. In this way the theme of the novel is developed by a mirroring of successive stages in the hero's changing consciousness. In addition, not only a formal theory of aesthetics is embodied in the narrative but also an act of creation. Stephen shapes his experiences in love into a villanelle, written in the style of Joyce's early poetry. The hero is thus portrayed growing up, creating a poem, and formally stating his ideas on art. The inner life of the artist is what is significant. Whether or not one may feel that some of the writing is dated, the style, the perspective, the organization of the novel all seem to harmonize beautifully with its content.

The *Portrait* is widely regarded as one of the major modern novels dealing with adolescence and youth. But this view calls for qualifications. Almost from childhood, Stephen is an exceptional character. He is separated from others.. He is aloof, lonely, different. His childhood is not a normal one in which he shares the common experiences of give-and-take among boys. He seldom participates in games; he is bookish, introspective. By the time he has become a university student his mind is monkish, cloistered, and he regards it as such. Not only is he superior to his environment, his companions, the members of his own family; he feels he is superior. At the same time he is, until his loss of faith, more tractable than the other boys. His religious faith is deeper than theirs. His pride, his isolation, and his difference from others are marked even in his religious emotions. He can perform spiritual exercises, but he cannot really feel a sense of communion with others.

At an opposite pole, he sins alone. He goes to brothels not in a group but by himself. Instead of discussing his sins with others—something so many youths do—he embroiders them with languorous and conventionally poetic thoughts. He exists on a higher level of consciousness than do others of his own age. He does not have real friendships. He reveals his intellectual domination in one-sided conversations.

Stephen's temperament is further revealed by the way in which we see him suffer. A great deal of his suffering is described not in terms of its immediate impact but through thoughts and images which reflect the assimilation of his experiences. His greatest torments come from images, images of the tortures of the damned in Hell. His pangs of rejected adolescent love, his feelings of shame and humiliation, are reproduced principally in this manner. Thus the *Portrait* typifies a major strain in Joyce's writing.

Stephen is not only different from his own peers, he is different from many of the young heroes of nineteenth-century fiction, for instance, the youths of Tolstoy. No matter how superior a Tolstoyan young man may be, he generally goes through the normal experiences of his generation and of his circle. He is not socially alienated; he does what others do, shares experiences, and participates in the social life of his class and group. His sensibility may mark him as superior to his comrades, but it does not set him apart from them as Stephen is set apart. But, although he is so different, Stephen is a young man who rises out of the tradition of nineteenth-century European literature.

It has often been remarked that in nineteenth-century European fiction the figure of the young man is used to dramatize the problems of the individual set against society and thereby of the moral, psychological, and personal consequences of the historic phenomenon known as individualism. Early in the century we see the young man—for instance, Julien Sorel of *The Red and the Black,* or Balzac's Lucien and Rastignac—seeking glory and fame. Their aim is success, and the plane of action is the objective one of society. In the Russian novel—Pierre of *War and Peace,* Levin of *Anna Karenina,* Bazarov of *Fathers and Sons,* and Dostoevski's Raskolnikov and Ivan Karamazov—there is a shift of emphasis. These young men probe for the meaning of life; they seek to harmonize their words and their deeds. And there is still another change of emphasis. We see the young man seeking freedom in the realm of feeling. This is the object of Frederic Moreau in *A Sentimental Education* —and of Des Esseintes (in a purely decadent fashion) in Huysmans' *Against the Grain.* Marius and Stephen are both of this line; they, too, seek freedom in the realm of feeling and of culture.

This brief outline reveals the evolving conditions of life in the nineteenth century. The character of public life changes and decreases the opportunities to be free. The idea of culture (as the realm of freedom) begins to grow. Thus, the logic of art for art's sake. The artist, crushed by the weight of contemporary culture, adopts the attitude that art is its own end, becomes the rebel artist. As the rebel, he gives expression to a profound despair, one that questions the whole moral sensibility of the times.

Such is the despair of a Flaubert, a Rimbaud, a Baudelaire. Stephen is the artist as rebel, questioning the whole moral sensibility of his age. The image of the artist he represents is that of a melancholy but sovereign creator who rises above his time and his own weakness and gazes down at the turgidly flowing river of time, seeking to construct, to mold, to fix what he sees in beauty and in sadness.

Further, Stephen's ideas of art for art's sake are purposeful ones. In artistic creation he will not only become an unfettered soul, he will also create with a loyalty to a superpersonal ideal of the truth. He will try to cast a shadow over the imagination of his race so that he may help it become more noble. He will strive to forge the conscience of his race, to connect all that produced him with the great streams of European culture. He dedicates himself with pledges of high purpose and without fears. And he says: "I do not fear to be alone or spurned for another or to leave whatever I have to leave. And I am not afraid to make a mistake, even a great mistake, a lifelong mistake and perhaps as long as eternity."

It would be pointless to try to discuss Joyce's later writing here, in a few final words. *Ulysses* is one of the literary masterpieces of this century, and the impression it has left on world literature promises to be felt for decades to come. And concerning *Finnegans Wake,* which I have made only preliminary efforts to study, on the basis of even these attempts I can say that I disagree with those who attack and denounce it. No writer has ever made such a bold attempt to penetrate the depth and density of man's unconscious mind. Today, on the whole, man stands in fear of his unconscious mind. But this will not always be so. Man will yet conquer his own unconscious mind as he will society, and, when that day comes, all art will be different. I believe that, for a new and future art of the fully free man, *Finnegans Wake,* with all its obscurity, may well be considered to have been one of the important books of this age. In any case it can be said in conclusion that in his later creative life James Joyce kept Stephen's pledge of dedication. He remains in literature a living inspiration not only because of his great constructive genius but also because of the living force of his example, his tireless labor, despite his failing eyesight, on major projects, his intensely creative activity, his dignity, and his artistic daring. Great as is his influence upon the technique of his art, that of his very example is likely to be equally important for writers of the future.

POSTSCRIPT ON *STEPHEN HERO*

The foregoing essay was written before the publication of *Stephen Hero*,[4] a fragment of the first draft of *A Portrait of the Artist as a Young Man*. Needless to say, it would be pointless to judge this fragment as one might a finished work. But it is of incalculable value for all students of Joyce.

I have already suggested that in the *Portrait* Joyce's realism was of the mind, of the consciousness. *Stephen Hero* is written in the traditional "realistic" or "naturalistic" manner. It contains many indications of the later *Portrait* but is different stylistically and in terms of the perspective from which it is written. The material is presented as though from the standpoint of an impartial observer looking at the characters. Whereas in the *Portrait* Joyce was intensely and specially selective, in the earlier draft he seems to have been concerned with presenting details more copiously. *Stephen Hero* contains many details of life in Dublin which were omitted from the *Portrait*. The chapters in this fragment are organized in terms of generalized statements, descriptions, accounts of what happened, and analyses of Stephen and of other characters, and, interlarded with these, there are short scenes in which dialogue between various characters is set down. These short scenes are usually illustrative of the generalized narrative which makes up the greater portion of the fragment.

It has been noted that the *Portrait* is organized in terms of a series of catharses or purgations, which reveal Stephen rejecting the emotional ties and the values which interfere with his line of development as the young man becoming a priestly artist. The *Portrait* should be interpreted as a novel presenting a concept of aesthetics and of the artist, one which has historical roots. *Stephen Hero* also reveals Stephen to us as the youth whose artistic disposition is being forged. But in these pages he appears more clearly as the struggling adolescent. The emphases in the two versions are, thus, decidedly different. At the same time, I would add that I have found nothing in *Stephen Hero* which I would consider as demanding any change in my interpretation of the *Portrait*.

Stephen Hero shows Stephen as less set off from others than he is in the *Portrait*. For instance, there is more give-and-take in the discussions between Stephen and Cranly, and the latter is more independently characterized. There is also a close relationship between Stephen and his

---

4. James Joyce, *Stephen Hero, A Part of the First Draft of "A Portrait of the Artist as a Young Man,"* ed. Theodore Spencer (New York: New Directions, 1944).

brother Maurice. The two brothers look toward life with eager and curious young eyes; they take long walks together, and they have serious discussions. The subjects of these discussions are determined by Stephen's interests—as are those of the discussions with classmates in the *Portrait*. When Maurice's vision or ideas are insufficient, he adapts himself to those of his brother. Stephen is intellectually dominant in this relationship, as he is in his association with Cranly. But he is less sure of himself than in the *Portrait*. He is more open to self-doubt, and he is more heedful of what others say in discussion.

The Dedalus family receives more attention in *Stephen Hero* than it does in the *Portrait*. Mrs. Dedalus is characterized, and her relationship with her son is sufficiently developed so that she emerges in her own right as an independent characterization, one living in an aura of pathos and frustration. In my essay "Joyce and Ibsen" I allude to the conversation, between Stephen and his mother, in which Ibsen's work figures.[5] Here, Mrs. Dedalus confesses that she once read books and had more interest in life than she now has as the aging mother of a large family. She is deeply touched by Ibsen's work but cannot fully and honestly express her emotions. She hides behind generalizations and evasions. Her fate offers young Stephen proof to confirm his admiration for Ibsen; more fundamental than this, he gains added assurance that his road of rebellion is the proper one. The tragic fate of the sick sister, Isabella, is also recounted most movingly in *Stephen Hero*. Her death brings tragedy into the Dedalus home. She "enjoyed little more than the fact of life, few or none of its privileges."[6] A similar comment could be made about Mrs. Dedalus. This would suggest one of the differences of emphasis in these two versions. Stephen is superior and aloof in the *Portrait*. His development is steady and sure. His sufferings—as we have noted—are most intense when he hears and is frightened by a sermon which vividly depicts the torments of the damned in Hell. In *Stephen Hero*, the other members of the Dedalus family can scarcely do more than enjoy the "fact" of life; Stephen's struggle is one calculated to win for himself the privileges. *Stephen Hero* is organized by setting down the fact of life and by showing Stephen as an adolescent who wants to rise above the fact to the privileges. The young Stephen of this fragment is concerned with living more fully, more naturally. In the *Portrait*, Stephen purges himself of loathings and desires in such a way as to illustrate the theory of aesthetics he enunciates toward the end of the novel; here, Stephen wants to live according to the tenets of modern and emancipated ideas.

---

5. See below, pp. 62–63.
6. Joyce, *Stephen Hero*, p. 165.

His guiding conception in the *Portrait* is (let me repeat) that of the artist as the priest of the eternal imagination; in the earlier draft, his ideal is that of the natural man who determines to live a full life according to his instincts. He views the poet as "the intense centre of the life of his age."[7] The poet "alone is capable of absorbing in himself the life that surrounds him and of flinging it abroad again amid planetary music."[8] And he concludes that no one serves the generation into which he has been born so well as the person who, in life or in art, offers "the gift of certitude."[9] This gift is one of affirmation. But certitude to Stephen means an affirmation of the whole natural life of man; certitude in the *Portrait* is more refined. This refinement is to be seen in the parallel between Stephen's experiences as he forges his disposition as an artist and the Aristotelian theory he offers as an expression of his aims and his ideals. In the *Portrait,* Stephen himself is seen purging himself of desires; in *Stephen Hero,* he is more inclined to express as an aim the satisfaction of desires. The core of the adolescent nature revealed in *Stephen Hero* lies in the fact that Stephen is struggling with the priestly nature alluded to in the *Portrait.*

In *Stephen Hero,* Joyce attacked the Catholic Church more bluntly than he did in the *Portrait.* The former contains a number of explicit accusations hurled at the Church. The Church is viewed as a "plague." It stands in the way of people's winning the privileges of life: it allows them only to accommodate themselves to the fact. In consequence, it contributes toward the distortion of the human personality. That distortion is seen in the torturing and deforming of instinct. Thus the Church is described as narrow, bigoted, and intolerant. In conversation with his mother, Stephen tells her that if she were really a genuine Catholic she would burn him as well as his books. His feeling that his mother is insufficiently sympathetic to him, his anger at the failure and frustration in her own life, both become bound up with his revolt against Catholicism. And this revolt wounds his mother, who declares to him: "I little thought that it would come to this—that a child of mine would lose the faith."[10] To Stephen, Mrs. Dedalus is a living proof that the Church is a plague, denying people the privileges of life. Church and mother are thus linked together in his revolt. And in *Stephen Hero* he shows more anger than he does in the *Portrait.* This anger expresses both a feeling of sympathy for others and a disappointment in them.

---

7. Ibid., p. 80.
8. Ibid.
9. Ibid., p. 76.
10. Ibid., p. 133.

The antipathy to the father, Simon Dedalus, revealed in the *Portrait,* is also stamped on the earlier fragment. Simon is a man who "had his son's (Stephen's) distaste for responsibility without his son's courage." He hates his wife's maiden name; and his tirades at home, due to his economic decline, approach the monomaniacal. Mrs. Dedalus gives him Ibsen to read, but he is bored. This suggests the gulf between father and son. The other members of this family fade out of Joyce's later works. But, as we know, Joyce characterized Simon Dedalus in both the *Portrait* and *Ulysses.* The father-son theme in Joyce's work has, however, been commented on so often that we need not go into detail here. Suffice it to say that Simon Dedalus, the father, can stand as representative of the quality of men in Ireland. The gifted son, in rejecting his father, expresses his attitude concerning the quality of Irishmen; he finds, in place of the father, the apersonalized father image of Ibsen. Here we can see a perhaps unconscious symbolism. Simon Dedalus represents Ireland. Ibsen represents the escape from Ireland, the great continental tradition, and the ideal of freedom, emancipation, and self-expression. The bold thinker is described by Stephen in this fragment as the "irredentist."[11] Stephen's "irredentism" is expressed on the family plane as well as on those of society, of art, and of ideas. And, to extend the symbolism, the mother represents the Church. The revolt against nationalism involves the father; the revolt against Church involves the mother. And outlines of these revolts are laid down in *Stephen Hero.*

At the same time, Stephen has a penchant for scholasticism. Whereas he sees the Church in Ireland as a fetter, he regards Aquinas as a thinker who will aid him to gain intellectual clarity. His use of Aquinas as a source of aesthetic premises is presented in *Stephen Hero* and is more fully and clearly revealed in the *Portrait.*

In the treatment of Aquinas, as in everything else, we can see that these two versions dateline different stages of Joyce's own development. The *Portrait* is the mature revelation of the conclusions which are being hammered out in the adolescent period of *Stephen Hero.* There is a reduction of aim from *Stephen Hero* to the *Portrait.* We have already remarked on this difference. To repeat, in *Stephen Hero,* Stephen desires to become emancipated in the Ibsenian sense of the word; in the *Portrait* he refines this ideal to that of free and priestly artistic dedication. However, this apparent reduction of aim can also be interpreted as a difference between adolescence and maturity. The *Portrait* presents, as it were, the conclusions finally drawn from the period of searchings, probings, and

---

11. Ibid., p. 170.

agonies set down in *Stephen Hero.* More important, then, than the differences in emphasis between these two versions, there is the fact of their continuity.

Stephen Hero covers the same period of time as the final sections of the *Portrait,* but the manuscript ends before Stephen reaches any resolution. It presents something of the nature of the painful burden of reality of which I have spoken in the above essay. And it might be added that in *Stephen Hero* the scenes and references to Stephen's love for Emma Clery are presented more directly than in the *Portrait.* Stephen proposes that Emma give herself to him out of wedlock, and he is rejected. He sees in her, at the same time, both physical attractiveness and middle-class conventionalism. Her body appeals to him; her mind is a product of all from which he needs to escape. His sexual proposal to her, in *Stephen Hero,* is an expression of his desire to live and of those contradictions in his nature with which he is struggling in order to become free. And here, also, we see a somewhat different Stephen from the proud young man in the last pages of the *Portrait.* Disappointment in love, rejection, are there described in a reflected manner through his consciousness; they become the source of a poem. He licks his wound, works through his disappointment, and transmutes it into an illustration of his ideal of art and poetry. His relationship with Emma Clery also involves his attitude toward cultural nationalism. *Stephen Hero* contains scenes showing the young hero with the Gaelic-language group. However, since these scenes are quite in accord with what has been written by Herbert Gorman concerning Joyce's own life during this period, we need not comment on them here.

In *Stephen Hero,* Stephen is seen as a passionate youth, finding his way in solitude and loneliness but, at the same time, being pulled from his solitude by the claims and attractions of society. At the end of the *Portrait,* he has resolved the conflict which was presented in *Stephen Hero* in a raw state. Not only stylistically but also emotionally and intellectually the relationship between these two books is the obvious one. The fragment is raw material; the *Portrait,* the finished product. We can say, along with this, that the *Portrait* describes how Stephen has developed a concept of art both as a "character armor" and as a means of channeling all the aspirations of his nature. The publication of *Stephen Hero* helps us to see the significance of this concept all the more clearly.

Joyce and Ibsen[1]

I

It is commonly known that James Joyce, in his youth, was influenced by Ibsen's plays. Formally, this influence is most clearly revealed in Joyce's play *Exiles;* in fact, *Exiles* has often been criticized as being too imitative of Ibsen. However, the influence Ibsen exerted on Joyce was more than merely formal or technical.

Joyce admired Ibsen with deep sincerity. He even learned Norwegian in order to read Ibsen in the original. And, according to Joyce's friend Frank Budgen, Ibsen was one of the very few writers whose works Joyce read completely.[2]

For Ibsen was an artist who had achieved the kind of fame and influence Joyce, as a youth, desired. Young Joyce closely identified himself with Ibsen when he was breaking with his entire past. He saw himself both as one of the younger generation for whom Ibsen had spoken and as one of Ibsen's successors. Ibsen's plays became a banner for Joyce to wave in Dublin in proud defiance. He could demand that these plays, along with works of Hauptmann and Tolstoy, be presented by the Abbey group, which had then but recently been formed; he could defend Ibsen against ignorant and malicious attacks. And he could experience a vicarious feeling of triumph in the almost universal recognition Ibsen had received in the civilized world. Ibsen, already old, had won his battle. To Joyce he was beyond criticism. He was a great and dominating figure who belonged in the bigger world existing beyond Ireland. He was one of the men who had molded a great literary tradition.

In March 1901, on the occasion of Ibsen's seventy-third birthday, Joyce addressed a letter of felicitation to him. It is admiring, youthful, and self-conscious; and it approaches the presumptuous and even the unconsciously cruel.

---

1. Reprinted from *Reflections at Fifty and Other Essays* (New York: Vanguard Press, 1954), pp. 66–96. The essay also appeared in *James Joyce: Two Decades of Criticism*, pp. 95–131, in a somewhat different form and under the title "Exiles and Ibsen."

2. Frank Budgen, *James Joyce and the Making of Ulysses* (New York: Harrison Smith and Robert Haas, 1934), p. 181.

In it Joyce wrote:

I have sounded your name defiantly through the college where it was either unknown or known faintly and darkly. I have claimed for you your rightful place in the history of the drama. I have shown what, as it seemed to me, was your highest excellence—your lofty impersonal power. . . . And when I spoke of you in debating societies and so forth, I enforced attention by no futile ranting.[3]

In the same letter Joyce wrote of "what bound me closest to you":

What I could discern dimly of your life was my pride to see, how your battle inspired me—not the obvious material battles but those that were fought and won behind your forehead, how your wilful resolution to wrest the secret from life gave me heart and how in your absolute indifference to public canons of art, friends and shibboleths you walked in the light of your inward heroism.[4]

At the time, Joyce had already come through his own first inward battles. He had rejected religion; he had launched forth against "the rabblement"; he had asserted his views and his determination to be independent. This independence was seen in terms of an escape from Ireland —escape on the intimate and personal level, escape on the level of social restraints and sanctions, escape on the level of ideas and aspirations. He would move into the great stream of European culture.

Joyce's letter reveals lack of taste. For he also wrote to Ibsen:

Your work on earth draws to a close and you are near the silence. It is growing dark for you. . . . As one of the young generation for whom you have spoken I give you greeting—not humbly, because I am obscure and you in the glare, not sadly, because you are an old man and I a young man, not presumptuously nor sentimentally—but joyfully, with hope and with love.[5]

This letter is somewhat different from other expressions concerning Ibsen which Joyce wrote in the same general period of his youth. In *Stephen Hero,* for example, there is a poignant scene between Stephen and his mother in which Ibsen's work figures. This scene occurs in a chapter which reveals young Stephen in the process of developing and writing out his own conceptions of art. Stephen "was persuaded that no-one served the generation into which he had been born so well as he who offered it, whether in his art or in his life, the gift of certitude."[6] He was

---

3. Quoted in Herbert Gorman, *James Joyce* (New York: Rinehart & Co., 1939), p. 70.
4. Ibid.
5. Ibid.
6. James Joyce, *Stephen Hero, A Part of the First Draft of "A Portrait of the Artist as a Young Man,"* ed. Theodore Spencer (New York: New Directions, 1944), p. 76; the scene with Stephen and his mother is on pp. 84–88.

dubious concerning the claims of the patriots. His predilection was for the premises of the scholastics. Saturating himself in the life around him, Stephen was also intensely absorbed in himself. According to Herbert Gorman, Joyce, in the early 1900s, sent to William Archer a play which he had dedicated to his own soul. Stephen, in this manuscript, is of the belief that "the poet is the intense centre of the life of his age to which he stands in a relation than which none can be more vital."[7] Stephen's self-absorption can be seen as related to the conviction that he is preparing himself to have a *vital* relationship with the life of his own times. And he feels a need for intelligent sympathy. This is one of the motives impelling him in a state of agitation to give his essay to his mother to read.

After Mrs. Dedalus has read the essay, she speaks of Stephen's idol, Ibsen. Then she remarks that Ibsen must be a great writer. Stephen asks if she wants to read the plays. She tells Stephen that before her marriage she had read a great deal and had taken an interest in plays.

"—But since you married neither of you so much as bought a single book,"[8] Stephen says.

The mother also says: "—Of course life isn't what I used to think it was when I was a young girl. That's why I would like to read some great writer to see what ideal of life he has. . . ."[9]

After reading Ibsen, she tells Stephen that Ibsen is a wonderful writer. Stephen asks if she thinks the plays immoral. She replies that Ibsen treats of subjects of which she knows little; she doesn't know if it is or isn't entirely good for people to be ignorant of these subjects, but she thinks knowledge of them might do harm to some "uneducated unbalanced people." She begins to speak then of Stephen. He sidetracks her by asking if she thinks the plays are unfit for people to read. To Stephen, her reply is merely "well-worn generality." But Mrs. Dedalus gives some of Ibsen's plays to her husband to read. He selects *The League of Youth* with the hope that it will remind him of his own youthful roisterings. He abandons reading the play because it is too tedious. From neither of his parents does Stephen get allegiance.

Not only had Joyce read much of Ibsen and become familiar with the controversies that had raged around him, but we can also assume that he had some familiarity with the story of Ibsen's life as it was publicly known at the time. There are some interesting if general parallels in the lives of Ibsen and Joyce. One cannot be sure that Joyce consciously recognized these parallels or that he was, accordingly,

7. Ibid., p. 80.
8. Ibid., p. 85.
9. Ibid.

motivated by them. But the parallels are, in any case, highly suggestive.

Ibsen, like Joyce, grew up in a small country not directly involved in the main streams of European culture. He, also, lived his early life in a setting of provincialism and cultural backwardness. Just as the English shadow hung over Irish culture in Joyce's youth, so did the Danish shadow hang over Norwegian culture in Ibsen's youth. Ibsen, like Joyce, faced the problem of being an artist in such a country. The course of Ibsen's development demanded, as did that of Joyce's, that he burst all the bonds which threatened to confine him.

For many years Ibsen was a voluntary exile, as Joyce was later to be. During this exile Ibsen was bitter concerning the lives and conduct of his own countrymen. This bitterness was bound up with a feeling of national disappointment. In Joyce's case, this great national disappointment was the fall of Parnell. In Ibsen's life the disappointment was the failure of the Norwegians to join with Denmark when that country was attacked by Prussia. Joyce, like Ibsen before him, believed his own countrymen had lacked manliness. Spending years in his self-imposed exile, he maintained a firmly independent attitude.

In Joyce's early days, Ireland was beginning to express afresh desires for cultural autonomy. Irish culture was saturated with national ideas. Norway, during Ibsen's youth, also began to develop national cultural ideas, and Ibsen, at one stage of his career, played a role in this upsurge. Both Joyce and Ibsen rejected nationalist cultural premises, substituting for them broader European premises and concepts. The young Joyce thus described Ireland as an "afterthought of Europe."[10] Georg Brandes, the Continental critic who perhaps understood Ibsen best in his own lifetime and who was most sympathetic to him, wrote in *Creative Spirits of the Nineteenth Century:* "He [Ibsen] has . . . no consciousness of being the child of a people, a part of the whole, the leader of a group, a member of society. . . ."[11] Brandes also quoted from a letter of Ibsen expressing the latter's disappointment with the conduct of his countrymen during the Schleswig-Holstein war. Ibsen wrote Brandes: "We should have been brought into the movement, should have belonged to Europe. Anything in preference to remaining isolated."[12] And in a speech to students in Christiania, delivered in 1874, Ibsen declared: "A poet belongs by nature to the race of the long-sighted. Never have I seen

---

10. Ibid., p. 135.
11. Georg Brandes, *Creative Spirits of the Nineteenth Century* (New York: T. Y. Crowell Co., 1923), p. 357.
12. Ibid., pp. 316–17.

home, and the living life of home, so distinctly, so circumstantially, and so closely, as from a distance and in absence."[13] Independence and dissatisfaction—a dissatisfaction both on the personal level and on that of ideas—are here bound up with the rejection of nationalism and the looking outward to Europe.

II

Joyce's early article "Ibsen's New Drama" deals principally with *When We Dead Awaken*, although it contains references to other Ibsen plays and expresses a general admiration and enthusiasm for Ibsen's work. After outlining the plot of *When We Dead Awaken*, Joyce comments:

> Ibsen's plays do not depend for their interest on the action, or on the incidents. Even the characters, faultlessly drawn though they be, are not the first thing in his plays. But the naked drama—either the perception of a great truth, or the opening up of a great question, or a great conflict which is almost independent of the conflicting actors, and has been and is of far-reaching importance—this is what primarily rivets our attention. Ibsen has chosen average lives in their uncompromising truth for the groundwork of all his later plays.[14]

He sees the key to the play in the following words of the character Irene:

> I was dead for many years. They came and bound me—laced my arms behind my back—. Then they lowered me into a grave-vault, with iron bars before the loop-hole. And with padded walls—so that no one on the earth above could hear the grave-shrieks—. But now I am beginning, in a way, to rise from the dead.[15]

This can be connected with the following lines, also spoken by Irene:

> I should have borne children into the world—many children—real children —not such children as are hiding away in grave-vaults. That was my vocation. I ought never to have served you—poet.[16]

Joyce comments on these latter lines as follows:

---

13. *Letters of Henrik Ibsen*, trans. John Nilsen Laurvik and Mary Morison (New York: Fox, Duffield & Co., 1905), p. 27.

14. James A. Joyce, "Ibsen's New Drama," *The Fortnightly Review*, April 1900, p. 586.

15. *The Collected Works of Henrik Ibsen*, 12 vols. (New York: Scribner's, 1924), 11: 367–68.

16. Ibid., p. 419.

The thought that she [Irene] had given up herself, her whole life, at the bidding of his false art, rankles in her heart with a terrible persistence.[17]

The large problem treated by Ibsen, we can deduce, is one concerning the relationship of life to art, and this involves guilt in the love relationships of men and women. Selecting these particular lines as the keynote of *When We Dead Awaken,* Joyce would suggest that he accepted the idea of creativity and freedom as being central to the play. Irene's heart rankles because she has been "used" by the artist for the sake of art. But Joyce does not really attempt an interpretation of the play. He remarks that Ibsen's "analytic method is made use of to the fullest extent, and into the comparatively short space of two days the life in life of all his characters is compressed."[18] He adds that in the conversation of Rubek with Irene

> there is involved an all-embracing philosophy, a deep sympathy with the cross-purposes and contradictions of life, as they may be reconcilable with a hopeful awakening—when the manifold travail of our poor humanity may have a glorious issue.[19]

Joyce emphasized a note of hopefulness in his essay. *When We Dead Awaken* does not end with any hope for Rubek and Irene, although Maia goes off singing of her freedom. Rubek is not hopeful. Rubek and his model, Irene, awaken to life too late. Thus, Joyce's emphasis suggests, as did the letter, his own youthful hope and ambition.

Joyce also declared in his essay that "it is doubtful if any good purpose can be served by attempting to criticize"[20] *When We Dead Awaken.* For "Henrik Ibsen is one of the world's great men before whom criticism can make but feeble show."[21] And:

> Appreciation, hearkening, is the only true criticism. . . . When the art of the dramatist is perfect the critic is superfluous. Life is not to be criticized, but to be faced and lived.[22]

Here Joyce again states an attitude similar to one expressed in *Stephen Hero:* "The poet is the intense centre of the life of his age. . . ."[23] Ibsen, one of the world's great artists, has revealed life in its intensity in a drama which, the young Joyce thought, did not contain one superfluous word. Art, when it is such an intense and perfect expression of life,

---

17. "Ibsen's New Drama," p. 583.
18. Ibid., p. 576.
19. Quoted in Gorman, *James Joyce,* p. 67.
20. Ibid.
21. Ibid.
22. Ibid.
23. Joyce, *Stephen Hero,* p. 80.

becomes life itself. It should be appreciated, lived, hearkened to, not criticized. Joyce here reveals himself as the artist. At this time he was highly critical of the Irish writers of the renaissance, and, in contrast to them, he would cite such European writers as Ibsen, Turgenev, Tolstoy, Hauptmann, and Flaubert. His concept of art as the most intense form of life was satisfied by the masters of Continental literature. Ibsen was one of these masters.

Joyce did not see Ibsen in a national, or a Norwegian, setting. In Joyce's eyes, Ibsen wrote about life itself, not merely about life in Norway. This approach, this absence of nationalistic or localistic emphasis in his critical piece, is meaningful. For at the time the Dublin literary scene was highly exciting. The seeds of Sinn Fein had already been planted. Many were studying Gaelic, and even Joyce had taken a few lessons. But in *Stephen Hero* Stephen insists that the artist cannot give patriotic allegiance. And in his essay "The Day of the Rabblement," Joyce wrote:

> The Irish Literary Theatre must now be considered the property of the rabblement of the most belated race in Europe. . . . The censorship is powerless in Dublin, and the directors could have produced "Ghosts" or "The Dominion of Darkness" if they chose. . . . A nation which never advanced so far as a miracle play affords no literary model to the artist, and he must look abroad.[24]

To him, "the new impulse" in Ireland "has no kind of relation to the future of art."

Joyce, in this same essay, tried to define his own position. He wrote:

> If an artist courts the favor of the multitude he cannot escape the consequences of its fetichism and deliberate self-deception, and if he joins in a popular movement he does so at his own risk.[25]

Until the artist has

> freed himself from the mean influences about him—sodden enthusiasm and clever insinuation and every flattering influence of vanity and low ambition—no man is an artist at all.[26]

Briefly, the artist must not allow himself to fall into any kind of bondage. And there are examples of such artists. For:

> Elsewhere there are men who are worthy to carry on the tradition of the old master who is dying in Christiania. He has already found his successor

---

24. Quoted in Gorman, *James Joyce*, p. 72.
25. Ibid., p. 73.
26. Ibid.

in the writer of "Michael Kramer," and the third minister [we must assume that this is Joyce himself] will not be found wanting when the time comes. Even now that hour may be standing by the door.[27]

This is dated October 15, 1901.

In his youth, Ibsen had been democratic. He had been intensely excited by the events of 1848. The decline of revolutionary fervor, the failure of 1848, played a significant role in his career. The realistic plays of his latter period were, at least partly, motivated by a disillusionment with politics. They are related to the general course of politics in Continental Europe during Ibsen's lifetime. Although Ibsen was not a propagandist, his plays were critical of many aspects of the life of his times. He exposed the character of the *petite bourgeoisie* and the *bourgeoisie,* and his dramas were interpreted politically by others. His emphasis on independence became a dominant note; it is clearly registered in the final scene of *An Enemy of the People.* Dr. Stockmann, a character who bears a definite resemblance to Ibsen himself, declares, "The strongest man in the world is he who stands most alone."[28] Ibsen's disillusionment is not a matter of mere guess or deduction. In a letter to Brandes, written from Dresden on December 20, 1870, he wrote:

> The great events of the day occupy my thoughts much at present. The old, illusory France has collapsed: and as soon as the new, real Prussia does the same, we shall be with one bound in a new age. How ideas will come tumbling down about our ears! And it is high time they did. Up till now we have been living on nothing but the crumbs from the revolutionary table of the last century, a food out of which all nutriment has long been chewed. The old terms require to have a new meaning infused into them. Liberty, equality, and fraternity are no longer the things they were in the days of the late-lamented guillotine. This is what the politicians will not understand; and therefore I hate them. They want only their own special revolutions—revolutions in externals, in politics, etc. But all this is mere trifling. What is all-important is the revolution of the spirit of man.[29]

When Dr. Stockmann declares that "the strongest man in the world is he who stands most alone," he is suggesting the same thought. Here is the "inward heroism" that attracted Joyce to Ibsen. Ibsen's attitude can be described as one strongly asserting the individuality of a proud man. There were similar traits in Joyce's own character. The story of the forging of Stephen's disposition as an artist, as told in *A Portrait of the Artist as a Young Man* and additionally illuminated by the material of *Stephen Hero,* shows him developing as an artist of intense and uncompromising individuality.

---

27. Ibid. *Michael Cramer* was a play written by Gerhart Hauptmann.
28. *Collected Works of Ibsen,* 8:188.
29. *Letters of Ibsen,* p. 205.

It is clear that the proud and rugged character of Ibsen drew the young Joyce to him. The parallels in their experiences undoubtedly were important here, although we have no means of defining this importance precisely. The similarities in the problems which both Joyce and Ibsen faced called forth a strong expression of similar traits of character. Ibsen's pride and independence helped him to break away from the fetters of localism and of a binding nationalism. Joyce had already gained a clear idea of what he must escape from in order to achieve his destiny as an artist. It should, therefore, be easy to understand why Ibsen exerted such a magnetic attraction on him.

III

What does Ibsen's "naked drama" really involve?[30]

In Ibsen's plays, there is a symbolization of nature, of air and sun and mountains, which signifies freedom. (Joyce observes this but does not evaluate it. He points out that some of Ibsen's earlier plays—*Ghosts*, for example, and *The Doll's House*—are set inside rooms. The last scene of *The Master Builder* occurs outside, in the open air. And, as Joyce noted, all of *When We Dead Awaken* occurs out-of-doors.) Oswald, for instance, in *Ghosts*, speaks of the sun. John Gabriel Borkman goes up into the mountains. Solness falls climbing to the high tower where he is to put a wreath for Hilda Wrangel. And Rubek and Irene, the awakened dead who have not lived and loved as they might, climb to the mountain heights in the face of the storm: They climb in order to live. One of Ibsen's central emphases or motives is the desire for happiness, symbolized by the desire for the mountains, for the air and the sun.

The reason for the lack of happiness in Ibsen's world is to be found in life itself, life subject to laws of determination. There are strong suggestions of heredity in the plots of his plays. Heredity, the ghosts of the past forever recurring to become a troubling source of conscience and of guilt—these are the factors which turn humanity's dreams of happiness into mere metaphors; the gales, the sun, the mountain heights, and the pure clean air become sad symbols of yearning.

Ibsen as a playwright was pursuing an image of the truth; the role of the truth in human relationships was one of his themes. Lies, broken words, broken contracts affect the new generation. The truth is necessary for freedom. And yet it does not always make men free, or happy.

---

30. "Ibsen's New Drama," p. 586.

Thus, in *The Wild Duck,* Gregers Werle, the perpetual thirteenth man at the table, insists on telling the truth to characters who cannot assimilate and bear it. Picturing the lives of men and women in their personal relationships, Ibsen showed how they were sometimes broken because they did not know the truth, and how, on other occasions, knowledge of the truth was an integral factor in their tragedies. The ideal is not real. The realist of the later plays is negating some of the hopes of the earlier romanticist. Truth and freedom are component parts of this ideal which, in the end, becomes only a metaphor of desire. There is a deep pathos in the disillusioning aspects of Ibsen's later plays. And involved in the incapacity of people to be happy there is also the factor of age. Solness, the master builder, and Rubek, the sculptor, two of Ibsen's last major characters, are middle-aged. They have not found satisfaction in their work. Solness also hates and fears youth.

Creating his own world, Ibsen projected his own psychological life cycle. The note of disillusionment becomes more emphatic in his last periods than it is in any of his earlier plays.

But Joyce, in his youth, did not share this disillusion. He knew that he had his own destiny to fulfill. The disillusioning features of plays like *When We Dead Awaken* and *The Master Builder* did not weaken Joyce's own enthusiasm. The full example of Ibsen's life and work served to give him an added determination to fulfill himself as an artist. Even when he was the "dying master in Christiania," Ibsen's example carried a message of youth and moral courage to Ireland's most gifted literary young man.

IV

Joyce's play *Exiles,* written in 1914, has been criticized more than have his other writings, with the possible exception of *Finnegans Wake.* Many admirers of Joyce's work speak of this play with reservations. Dramatic critics and other theatrical persons have frequently asserted that it will not "play." It is at least obvious, however, that *Exiles,* if played at all, could be presented only to a highly alert and sensitive audience.

The relationship of *Exiles* to Ibsen's dramas is also a commonplace in the commentaries on Joyce. Joyce's description of the "naked drama" in Ibsen can be applied to *Exiles.* The great question which *Exiles* purports to open up is that of human freedom and human dignity; in this instance, in a marital relationship.

The major character of *Exiles* is Richard Rowan, an Irish writer who has returned to Dublin after living abroad for a period. I think we are justified in observing that there is some relationship between Richard Rowan and Joyce himself, although not perhaps so close a one as that between Joyce and Stephen Dedalus. Richard Rowan is a man of the same cast of personality as Joyce seems to have been. He is out of the swim of Irish life, and he has studied Aquinas. When younger, he had some roistering experiences with his friend, the journalist Robert Hand. Motivated by the desire and the determination to be a free man, he had gone abroad with Bertha, who is culturally and intellectually inferior to him. He has molded her character so that she seems to have become something of an image of what he had wanted to make of her. It would almost seem that Rowan had approached Bertha and lived with her not only as a mate and lover, but also as an artist who had re-created her very personality. The creation of art is a central, thematic motif in Joyce's writings.

Bertha and Richard have one child, Archie. Richard is not too attentive to him because he is too absorbed in himself and in his own problems. Bertha, a good wife and mother, is more or less submissive to Richard, the center of the household. Beatrice Justice, a cousin of Robert Hand and Archie's music teacher, is a rather pathetic creature. There exists between her and Richard a kind of spiritual or Platonic affinity. While he was away from Ireland, her letters had inspired him. She, more than his wife, is in his mind when he writes. She understands him better. Bertha cannot understand her husband, just as the Dedaluses could not understand their son.

Richard's old friend Robert Hand comes to see the Rowans. He is less intense, less logical, less penetrating and talented than Richard. He wants Richard to remain in Ireland and attempts to get him a job. He flirts with Bertha and tries to arrange a rendezvous with her at his cottage. In the old days, he and Richard had used this cottage for parties and for liaisons. The failure of the rendezvous, Richard's visit to this house and then his wife's, suggest the Ibsenian drama with the recurring ghosts of the past.

If this play is to be located in a tradition, it is obviously that of Ibsen. Structurally, *Exiles* bears many resemblances to Ibsen's plays. In describing Ibsen's dramas, Joyce remarked that the time is usually a short span of a day or two. The time sequence of *Exiles* is similarly short, with all the action and revelations taking place in two days. In referring to Ibsen, Joyce used the phrase "the analytic method," by which he meant that form of combined retrospective analysis and revelation ("epiphanies") whereby the characters explore the past, tell one another what they thought and why they acted as they did, and in this way reveal a past relationship which colors their present situation. This method also served Ibsen as a means of characterization. It allowed him to establish his characters and to endow them with added depth and credibility. At the same time, this analysis served as a means whereby he laid out his plot or problems. No theoretical method is of much meaning without its application, and in writing—especially, perhaps, in playwriting—application demands insight. We cannot fully explain Ibsen's penetrating insight by his method. But we can say that his method was highly valuable and useful as a means for projecting his insight.

Joyce used an Ibsenian situation, but the insight applied to this situation shows many differences from that of Ibsen.[31] The organization of *Exiles* is rather similar to that of Ibsen's plays. Joyce tried to create "naked drama," drama which reveals life itself and is, in this sense, more than mere characterization. We have written evidence this was Joyce's purpose; but a comparison of *Exiles* with Ibsen's plays would also make this obvious. The "naked drama" of men and women seeking freedom and dignity and faced, in their effort, with the pressure of social convention, is focused in the attention paid to the hero, Richard Rowan. Richard Rowan dominates the play. He is the most perceptive character in this small group. He knows more about what is going on than do any of the others. He insists on utter frankness. Bertha must know him as he is; he must know her as she is. There must be no secrets between them. Thus, the effort of Robert Hand to seduce Bertha is no secret to Richard, although Robert is not aware of Richard's knowledge.

A considerable portion of Richard's dialogue is concerned with questioning the other characters and ascertaining their motives. Within the play, Richard serves as a vehicle for the author. But he is different from Dr. Stockmann in *An Enemy of the People*. The latter goes through a

---

31. FARRELL'S NOTE: For another discussion of the relationship of Joyce and Ibsen, see "The Influence of Ibsen on Joyce," by Vivienne Koch Macleod, *PMLA* 60:3 (September 1943): 879ff. Vivienne Koch Macleod discusses *Exiles* mainly in relationship with *Brand, Peer Gynt*, and *Love's Comedy*. She points out that there was a definite parallel between Ibsen's relationship with his parents and Joyce's with his. She explains why *Exiles* is not "successful" by stating that it "involves profound issues" but that "its implications are narrowed by centering them in the fairly negligible matter of a seduction." My own analysis of *Exiles* would indicate that I do not accept this judgment. However, I would add that my own analysis, completed before I had read Miss Macleod's, is, in various details, similar to hers. Miss Macleod sees thematic similarities between Joyce and Ibsen in their treatments of "the nature of the artist as man and as citizen." I would accept this, if my own points concerning differences such as those I will make concerning Richard Rowan and Rubek are also considered. I would suggest that the interested reader see Miss Macleod's essay.

cycle of experiences which motivate and justify his final decision, expressed in the remark that "the strongest man in the world is he who stands most alone." But to Richard knowledge comes instead through verbal questioning, analysis, and moral discussion, this last partly based on his training in Aquinas. Whereas in *A Portrait of the Artist as a Young Man* Joyce utilized Aquinas as a means of presenting formal aesthetic ideas and a formal statement of Stephen's aims, here he partially relies on Aquinas in order to discuss the intimate emotional problems of men and women, to deal with these morally, and to establish and explain a concept of freedom and dignity. Of course, in Ibsen's plays, too, one character may be dominant. *Hedda Gabler* is an instance. Hedda dominates the play, and her moods and conduct control the actions of all the other characters. But Hedda does not dominate by intellectual superiority. In *The Master Builder,* Solness, the most intelligent character in the play, does not completely dominate the plot or the actions of the other characters. In fact, he is influenced by Helga Wrangel. But Richard does dominate and influence. His thoughts, desires, and determination, his inner problems, dictate the events in *Exiles.*

Joyce introduces a character who is more "subjective" than any of the leading characters of Ibsen. The present attitudes of Richard constitute the basis of the play. And these grow out of a tenuously adumbrated emotional conflict within his own nature. He wants to be free and wants his wife as free as himself. He is pushing her into accepting or rejecting the proposition of a liaison offered her by Robert Hand. He insists that he know of this, and that his friend Robert Hand know that he knows. At the same time, he is pulled and torn by jealousy. The woman he has molded, almost in the spirit and manner of an artist molding the character of a heroine in a novel or play, must now act on her own, in freedom and in frankness.

Another point of difference between Ibsen's plays and *Exiles* is to be seen in the way women are represented. In many of Ibsen's plays, woman is the victim; and the victimization of woman is tragic in the Ibsenian world. An instance is Hedda. She is really victimized because, as Ibsen stated in one of his letters, his "intention . . . was to indicate that Hedda, as a personality, is to be regarded rather as her father's daughter than as her husband's wife."[32] Her father is an unseen ghost influencing Hedda. She is living in a house that suggests her father's house. She plays with, and finally kills herself with, her father's pistols. Moreover, the yearning and need for freedom on the part of Ibsen's

---

32. *Collected Works of Ibsen,* 10: viii.

women comes from an inner impulse. Nora slams the door because she must be a human being, not her husband's doll. But the entire problem of personal freedom for Joyce's Bertha is imposed from without. And this imposition continues past the relationships between Richard and Bertha. Richard created her. He continues to mold her character during the course of the play. Truth, an integral element in the plays of Ibsen, is equally integral in *Exiles.* But it is something which concerns Richard Rowan alone. Bertha, Beatrice, and Robert Hand do not feel the same need of truth that Richard does. Whereas a character like Nora discovers the truth in spite of her husband, Richard is impelled to force truth on his wife, regardless of her own needs. He does this because he feels that he must know the truth. How Richard dominates the play so that his needs, his problems, and his concerns play a causal role in the actions of the other characters is partly to be seen in his interest in the truth. He must know what Robert Hand has said to his wife and what she has said; whether he has kissed her or not, and how he has kissed her. And he must also know whether or not she consents to a liaison. But even though Bertha will tell him, still, as he says in the third act, he "will never know. Never in this world."[33] In his last speech, Richard tells Bertha that he desires her in "restless living wounding doubt."[34] And he had longed for something else—to hold her by no bonds, not even by those of love. He had wanted to "be united" with her "in body and soul in utter nakedness."[35] But he is tired, tired by his wound. And she in turn asks him to forgive her, asks him, her "strange wild lover,"[36] to come back to her.

The emotions of the play also involve guilt. The element of guilt was integral in Ibsen's plays. Actions in the past have injured those who are living in the present. Rubek, in *When We Dead Awaken,* feels the pincers of guilt, and Irene deepens this feeling. He had killed her human, womanly love for the sake of the statue he made of her. It would seem that Joyce, in his characterization of Richard Rowan, deals with guilt at the point where Rubek left off. Richard's concern with truth—his demand to know, his stringent insistence on permitting his wife to be free —all this suggests an effort so to act in the present that he will not, when he is older (when he is middle-aged, like Rubek), be faced with an Ibsenian ghost of conscience. He does not want to make his wife's life poorer in love. When he speaks with Robert Hand about Bertha and his

---

33. James Joyce, *Exiles* (Norfolk, Conn.: New Directions, 1945), p. 139.
34. Ibid., p. 154.
35. Ibid.
36. Ibid.

own attitudes, there are references to the law of change in nature. This conversation also deals with moral fear, and Richard accuses Robert, whom he has known since boyhood, of not understanding moral fear. Richard's fear is a moral one; it is guilt. Richard tells Robert:

> She is dead. She lies on my bed. I look at her body which I betrayed— grossly and many times. And loved, too, and wept over. And I know that her body was always my loyal slave. To me, to me only she gave.[37]

At this point he breaks off, because he is unable to continue. Robert tries to give him assurance. Turning almost fiercely toward Robert, Richard declares that he is not afraid, not fearful that she has not loved him loyally. His real fear is

> that I will reproach myself then [when Bertha is dead] for having taken all for myself because I would not suffer to give to another what was hers and not mine to give, because I accepted from her her loyalty and made her life poorer in love. That is my fear. That I stand between her and any moments of life that should be hers, between her and you, between her and anyone, between her and anything.[38]

For these reasons, then, he dares not stand between Robert and Bertha. But nonetheless he does stand between them. He demands to know the truth, insisting that only if he knows will any act of his wife be free and open rather than dark and secretive.

This situation has further parallels with *When We Dead Awaken*. Rubek has killed the soul of Irene by making a cold statue of her. There is a duality in the woman Irene and the statue fashioned by Rubek. In *Exiles* there is also a duality. Bertha, Richard's wife, is also his creation. Richard tried to give his wife new life, and he tortures himself, in the presence of his friend, by declaring that he has taken "her girlhood, her laughter, her young beauty, the hopes in her young heart."[39] Further, there is the shadow of Richard's dead mother. And here is the real duality in *Exiles*—Bertha and the dead Mrs. Rowan.

In the first act, when Rowan is talking with Beatrice, she says that it is difficult to give oneself wholly and freely. Richard speaks about what he is, at the very moment, suffering. He suffers for the frustration of Miss Justice and, even more, for himself. Then, with *"bitter force,"* he cries out: "And how I pray that I may be granted again my dead mother's hardness of heart!"[40] His mother had not sent for him when

---

37. Ibid., p. 86.
38. Ibid.
39. Ibid., p. 84.
40. Ibid., p. 12.

she died. "She died alone, not having forgiven me and fortified by the rites of the church."[41] She had written a letter before her death, warning him, bidding him to "break with the past."[42] She turned aside from him and from his.

> How can my words hurt her poor body that rots in the grave? Do you not think that I did not pity her cold blighted love for me? I fought against her spirit while she lived to the bitter end.[43]

Then he presses his hands to his forehead before saying: "It fights against me still—in here [his head]."[44] And he goes on:

> She drove me away. On account of her I lived years in exile and poverty too, or near it. I never accepted the doles she sent me through the bank. I waited . . . not for her death but for some understanding of me, her own son, her own flesh and blood; that never came.[45]

He needs the spirit of this old woman, now dead—his mother. He can neither possess fully nor can he relinquish his possession. Here he is explaining the motivation for the wounded doubt to which he gives voice in the final scene. He needs the hardness of heart he saw in his mother, for it is, in his case, linked with intelligence. He is a modern man, seeking to bring the light of reason into the most intimate and complicated personal relationships. He wants to be logical about human emotions. Briefly, Richard has never resolved his emotional conflict concerning his dead mother, the "ghost" of *Exiles*. He is bitter and hurt. In his youth he was misunderstood.

We can assume that Richard's nature is akin to that of his mother. His logic and intelligence are cold. (How different this is from Dr. Stockmann's temperament and faith in truth!) In effect, Richard relates hardness of heart with rationality. This is cleverly revealed in the first act, when he thinks of his father. Talking with Beatrice, he points to a picture of his father on the wall. He asks her, "Do you see him there, smiling and handsome . . . ?"[46] He remembers the night his father died, and the man's last thoughts. Richard was then a mere boy of fourteen. The father called young Richard to the bedside, knowing that the boy wanted to go to the theater to hear *Carmen*. He told the mother to give the lad a shilling. Richard kissed his father and left. "Those were his last

---

41. Ibid., p. 13.
42. Ibid.
43. Ibid., p. 14.
44. Ibid.
45. Ibid.
46. Ibid., p. 15.

thoughts as far as I know."[47] He asks Beatrice, "Is there not something sweet and noble in it?"[48] This remark is put in the form of a question, rather than of a positive declaration, for, almost immediately after speaking these lines, he says, "No, no. Not the smiler. . . . The old mother. It is her spirit I need."[49]

Richard is his mother's son. And the "ghost" of his dead mother somehow shows up in Beatrice. There is something of the same chill in her Protestant nature that there is in Richard's Catholic nature. She cannot give herself wholly and freely. Seeing Beatrice on his return to Dublin, Richard unburdens himself of his guilts and feelings. He has returned to scenes that remind him of his mother. She was alive when he left; she is now dead. He is bitter because she did not call for him, forgive him. But the play makes it clear that by leaving Ireland he was escaping from her; he ran off in such a way as to suggest that he did not want forgiveness. Now he is bitter because he did not get what he did not want.

Richard could not speak in this fashion to Bertha, but he can to Beatrice. In the last act, Bertha tells Beatrice:

> I do not understand anything that he writes. . . . I cannot help him in any way, when I don't even understand half of what he says to me sometimes.[50]

This would suggest that the basis of the misunderstanding between Richard and Bertha is cultural. But he ran off with her rather than with Beatrice Justice, who, like Richard, is Bertha's cultural superior. And Bertha senses that there is more to the misunderstanding between Richard and herself than her lack of understanding of his ideas and his writings. In the final part of the third act, Bertha reveals this fact. She tells her husband that Beatrice is the person for listening to him, not she. Richard accuses his wife of having driven Beatrice away. Bertha answers:

> I think you have made her unhappy as you have made me and as you made your dead mother unhappy and killed her. Woman-killer! That is your name.[51]

Bertha curses the day she met Richard and calls him a stranger. Agitated, and after a burst of tears during which she has sunk to the floor, she says she is "living with a stranger."[52]

---

47. Ibid.
48. Ibid.
49. Ibid., p. 16.
50. Ibid., p. 132.
51. Ibid., p. 140.
52. Ibid., p. 141.

We can easily deduce that, culturally, Bertha is on the level of Richard's mother rather than of Beatrice, whom she describes as "everything I am not—in birth and education."[53] Also, we can justifiably assume that her nature is more maternal than was his mother's. He has taken this nature and tried to re-create it. He has put something of his own chill into it. The play makes clear that his basic image of womanhood has been given to him by his mother. The woman he has so loved and created, he now wants to set free from bondage. He is, in effect, giving her away to a lover and, at the same time, tearing himself with acute agony because he is doing so. His friend Robert Hand says to Bertha:

> He longs to be delivered . . . from every law . . . from every bond. All his life he has sought to deliver himself. Every chain but one he has broken and that one we are to break, Bertha—you and I.[54]

Here is the crux of Richard's emotional struggle. He is delivering not only Bertha but himself.

This suggests another difference between *Exiles* and *When We Dead Awaken*. Rubek's feelings and problems are integrally linked with his art. His guilt feelings are bound up with his career as an artist. He has had a different relationship with Irene from that which Richard has had with Bertha—a professional relationship. Concerned with his own aesthetic aims, he has poured his own love and humanity into his creation. He and Irene then part, and he has lost his inspiration. He has done no more work that satisfies him. He has done many portraits, and in these he has subtly made his subjects look like pigs. Moreover, he talks more of his art than Richard does. We get a clearer idea of what kind of artist Rubek is than we do in the case of Richard.

The problems Ibsen treated, not only in *When We Dead Awaken* but also in many of his other plays, are more equitably distributed among the characters than are the problems in Joyce's *Exiles*. Rubek's problems, his guilt, and his hopes are not rendered dramatically important at the expense of Irene or Maia. But in *Exiles* Richard's problems are stated at the expense of other characters: the concerns of Richard overwhelm those of the other characters. Herein lies, I believe, the real reason why so many critics have frequently expressed dissatisfaction with *Exiles* as a play. This dissatisfaction has often been voiced in the charge that Joyce has no dramatic talent. His main drama is the subjectivized, psychological drama of Richard Rowan. This subjectivized, psychological

---

53. Ibid., p. 140.
54. Ibid., p. 115–16.

drama is projected onto the other characters, and the conflict of the play itself remains unresolved, for at the end Richard is still as torn as he was at the beginning. The cultural distance between Richard and Bertha is great, and this preys upon his mind.

Richard's lack of success in his own creation is revealed as Bertha's latent bewilderment is brought into the open. With Bertha he has failed. He must remain wounded by doubt or else see his failure nakedly. He remains wounded by doubt. He is not delivered; he cannot bring deliverance to himself. He has created Bertha on the basis of his own divided soul. Here is his real wound. Bertha wants only his love. The implication is, then, that Richard is too wounded to give her the love she craves. They stand facing each other in the Dublin home to which they have returned, spiritual exiles from each other.

It would seem that Richard Rowan, trying to avoid the dangers of a sick conscience, in the end finds himself with precisely what he has sought to escape. Ibsen's denouements were more definite than this. But the difference between Ibsen and Joyce here is not merely one concerning the denouement. It is a difference in insight. Richard Rowan could not be called an Ibsenian character. This suggests that, while there are parallels between Ibsen's plays and *Exiles* in structure and in the type of situation used, there is a definite difference in inner content.

V

Edmund Gosse, in his life of Ibsen, quotes a remark of Hazlitt: "The progress of manners and knowledge has an influence on the stage, and will in time perhaps destroy both tragedy and comedy. . . . At last there will be nothing left, good nor bad, to be desired or dreaded, in the theatre or in real life."[55] Hazlitt's observation is suggestive. If anything, the progress of knowledge exerted an increasingly great influence on drama, on all art, during the nineteenth century. But Ibsen's later plays demonstrate that the theater was not killed as Hazlitt forecast. Ibsen's dramas would be unthinkable without the growth of science. The role of truth and of heredity as Ibsenian motifs show this to be the case. Ibsen's dramatic situations are those all of us could meet in our lives. Ibsen's characters exist on the same level of experience as we ourselves do. The same sort of spiritual and social catastrophes that overwhelm

---

55. Edmund Gosse, *Henrik Ibsen* (New York: Scribner's, 1917), p. 54.

some of his characters could overwhelm us. Ibsen's characters have a representative quality: they are like many people who have lived, and who still live, in the real world. To use words which have now become mere abusive terms, Ibsen's plays are realistic and naturalistic. A considerable knowledge of men and women, of characters and events, stands behind these plays.

With these facts in mind, we can attempt to indicate an additional significance to Joyce's phrase "naked drama." Ibsen's use of a method of retrospective analysis and revelation permitted him to show us people on the stage as they were engaged in the process of discovering some of the secret and mysterious meanings of their own lives. They pressed closely toward gaining a clear conception of their own aims, aspirations, and desires. In other words, their hidden impulses were brought into the open. These hidden impulses are the major source of dread, if we interpret dread to mean anxiety in the Freudian sense of the term. Through the development of what is loosely called naturalism and realism, writers have for many decades been tending to unveil the psychological mysteries of man, even to use this very process of unveiling as part of the stuff of drama. In this sense, one can say that Ibsen's plays are describable as "naked drama." And, in aim, *Exiles* is similar. It is a psychological play, concerned with stating, dramatically and realistically, the secret drives of its characters. This is done in a setting of reality.

Thus Joyce was seeking to achieve the kind of effects Ibsen did. Ibsen was concerned with creating real and plausible people, with showing them to us as they lived in a world as real as our own. It is a commonplace now to say that his ability to achieve this artistic aim was uncanny. Many critics have already commented on the marvelous integration in his plays. Character and situation are so presented that an overpowering sense of reality is established. Even though this is all readily accepted in the literature on Ibsen, I should like to illustrate Ibsen's technical capacity with one example. Regardless of all other considerations, *The Doll's House* would lose its power of sustaining any dramatic illusion if the author had not provided for the care of the children after Nora slams the door. If Nora left a home in which the children were orphaned, threatened with the danger of having no love, no security, no proper care, then audiences all over Europe would have reacted to this play with disgust. The motivation of Nora would have been destroyed. Her actions would have seemed unjustified. Ibsen did not place undue stress on the Helmer children. Casually, almost as though it were not even noticed and as though the author had never thought of this problem, the situation of the children in the Helmer home is integrated into the play. The nurse is stamped as a nurse. Thus, when Nora leaves, one doesn't think that now the children are left so orphaned as to have their lives ruined. The children do not seem to be the real victims when Nora slams the door in order to express her driving need for freedom, maturity, dignity, and individuality. Ibsen's dramas are marked by their internal consistency. Internal consistency in so-called naturalistic drama is extremely difficult to maintain, for one has fewer tricks, devices, off-stage aids at one's command. What happens must happen as though it were taking place not on a stage but in real life.

George Bernard Shaw—who, in my opinion, understood many of the salient aspects of Ibsen more clearly than a number of other critics and commentators—remarked, in *The Quintessence of Ibsenism:*

> People cannot be freed from . . . failings from without. They must free themselves. When Nora is strong enough to live out of the doll's house, she will get out of it of her own accord if the door stands open; but if before that you take her by the scruff of her neck and thrust her out, she will only take refuge in the next establishment of the kind that offers to receive her. Woman has thus two enemies to deal with: the old-fashioned one who wants to keep the door locked, and the new-fashioned one who wants to thrust her into the street before she is ready to go.[56]

Exiles, as concerned as it is with the freedom of a woman—Bertha —does not show Bertha freeing herself because she is ready; nor does it clearly show her loyally rejecting a proposal to be free—to have an extramarital relationship—because she is a free spirit and decides against taking such action. Thus, behind the theme of freedom and dignity in *Exiles* we see the factor of control, the control of another destiny. Richard Rowan is intelligent; at the same time, he is a busy-body. And it is in this fact that *Exiles* differs from Ibsen's outstanding dramas. The characterization of Richard is not of a type to carry the weight of the theme of freedom and dignity. Richard really destroys some of the dramatic intensity of the play. The Ibsenian bones of *Exiles* are more apparent than is the Ibsenian spirit.

As Shaw demonstrated with admirable clarity in *The Quintessence of Ibsenism,* Ibsen's plays imply an attitude of moral relativity. The theme of *Exiles* also implies moral relativity. But the main character, who gives expression to this theme, is prevented by his nature from practicing moral relativity. His ideals of freedom are incompatible with those elements of his character which stamp him as his mother's son. And the

---

56. George Bernard Shaw, *The Quintessence of Ibsenism* (New York: Dodd, Mead & Co., 1917), p. 104.

naked revelation of the play, the "epiphany," if we use a phrase Joyce was fond of in his youth, is really to be seen as the exposure of Richard's wound. *Exiles* is concerned with "the naked drama of life." But the hero —one who is intensely subjectivized—is, at the end, spiritually wounded. Consequently the play is not sufficiently resolved: the ending is inconclusive. It lacks the catharsis which the situation calls for. *Exiles* is really a problem play which ends in a mood. This is insufficient. If *Exiles* is to be accepted as a play stating a problem and exposing and focusing its inner essences, then it needs to be pointed out that the terms of this problem are distorted by the specific characterizations. Richard Rowan distorts the general problem with his own wounded spirit: Bertha is not ready for the freedom he would give her. The problem melts into a psychological dilemma.[57]

VI

This analysis does not permit us to come to one *single* conclusive explanation of Ibsen's influence on Joyce. That influence is too broad. But it does suggest that there were both definite affinities and definite differences between the temperaments of Joyce and Ibsen. Both were independent and stood alone. And it might be said that each in his lonely independence had an exiled consciousness. Ibsen's honesty, his independence, his stress on freedom strongly attracted the young Joyce. Ibsen began as a poet, utilizing old Scandinavian legendary material as his source. For a short time, but without fanaticism, he was a cultural nationalist. His youthful ideal was one of sacrifice, of heroism, and of romantic action. Living in Norway, he was stirred by the revolutions of 1848. In veering from poetic drama to naturalistic plays, he developed themes of defeated idealism and of the relativity of truth and morals.

---

57. FARRELL'S NOTE: Francis Ferguson, in his introduction to the New Directions edition of *Exiles,* argues that in *Exiles* Joyce created an image that is a "timeless artifact," and that "the tragic flaw is not in him [Richard Rowan] but in his metaphysical situation." While I do not question Mr. Ferguson's seriousness, I would point out that this kind of conception reveals how literary and dramatic critics often sentimentalize and distort the significance of works of art. What metaphysical situation exists in *Exiles* in which there is a tragic flaw? And what does it really mean, if anything, to declare that Richard Rowan should be described as an image to be seen as a "timeless artifact"? My own analysis runs counter to all such interpretations of Joyce's *Exiles,* or, for that matter, of the drama as a whole. With such an interpretation, the dramatic quality of *Exiles* is reduced, and it seems to be a talky play, even though it contains characterizations which are drawn with a remarkable clarity and honesty.

Out of a world of contrasts, of guilts and broken words and catastrophic personal disasters, there comes forth a yearning for freedom and for the ideal.

If we consider the question of freedom in Joyce's work, and if we look outside of *Exiles,* we can note that freedom has not precisely the same significance for him as for Ibsen. The problem of Stephen Dedalus is that of freedom. But freedom for him is to be found in priestly dedication to the ideal of art. And art, as he conceives it, permits a purgation of all emotions but those of pity and terror. There is a difference between Joyce and Ibsen, but it need not be seen as a criticism of either. Ibsen's freedom is the freedom of man; Joyce's is the freedom of the priestly artist. Ibsen, as it were, symbolically climbed the heights: he saw the eagle in the sun. But there is the restraining disillusionment in his work: life is not the ideal. Joyce deliberately chose the name of Dedalus. Stephen Dedalus, the son, would fly away to the sun of freedom. In *Stephen Hero,* the young Stephen wants to experience all of life. In *A Portrait,* his goal is art, the life of art. For him, art is a form of living; art is freedom. The difference in temperaments between Ibsen and Joyce is suggested in their work. Rubek, in *When We Dead Awaken,* is disillusioned with art. Stephen goes from the disillusionments of his home life and his Irish experience to the ideal of art. His priestly dedication to art is one of purgation, purgation of all that would have led a Rubek to go to the highest mountain with Irene in a snowstorm. Encouraged, inspired, moved by the example of Ibsen, Joyce, as a youth, was moving in a dialectically opposite direction. He was seeking his own self-fulfillment. That self-fulfillment, insofar as it is mirrored in his work, is to be seen more clearly delineated in his other writings than in *Exiles.* The play is much more significant as a document concerning Joyce, as a means of checking the influence on Joyce of Ibsen, as a personal "epiphany" of the author, than it is in the history of the drama.

Ibsen also exerted a technical influence on Joyce. We have seen that young Joyce commented on how many of Ibsen's plays occur in the short space of a day or two. *Exiles* has the time span of two days; *Ulysses* has a time span of a day; *Finnegans Wake,* of one night. Joyce's remark in his essay is insufficient to establish the fact that the time span of Ibsen's plays influenced Joyce's writing. But the remark, plus these parallels, does suggest that this question of time span was on Joyce's mind. Also, it well might be that Ibsen stands behind Joyce's use of dialogue. There is, for instance, a certain brevity and sharpness to Joyce's dialogue. The dialogue of *Stephen Hero,* with this sharpness and brevity, and with many subtly characterizing touches, was undoubtedly influenced by Ibsen. And the dialogue here forecast much of the use of dialogue in *A Portrait* and in *Ulysses*. But much more important than these or other possible influences there was the example of Ibsen. Edmund Gosse, in his biography of Ibsen, wrote: "To a poet the achievements of his greatest contemporaries in their common art have all of the importance of high deeds in statesmanship and war."[58] Ibsen's accomplishments were among the high deeds inspiring Joyce.[59] The young poet, destined to be one of the great writers of the twentieth century, found for his model one of the truly great writers of the end of the nineteenth century. The influence of Ibsen on Joyce further bears testimony to the continuity and to the international character of art. Ibsen, breaking the bonds of nationalism to become one of the great European writers of his age, in turn inspired the young Joyce to yearn for a place in the great European stream of culture rather than merely that of Ireland. And by moving forth into the great stream of world culture, each artist in turn became one of the greatest writers of his own country.

---

58. Gosse, *Henrik Ibsen*, p. 76.

59. FARRELL'S NOTE: Shaw's *The Quintessence of Ibsenism* was published in 1891. It contains an appendix on acting, in which Shaw indicated the influence of Ibsen in England at the time. He wrote: "Playwrights who formerly only compounded plays according to the several prescriptions for producing tears or laughter, are already taking their profession seriously to the full extent of their capacity, and venturing more and more to substitute the incidents and the catastrophes of spiritual history for the swoons, surprises, discoveries, murders, duels, assassinations, and intrigues which are commonplace of the theatre at present" (p. 149). The example of Ibsen served as an influence on ordinary run-of-the-mill playwrights. On the basis of this fact, we can well sense how much more intensely this example would affect an ambitious young genius. Ibsen's very work helped to give added dignity to the vocation of art. Thanks to men like Ibsen, it was easier for Joyce to dedicate himself to the life of art.

A Note on
Ulysses[1]

We can, perhaps, most clearly realize the literary significance of James Joyce by juxtaposing him with another modern writer of indisputable greatness—Proust. Considering their work together one is struck by the narrowness of range in Proust's characterization, and by his repetitive succession of agonies of heart. In contrast, one is doubly impressed by Joyce's rigorousness, restraint, and stern dignity. Proust gave to literature the picture of a dying class; Joyce recreated a world.

And Joyce's world is a melancholy and dying one. In fact, *Ulysses* is one of the most melancholy of books. The funeral scene, and the chapter describing eighteen simultaneous incidents fill one with a profoundly apprehensive sense of the limitation of possibilities for any human being, and with a realization of the inevitable passage of time that carries every one to an inescapable death. In the midst of this world the protagonist stands, betrayed by a whole system, crying, with a feeling of the oppression of the past, that "all history is a nightmare to me," and finding no values or sources of faith in the present other than one of personal integrity. Three elements in the world which betrayed Stephen Dedalus might be noted: religion, Irish nationalism and a feeling of race, and romantic love and sex. They are represented concretely by Joyce's struggle with the Holy Trinity, his parodying of romantic love and his drastically realistic picture of sex, and an expressed bitterness toward the Ireland that permitted the Parnell fiasco.

Ulysses is also a glittering representation of the surface of a city's life, with its sights, sounds, odors, and casual characters. And it is studded with powerful and moving passages that are the hand of a master. Of such a character is the scene of Stephen by the seashore, remembering his dead mother, with "a faint odor of wetted ashes." Finally, it might

---

1. Reprinted from "Rescued at Last," *Scribner's Magazine* 95 (February 1934): 16, 19. The present title is supplied for this edition.

be stated that parts of *Ulysses* seem like stunt performances to permit the author the luxury of showing off. I feel that the question and answer chapter is of such a nature. But such performances remain the privilege of genius. Thanks to the action of Judge Woolsey the book is now available in this country.[2]

---

2. Judge John M. Woolsey's decision on 6 December 1933 had lifted the ban on importation of *Ulysses* into the United States.

On Some Marxist Critics of Joyce[1]

Often, when they have contrasted bourgeois and proletarian literature, revolutionary critics have been pressed into a dilemma. Bourgeois literature, so-called, has developed through a long tradition, and its heritage now includes a number of great works. Proletarian literature, so-called, has not had that same historical development. Revolutionary critics, proceeding in terms of these categories, have therefore been forced to counter what has been accomplished in bourgeois literature with faith in the prospects and potentialities of proletarian literature. Through many prognostications, much theorizing, countless prophecies, we have found these critics again and again cooking up recipes for tomorrow's "great" literature. Mr. [Granville] Hicks' description of a future proletarian Proust, greater than Marcel Proust himself,[2] is one of many such prophecies. These efforts suggest a remark of Louis Grudin's. Speaking of the critic who applies standards of measurement instead of criteria of judgment, Mr. Grudin comments:

> His procedure has been that of an excursion for words and notions to support his claims, wherever he could find them; and he has had to trust to the meanings he could read into already available odds and ends belonging to various fields and gathered into a makeshift critical doctrine.[3]

---

1. Excerpted and adapted from *A Note on Literary Criticism* (New York: Vanguard Press, 1936), pp. 82–85, 97–106. The present title is supplied for this edition. In *A Note on Literary Criticism*, Farrell addressed some questions current in leftist literary magazines and books during the early and middle 1930s. The book combines his philosophical grounding in Mead and Dewey with Marxist ideas derived largely from Leon Trotsky's *Literature and Revolution*, which Farrell had read in 1932. In general, the thrust of Farrell's book is to refute dogmatic and pedantic applications of Marxist categories to literary criticism and to reassert the importance of tradition and experience as critical values. In the course of these discussions, he makes special reference to the work of Joyce, which he defends against the mechanical attacks of Marxist writers. On the political context of these critical skirmishes, see Alan M. Wald, *James T. Farrell: The Revolutionary Socialist Years* (New York: New York University Press, 1978), esp. chap. 2.

2. Granville Hicks, "Revolution and the Novel," *New Masses,* 22 May 1934, p. 25.

3. Quoted by John Dewey, *Art as Experience* (New York: Capricorn Books, 1958), p. 308.

We can gain a further sense of the confusion in this aspect of the critical problem by considering the views of D. S. Mirsky on James Joyce.[4] After describing the social and ideological backgrounds and the personal history of Joyce, and proving that Joyce was introduced as a figure into the world of the international bourgeoisie by two millionaires, Mirsky asks the question whether or not Joyce offers any model for revolutionary writers:

> The answer is that his method is too inseparably connected with the specifically decadent phase of the bourgeois culture he reflects, is too narrowly confined within its limits. The use of the inner monologue (stream of consciousness method) is too closely connected with the ultra subjectivism of the parasitic, rentier bourgeoisie, and entirely unadaptable to the art of one who is building socialist society. Not less foreign to the dynamics of our [Russian] culture is the fundamentally static method in which the picture of Bloom is composed. . . . There remains still the most fundamental element of Joyce's art, his realistic grasp, his amazing exactness of expression, all that side in which he is of the school of the French naturalists, raising to its ultimate height their cult of the *mot juste*. It is this exactness which gives Joyce the wonderful realistic power in depicting the outer world for which he is famous. But this has its roots on the one hand in a morbid, defeatist delight in the ugly and repulsive and, on the other, in an aesthetico-proprietary desire for the possession of "things." So that even this one realistic element of Joyce's style is fundamentally foreign to the realism towards which Soviet art aims, mainly a mastery of the world by means of active, dynamic materialism—with the purpose of not merely understanding but also changing the reality of history.[5]

These quotations reveal the widespread confusion that has accompanied the applications of such categories to literature. Mirsky assumes such a direct tie-up between economics and literature that he finds Joyce's exactitude in description to be an acquisitive and an aesthetico-proprietary desire for "things"; and that Joyce's utilization of the interior monologue is too closely connected with a parasitic element of the bourgeoisie to be usable by revolutionary writers. Such discoveries enable Mirsky to legislate for writers at wholesale on what will or will not influence them.

Michael Gold, seeking to apply these categories, extends them to the audience, applies them retroactively to dead authors, and calls upon the subconscious for abetment in his damnation of bourgeois art. And Granville Hicks, in order to establish the importance of proletarian

---

4. D. S. Mirsky, "Joyce and Irish Literature," *New Masses*, 3 April 1934, pp. 31–34.
5. Ibid., p. 34. "Mirsky's remarks on Joyce," Farrell notes, "might be contrasted with Edmund Wilson's analysis in *Axel's Castle*" (New York: Scribner's, 1936), pp. 191–236.

literature, even relies on such baldly subjective evidence as the flat statement that no bourgeois novel will provide him with a unified aesthetic experience. The proper duties of criticism are ignored, and the carry-over value of literature is almost completely disregarded. Functional extremism rampantly leads to one-sided formulae, the rationalization of prejudices, and the concoction of meaningless recipes for the novelist of the classless society of the future.

Here it becomes necessary to re-emphasize a fairly apparent fact. The "bourgeois" novel has had a long history. It is possible to examine that history, to note the various types of novel that are included within the category, to arrive at some fairly accurate definitions, and even to make some fairly accurate descriptions of its growth and its methods. But with "proletarian" literature this cannot be done, because that literature is now only at the beginning of its history. It will grow and develop as part of the development of literature in general. It will not grow from the definitions of critics. In its growth it will—for some time to come—be constantly influenced by "bourgeois" literature. The assimilation will not be even and regular: it will not proceed according to the dictates of critical legislation. And since literature is a qualitative matter, and since it is aesthetic and subjective as well as functional and objective, the growth of future proletarian literature will not *per se* prove the failure of Joyce or Proust, let alone the failure of Dreiser or Melville. A proletarian classic in the future will not necessarily give rise to dispraise of *Ulysses,* any more than *Macbeth* can logically be cited in dispraise of Dante's *Divine Comedy,* or than Milton's *Paradise Lost* can be used to prove the failure of the author of *Beowulf.*

A generalized description of one of the roles played by literature is that it is a record of how people feel at different times. John Strachey writes:

> "Literature" is perhaps the most remarkable of all the ideal constructions which the human mind has begotten. It is a great sea into which for centuries have been poured all those thoughts, dreams, fantasies, concepts, ascertained facts, and emotions, which did not fit into any of the other categories of human thought. Into literature have gone philosophical ideas too tenuous for the philosophers, dreams too literal for plastic expression, ascertained facts too uncorrelated for science, and emotions too intertwined with the particular instance to find expression in the glorious and precise abstractions of music.[6]

---

6. John Strachey, *The Coming Struggle for Power* (New York: Covici-Friede, 1933), p. 186.

It is characteristic of life that it constantly tends to overflow the intellectual categories which are set up as the basis for apprehending, organizing, understanding, controlling and changing it. Strachey's definition here is an elaboration of the role that literature plays as a reservoir for this overflow.

Strachey goes on thus: "Literature, for the most part, attempts to illuminate some particular predicament of a particular man or a particular woman at a given time and place."[7] Literature, in this aspect, can conceivably permit a great diversity in method, in procedure, and in content. Time was when "leftist" critics tended to deny such a variety; but they are now ready to grant it, at least as a possibility. Granville Hicks says that revolutionary literature can have diversity. He speaks of "the most important differences of all, the differences that are inherent in the nature of revolutionary literature. If all bourgeois survivals could be miraculously obliterated, and if the same high talent everywhere prevailed, monotony would by no means be the result."[8]

However much this variety may be granted in a general statement, it has not been sufficiently revealed in specific literary criticism, in reviews, and in editorial policies. A kind of self-consciousness on the part of writers persists as a hangover from the days when leftists strove to legislate themes and subject matter; often an admirer of a book, in reviewing it, would be required to emphasize that even though it contained no strike scenes or demonstrations, it was nevertheless revolutionary—or, at least, a valuable piece of "exposure" literature. Similarly, again and again, there have been book reviews complaining that the author of a particular book was all right as far as he had gone, but that he had not gone far enough. And recently, Clifford Odets, arguing in defense of propaganda, declared that propagandists do not "excuse" James Joyce for "his *bad* themes."[9]

Dealing with James Joyce, Karl Radek has revealed a similar tendency, and I think that it is worth our while to present and analyze his judgment.[10] Radek contends that

> it does not lie within the power of bourgeois art to imitate the realism of Balzac, who endeavored to paint a picture commensurate with the epoch in which he lived. For a full picture of life as it is would be a condemnation of moribund capitalism.[11]

---

7. Ibid.
8. Granville Hicks, *The Great Tradition* (New York: Macmillan, 1935), p. 299.
9. "All Drama Is Propaganda," *Controversy*, February 1936.
10. Karl Radek, "James Joyce or Socialist Realism?" in *Problems of Soviet Literature* (Moscow: Cooperative Publishing Society, 1935), pp. 150–62.
11. FARRELL'S NOTE: Naturalism in literature was an attempt to utilize scientific method in the novel. It worked more or less on the theory that character is the product

He goes on to cite Joyce as an example.

> His basic feature is the conviction that there is nothing big in life—no big
> events, no big people, no big ideas; and the writer can give a picture of life
> by just taking "any given hero on any given day" and reproducing him with
> exactitude. A heap of dung, crawling with worms, photographed by a
> cinema apparatus through a microscope—such is Joyce's work. . . . The
> picture that he gives . . . does not fit even those trivial heroes in that trivial
> life which he depicts. The scene of his book is laid in Ireland in 1916.[12] The
> petty bourgeois whom he describes are Irish types, though laying claim to
> universal human significance. But these Blooms and Dedaluses, whom the
> author relentlessly pursues into the lavatory, the brothel and the pothouse,
> did not cease to be petty bourgeois when they took part in the Irish insur-
> rection of 1916. The petty bourgeois is a profoundly contradictory phe-
> nomenon; and in order to give a portrayal of the petty bourgeois, one must
> present him in all his relations to life. Joyce . . . has selected a piece of life
> and depicted that. His choice is determined by the fact that for him the
> whole world lies between a cupboardful of medieval books, a brothel and
> a pothouse. For him, the national revolutionary movement of the Irish
> petty bourgeoisie does not exist; and consequently the picture which he
> presents, despite its ostensible impartiality, is untrue.[13]

Radek then concludes, among other things, that Joyce's method is
unsatisfactory for the presentation of themes of class struggle; Balzac

---

of environment. The first developments in such a direction would, by the very nature of
environment, treat of environment and the relationship of environment to character. The
first works of naturalism would more or less have to be extensive rather than intensive.
Also, naturalism was tied to the development of materialism. The earlier materialism was
mechanistic, and so environment was juxtaposed to character.

This is important in the development of naturalism as a method and an influence in
literature. Naturalism as a method would have to go on, and develop various implications.
Likewise, it would have to reveal a growing and changing method. The shift of emphasis
from the extensive to the intensive was, as a consequence, a somewhat necessary and
understandable development. If the world is a process, and the factor of change is a
noticeable characteristic of the world as process, then the attempt to embody the world
as process would become intertwined with naturalism. Two developments would flow out
of the potentialities of naturalism. One would be a shift in emphasis to a more intensive
method, and an attempt to embody precision of details and the like over a small area. This
we find in Joyce. The other would be an attempt to apply the conception of the world
as process to the individual consciousness, and this would result in psychological relativ-
ism. This we find in Proust and Joyce.

A literary method and tradition in time reacts on itself. It leads to the development
of various potentialities wrapped within whatever fundamental assumptions it possesses
either implicitly or explicitly. These fundamental assumptions would not be directly the
product of economics and the base of a society. They would be the products of that,
connected with ideological strains of development, reacting to form the basis for a view
that would lead to the beginnings of a literary method and a tradition; and in addition,
there would be intertwined with it past literary methods and traditions.

Radek here tends to leave out links in the relationship, and thus arrives at an
interpretation which I consider too simplified, and therefore, too schematized.

12. FARRELL'S NOTE: This is an error of fact. The story is laid in June 1904.
13. Radek, "James Joyce or Socialist Realism?" pp. 153–54.

and Tolstoy are more appropriate models for the Soviet writers. In rebuttal of disagreements with his interpretation, Karl Radek says:

> All that appealed to Joyce was the medieval, the mystical, the reactionary in the petty bourgeoisie—lust, aberrations; everything capable of impelling the petty bourgeoisie to join the side of revolution was alien to him.[14]

The basis of this criticism is, I think, that Joyce failed to write what Radek, retroactively, desires him to have written. Radek is applying not criteria of judgment but standards of measurement; these standards of measurement relate to class phenomena, and he is proving Joyce a bourgeois writer and then condemning him because he is not the kind of bourgeois writer that Balzac was. Radek applies the standard that a writer must treat the whole of the life of his characters. But Joyce did not treat the whole of the life of the petty bourgeoisie. No writer can succeed in presenting all of life nor all of one class in a book or even in many books. A writer does not surmount all the limitations of his time, his heritage, and many other humanly and socially qualifying factors and conditions. Radek's criticism is of a type that is irrelevant and unreasonable.

One of the ideological and social backgrounds of Joyce's work is Irish nationalism, to which we find him antagonistic. His revulsion goes back to the Parnell episode, which shook Irish history and bitterly split the Irish nation. Instead of condemning Joyce, however, it would be more fruitful for us to investigate this antagonism as it is refracted through his work, by making a genetic approach to its sources. Such an approach would provide us with an emotional awareness of this feature of Irish life; and it would furnish us with much illustrative information.

A second ideological source in Joyce is Roman Catholicism, which connects closely with Irish nationalism. Ireland is a Church-ridden country, and the clergy played an important—and infamous—role in the Parnell case. Ireland is strongly Catholic, belligerently Catholic, furiously Catholic; and, whether or not the reactionary elements of the petty bourgeoisie appealed to Joyce, his attack on Catholicism in Ireland has banned his works from his own country and made him a pariah.

Has a Marxist, then, any right to take a position like Karl Radek's on Joyce? Is a Marxist warranted in judging from so philistine a viewpoint while failing to consider the relation of Irish Catholicism and nationalism to Joyce's work?

---

14. FARRELL'S NOTE: Karl Radek praises Dostoevski, to whom these same aspects appealed. Dostoevski consciously affirmed even the mystical and the reactionary; and the phenomena of aberration are curiously important in his writings.

Finally, the relation of Joyce to Irish literature must be considered; there we find him among the first to utilize the urban life of Ireland as the material for Irish writing. In the main, his predecessors utilized material from native folklore, from the life of the peasantry, and the like. This fact was a tremendous step forward in the history of Irish literature. All such factors are ignored by Radek in order to enforce a blanket condemnation.

The Irish revolution and Civil War have both been given extensive treatment in Irish literature. I might cite the following works: *The Clanking of the Chains,* by Brinsley Macnamara; *Juno and the Paycock, The Shadow of a Gunman,* and *The Plough and the Stars,* by Sean O'Casey; *The Informer* and *The Martyr,* by Liam O'Flaherty; *Guests of the Nation,* by Frank O'Connor; *Midsummer Night Madness* and *A Nest of Simple Folk,* by Sean O'Faolain. None of these writers, be it noted, attempts to describe all of the life of Ireland. They utilize some of its features, and some aspects of the life of the petit bourgeoisie; and their works relate to the national revolutionary movement and the Civil War. These works, along with *Ulysses,* refract a sense of Irish life. In some of these works (such as *The Clanking of the Chains,* and also a much more effective novel of Macnamara's, *The Valley of the Squinting Windows*) we find a revulsion from Irish life as strong and as intense as it is in *Ulysses.* Does this not suggest to us that here are the phenomena of Irish life refracted through Irish literature, and that the picture warrants our investigation? In literature as well as in politics, local peculiarities find any number of expressions and reflections, and these must be considered when one indulges in literary criticism. All such features are ignored in Radek's criticism of Joyce, and in consequence we get a one-sided view. And further, there is the fact that Joyce has influenced several writers who have to some extent treated the national revolutionary movement; and it is not unsafe to prophesy that, when and if a novel dealing with the revolutionary movement in Ireland is written so as to satisfy Mr. Radek's thesis of socialist realism, it will be shown to have been influenced—most likely profitably—by Joyce's *Ulysses.* [15]

Besides being an attack on leftism, socialist realism represents a vital and healthy tendency. Still, it has not freed itself of the vice of

---

15. FARRELL'S NOTE: For a statement agreeing with Radek's interpretation of Joyce, see Edwin Seaver's review of *Problems of Soviet Literature* in *New Masses,* October 22, 1935. Mr. Seaver writes: "I remember, when first reading the abbreviated report of Karl Radek's address on contemporary world literature, resenting his attack on James Joyce as the antithesis of socialist realism. I must admit, however, that a closer examination of Radek's speech, and especially his answer to the discussion which followed, reveals a cogency of argument that is pretty hard to refute."

functional extremism. Radek's criticism of Joyce shows us that vice in a naked light. He measures Joyce by extra-literary standards, mixing essential and nonessential references in order to treat Joyce in purely ideological terms. What is essentially unsound in Radek's criticism is, I think, his failure properly to apply a concept of necessity in literary judgment, and—consonantly—his inability to make essential rather than nonessential references from Joyce's work to its ideological and social backgrounds.

A principal criticism of the "line" of socialist realism is that it seems to be developing a literary eschatology in advance of the development of the literature itself. It presents not only a directive emphasis but also definitions, and these become standards. The standards are used as external measurements. The work of literature is then measured to fit the standards, and the result is extra-literary criticism.

The reasoning presented in exposition and defense of a "line" of socialist realism simplifies processes. It skips several phases of interrelationships in the literary process, and in the connection of that process with others. Literature reacts on itself. In reacting upon itself, it reveals many streams of influence and counter-influence. Insufficiently apprehending the myriad reactions of literature upon itself, the proponents of socialist realism simplify literary influences. An example is Radek's argument that Balzac would be a healthier influence on Soviet writers than Joyce, because Balzac wrote at a time when the middle class was healthy, and Joyce writes of the middle class at an opposite historical pole. To arrive at such a simplified formulation, Radek merely skips seventy-five or a hundred years of literary development and of the reactions of literature upon itself.

Such simplifications lead him and other champions of this "line" to give writers wholesale advice on how they can and should be influenced. They also make the false assumption that literary masters are always the best influences for a writer—which is not necessarily correct. There are literary masters whose work will have eternal charm for a writer. There are masterpieces which a writer will recognize as such, without being importantly influenced by them. And there are various types of literary influences—technical, psychological, ideological, stimulating, suggestive. Critics like Radek ignore these matters.

Frank O'Connor's
The Saint and Mary Kate[1]

Since the Celtic Renaissance, there have been two parallel strains in Irish writing. The older of these has found its orientation in the ancient legends and has been largely characterized by mystical attitudes. A newer and now more vigorous strain can be described by a general word like "realism." The material of the realists is contemporary—life in cities and rural areas, industrialization, the social problems that result from the Civil War, and the like. The writing of most Irish realists is strongly confessional. One feels that even when the authors do not intrude themselves as characters, their books are a direct treatment of personal problems and an almost unqualified expression of their own prejudices. Hence, that note of sardonic bitterness and that tendency towards self or racial destruction to be noted in Joyce and O'Casey, in the melo-dramas of O'Flaherty, and in books like Macnamara's *The Valley of the Squinting Windows* or even Stephens' *Etched in Moonlight*. A variation from this confessional realism is exemplified in the novels of Peader O'Don-nell, in Corkery's *The Threshold of the Quiet* and, now, in *The Saint and Mary Kate*.

There is a sensitive tenderness in Mr. O'Connor's book that over-rides its patches of irony. Likewise, because of his skillful use of indirec-tion, he is able to portray that melodrama and extravagance so apparent in many Irish lives without being himself melodramatic. The back-ground of his novel is a tenement in the town of Cork that bulges with the sorrows and pitifulness of the poor. The two principal characters are Mary Kate and Phil, whose hopeful youth stands out in contrast to the frustrations of the older people they know.

Mary Kate McCormick, born out of wedlock, has been allowed to spring into womanhood without care from her babyish, anti-social, trivial mother and her slatternly aunt. She loves Phil Dinan, the son of a charwoman. His mother literally kills herself by working in loneliness

---

1. Reprinted from an untitled book review in *The New Republic* 72 (26 October 1932): 301. The present title is supplied for this edition.

to give Phil an education. Mary Kate goes to Dublin to live with her ostensible father, and she gets on there, but Phil, reading her letters, is scandalized by the life Nick McCormick has opened up for her. He journeys to Dublin and rescues her, and they tramp home to Cork. On their return journey, they sleep in a deserted castle. The corpse of a vagabond musician is dropped, almost at their feet. A crone comes in with her feverish daughter. The daughter has just had a baby, and Mary perceives that the crone has drowned it. This sudden revelation of the unpleasantness of life is a shared experience tending to draw the boy and girl together and, when they return, their love almost flowers. But Phil, the Saint, is driven by a strong Catholic devotion; and he is intensely striving to build his will power so that he can control his passions. Mary Kate and his experiences on the road threaten to destroy his methodical habits, and he leaves, incognito, to rebuild them.

Mr. O'Connor's book is serious and genuine. Its strongest pages are those which retail the pitiful and almost heartbreaking lives of the poor. He is, unquestionably, an Irish novelist who should be read.

Ireland in Its Novels[1]

How often have the Irish started to try and achieve something, and every time they have been crushed, politically and industrially! By consistent oppression they have been artificially converted into an utterly demoralized nation, and now fulfill the notorious function of supplying England, America, Australia, etc., with prostitutes, casual laborers, pimps, thieves, swindlers, beggars and other rabble.[2]

These lines are quoted from a letter which Friedrich Engels wrote to Karl Marx in 1856, following a journey through certain portions of Ireland. They describe almost an entire epoch in the bitter and tragic history of the Irish people. They open like a vista upon the historic background out of which modern Irish literature has grown. Synge's *The Playboy of the Western World* comes immediately to mind. The bitterness that exudes from such a fine novel as Brinsley Macnamara's *The Valley of the Squinting Windows* is understandable as one of the poisoned outgrowths of Irish history. The anti-nationalistic revulsion to which Joyce's Stephen Dedalus gives expression falls into perspective. Even the literature of the Irish on foreign soils comes into clearer focus. Pat O'Mara's magnificent book *The Autobiography of a Liverpool Irish Slummy* becomes more than the story of one man's life, and one man's people. His characters reemerge as part of that pathetic international rabble which age-long tyranny and oppression has flung into our century.

A reflex of the condition which Engels summarized is to be found in the stage Irishman created in the popular literature of the last century by such men as Lever and Lover.[3] Between a privileged group or class and an oppressed group or class, a set of conventions always develops as a guide to interclass and intergroup relations. In time, members of the privileged class will tend to identify these conventions, and the neces-

---

1. Reprinted from *The New Republic* 88 (14 October 1936): 285–86.
2. Engels to Marx, 23 May 1856, in *Correspondence of Marx and Engels, 1846–1895* (New York: International Publishers, 1934), p. 94.
3. Samuel Lover (1797–1868) and Charles James Lever (1806–1872) wrote novels of stereotyped Irish characters.

sary habits they create, with the assumedly essential human nature of the oppressed class. They will then view the conduct that is canalized by these conventions as deriving, not from objective social relationships and situations, but from a myth called the fundamental characteristics of the members of the oppressed class or group. Hence the unreal Handy Andys, the servile and obsequious Paddys and Tighes. Such "characterizations" are a wish-fulfilment of what the English oppressors and their allies among the Irish upper classes would have liked the Irish to be. Any elements of truth behind such images were the products of the demoralization caused by terror, evictions, prisons and starvation. We have a parallel image in American popular writing, the stage Negro. At a later date, we can also trace connected variations of this development. Donn Byrne romanticized the fox-hunting gentry. A contemporary Irish writer, M. J. Farrell, has treated this social level in terms that reach silliness and banality.

Just as a disunified Germany produced a classical philosophy tending to compensate for a lack of material and national unity by striving toward a conception of spiritual unity that reached its apex in Hegel, so a disunified and oppressed Ireland has produced a literature of cultural nationalism and Gaelicized folklore. The fires of cultural nationalism which Standish O'Grady lighted with his sturdy and beautiful recreations from Irish mythology still burn. Cultural nationalism soon fused with the revolutionary movement. If Irish culture was to be free, then Ireland must attain its independence. It was through cultural nationalism that Padraic Pearse came to the Irish national revolution.

Pearse, along with James Connolly, was a leader in the abortive revolution of 1916. The story of this rebellion is now told for us in a brief but vivid and exciting narrative, *Easter Week,* by Brian O'Neill. He is an Irish Communist who has been deeply influenced by James Connolly. A previous book of his, *The War for the Land in Ireland,* can be taken as a companion volume to Connolly's *Labor in Ireland.* Both constitute the basis for a Marxist analysis of Irish history. And unless such an analysis be made, Irish history becomes—in the words of James Connolly—"but a welter of unrelated facts, a hopeless chaos of sporadic outbreaks, treacheries, massacres, murders and purposeless warfare."

In *Easter Week,* O'Neill describes how the two groups which joined in the Easter Rebellion came together. The larger of these was the Irish Volunteers, typified by Pearse, the mystic poet and Gaelic scholar. The smaller was James Connolly's Citizen Army, an outgrowth of the famous Dublin transport strike led by Jim Larkin in 1913. While paying due tribute to the other martyred leaders, O'Neill makes it clear that the greatest historic role in the rebellion was played by James Connolly. At the outbreak of the War, Connolly adopted a position analogous to that of Lenin. Before the rebellion, he told his Citizen Army: "Being the lesser party, we join with our comrades of the Irish Volunteers. But hold your arms. If we succeed, those who are our comrades today we may be compelled to fight tomorrow." Free of Pearse's mysticism, he was the man most equipped to be the political and the military leader of the rebellion, and to drive on through to the logical conclusion of fighting for a socialist Ireland. Despite his final reconciliation with the Catholic Church (which O'Neill neglects to mention) he belongs to the revolutionary movement, and not to Rome. Almost all Irish atheists are Catholics in their last hour.

Brian O'Neill also deals with the essential causes of the defeat. Casement's expedition to land German arms failed. Eoin MacNeill betrayed his comrades by issuing countermanding orders to the Irish Volunteers, calling off their mobilization. The rural districts did not answer the call. The small band in Dublin was trapped, and forced to face an entire British army. They were heroes. But God was on the side of the biggest battalions. Connolly and Pearse, both wounded, surrendered in order to save their comrades from decimation. All of the leaders were executed. Ireland was again crushed. Karl Radek, from the Continent, criticized the revolt as a "Putsch." Lenin replied in defense of Connolly, describing Radek as "monstrously doctrinaire and pedantic." O'Neill's account of these events is excellent.[4]

Connolly, Pearse and their comrades banged loudly on the doors of history. The Easter Rebellion was followed by the Black and Tan and the Civil Wars. New generations of writers drew upon these struggles for their material. One of the younger novelists who has utilized these sources is Rearden Conner. Like Pearse, he is half-Irish and half-English. His father was a British secret-service man whom the Irish Republican Army assassinated. Conner's first novel, *Shake Hands with the Devil,* was a tale of the horrors of the Black and Tan, and his entire emphasis was purely sensationalistic and melodramatic. The members of the IRA whom he described were all treated as ignorant yokels, or else as pure terroristic demons. The hero was a prig. The height of fatuity in the book was reached when the hero suggested to a member of the IRA that the Irish should, instead of landing arms at a certain spot on the coast line, turn that section into a tourist resort; they could then advertise for the English tourist trade.

Conner's new novel, *Time to Kill,* is a story of the Irish slums set

---

4. Farrell's view of O'Neill's excellence had changed by 1948. See below, n.12, pp. 119–20 in "A Portrait of James Connolly."

against the background of the depression. The principal figure, Timmy Morgan, is so driven and demoralized by unemployment and poverty that he becomes a maniacal terrorist murdering the rich, particularly those who consort with prostitutes. This novel can be described as an improvement upon its predecessor: however, one need go only a small distance to advance from zero. Conner's book has no roots in Irish life. It is commonplace as a story and the characters are stock. It is exceedingly bad Julian Green and William Faulkner with an Irish brogue.

All three of Sean O'Faolain's books are rooted in Irish life. The first, *Midsummer Night Madness,* was a collection of short stories of the Civil War. In these he displayed the technical mastery, evocative power, descriptive ability and sense of character that are so noticeable in his two subsequent works. Lenin somewhere quotes a Prussian general to the effect that a soldier on the battlefield does not pause to enjoy the beauties of the landscape. This comment can stand as a criticism of O'Faolain's short stories. Most of his characters were fugitives "on the run"; reading about them, one often wondered whether the characters were speeding past the scenery, or whether the landscape was rushing past them. Frank O'Connor's *Guests of the Nation,* dealing with similar subject matter, is a firmer and harder book merely because his fugitives are less interested in the loveliness of nature.

The novels of both Frank O'Connor and Sean O'Faolain genuinely recreate an Irish world. The two writers complement one another. The characters in O'Connor's *The Saint and Mary Kate* live in the tenements of Cork. O'Faolain's characters are several rungs higher on the economic ladder. Both writers have charm, the capacity to draw interesting and convincingly representative characters, descriptive talent, and the ability to render Anglo-Irish speech poetically. They also reveal the same kind of weakness. There is insufficient body to their novels. There is no underlying point of view around which the material is organized. They do not end stories conclusively. O'Faolain's major book, *A Nest of Simple Folk,* flows with Irish life. It is rich in characters and character vignettes. The hero, Leo Foxe-Donnel, is a Fenian whose career courses through representative aspects of the life of his times. For instance, the descriptions of the jails into which he is flung by the British read like concrete representations of those jails which caused the International Workingmen's Association to protest to the English government because of its mistreatment of Irish political prisoners. The very abortiveness of the insurrectionary attempts in which Donnel is involved is a reminder of how Ireland has tried so often to achieve something, only to be crushed. In this work, O'Faolain utilized all his resources; he produced a landmark in the Irish novel.

Bird Alone, his new book, is conceived in a minor key. It is the story of an old man remembering his youth and the tragic ending of his romantic love affair. After the death of his beloved, he became a bird alone. The theme is tenuous, and only O'Faolain's technical skill and sense of character save the book from banality. The novel has value because of its many peripheral features. There is a portrait of an old Fenian, Phil Crone, who is cut to the pattern of Leo Foxe-Donnel. There are many sidelights on Parnell's times. Some of the most moving pages are those which describe the old Fenian after the death of the Chief. The spirit and the emotional mood of the novel are Catholic. The pattern of the story is such that this spirit and mood are not untrue to the material. However, they make us wonder about the author. As William Troy has pointed out, O'Faolain himself seems to exist in a state of divided loyalties. He veers toward the spirit for which the Fenians stood; he retreats in the direction of Mother Church. He is permeated both with a sense of Irish life and with the proverbial Irish mists. The evocative moods which he establishes haunt one. But in this very power to haunt and evoke, he also softens. He seems to follow the line of least resistance, and to use his remarkable talents as a foil for his inconclusiveness. No Irish novelist since Joyce has possessed his skill; no Irish writer since Synge has rendered Irish speech as he does. And yet, he does not eat into the basis of one's consciousness, as do Joyce and Synge and O'Casey. He is a fine writer. But he has shown none of the real strength of literary greatness.

"How often have the Irish started to try and achieve something, and every time they have been crushed, politically and industrially!" The historic epoch of which Engels spoke has gone; a new one has come, and the Irish people have still to loose their chains. One of their few compensations has been that out of their poverty and suffering, their defeats and dreams and aspirations, their most talented sons have created a literature that is both bitter and beautiful, a literature that extends continuously from Carleton and Standish O'Grady to the new generation of O'Connor and Sean O'Faolain.

The Work of Frank O'Connor[1]

Frank O'Connor's first volume of short stories, *Guests of the Nation*, was published in America in 1931, and his novel *The Saint and Mary Kate* appeared here in 1932. These two works seemed to herald a new talent in Irish literature. His title story, "Guests of the Nation," is, in my opinion, one of the great modern short stories. The guests of the Irish nation are two British soldiers—veterans of the First World War, who have been captured by Irish Republicans, and are being held as hostages. Written in the first person, it contains clearly delineated characters, distinguishing the Irish guards, and contrasting differences in personality between the two British prisoners. A human relationship grows up between the captives and their guards. They come to like one another and the days pass in a cordial association with discussions, political arguments, and card games. A purely temporary situation, the consequence of war, deceives this small group. The war-time attitude of friend and foe is insidiously broken down, and, in its place, a human one grows up. Contact between these men results in a common human bond between Irish Republicans and British soldiers. And then the Irish get orders to execute their prisoners in reprisal for the shooting of Irish Republicans. This order is painfully carried out. The narrator of the story confesses that after the execution, "I felt very small and very lonely." He had gone into the struggle against the British with the feeling: "disunion between brothers seemed to me an awful crime." The preservation of a spirit of union between brothers in struggle leads to an execution which leaves him stricken with guilt. He feels small because the conditions of war and revolution had forced him into the role of executing men whom he had come to like, with whom he had learned to live, and these two men had seemed like his own equals. This story is written with a sharpness of vision, and a simplicity and honesty. It is a moving story.

---

1. Printed from an unpublished manuscript (n.d.) [2]. Parts of the essay appeared in "Novelist-Critic Praises Frank O'Connor for Accurate Portrayal of Modern Irish Life," *Philadelphia Sunday Bulletin Book Review*, 29 February 1948, p. 2.

I mention "Guests of the Nation" in detail here, not merely because it is such a poignant story, but also because, in the terms of a story and by means of contrasting characters in that story, Frank O'Connor, at the very beginning of his literary career, dramatized and focused features of Irish attitudes in new terms. In Ireland, thinking and feeling are organized and patterned within the framework of the Church and the Nation. Both institutionally and ideologically, the Church is impressed into the life of the Irish. Along with the concept of the Nation, the contents of consciousness of the Irish are pervasively affected. "Guests of the Nation" deals with psychological attitudes, deriving from the concept of the Nation, as these are expressed directly and immediately in a tragic situation. The concept of the Nation is translated into an attitude that "disunion between brothers seemed to me an awful crime."

In Frank O'Connor's first novel, *The Saint and Mary Kate,* the immediate actions and thoughts of the characters are related to the Church in the same way as the thoughts and actions of the story "Guests of the Nation" are connected with the idea of the Nation. The Saint is an Irish boy, destined by temperament for the priesthood. His relationship with his Irish mother is close and of the type which evokes guilt. For she centers all her love and emotion in her son, works for him without sparing herself. The dawning of emotion and love in the Irish boy from Cork and Mary Kate is traced, and it is set against a background of the life of the poor in Cork. There is real art here, as there is in practically all of Frank O'Connor's writing. However, the novel has an inconclusive character. Poetry, yearning, sadness surround the boy and girl as a kind of aura. They do not say, as does the narrator of "Guests of the Nation," that they feel small and lonely. But this feeling is there. The concept of the Nation and the ideas of the Church were, in these first writings of O'Connor, imbedded in his work, not conceptually or polemically, but in terms of mood, action, and thought, and in the context of human relationships which reveal pathos. The language of O'Connor's characters, not only in these works, but in other writings of his as well, is sometimes vigorous. The characters call one another off. But the emotions of his characters are not strong. It is because of this lack of stronger emotions that O'Connor usually achieves a note of pathos rather than tragedy.

The above remarks should, I believe, suggest how Frank O'Connor is a representative Irish writer. Excepting his early civil war stories, and his political play, *The Invincibles,* written in collaboration with Mr. Hugh Hunt, his stories deal with ordinary Irishmen living their daily lives. They fall in love and there are thoughts of money involved. They talk and brag at the pubs. They become sick and die. They eat and sleep and die. They indulge in boasting and bragging. It is by picturing types and by depicting very common features of Irish life that O'Connor gives an artistic treatment of the Irish, a treatment which, in the last analysis, leads back to Church and Nation. *The Invincibles* brings this out into the open. The Invincibles were a group of Irish terrorists, mainly working men, who committed the famous Phoenix Park murder of an English official. They were devoted men, determined to strike a blow for Ireland. The blow they struck resulted in their isolation. They were disavowed by Parnell. The Church turned on them. They died lonely but heroically. In the play about them which O'Connor wrote with Hugh Hunt (one of the most powerful and finest dramas in the entire repertory of the Irish drama) the Church and Nation are sharply focused, and strong criticisms of the Church, as a political factor in Ireland, are included in the lines. The Irish terrorists emerge from the play as both heroes and martyrs, and their martyrdom is tragic.

And this play might be contrasted with the spirit of O'Connor's novel, *Dutch Interior.* This is written in a realistic impressionistic manner. It covers a long span of time, but this sense of time, so important for the novel, is lost in the narrative. And the structure of the book explains why a sense of time is lost. *Dutch Interior* reveals modern Irishmen growing old too soon. They suffer, as it were, from a process of psychological attrition. They do not grow, do not gain an adequate sense of fulfillment, and do not even gain any adequate insight which would explain why. This theme is expressed in a novel of sharply drawn pictures running over a period of years. Each picture is realistically painted—the title is based on the work of Dutch painters—but the book as a whole is impressionistic. It lacks structure. The motif is one which embodies an idea of inevitability, but there is no inevitability in the novel. One of the characters declares: "All this drinking and talking and joking, it's all idleness, despair, putrification." The tragedy of the characters, though different from that of the Invincibles, is, in its own way, as profound. But the form and manner of the novel washes that tragedy out. A book which called for power is without power. This suggests, I trust, part of the nature of the pathos in the Irish world which O'Connor creates.

We might deal further with these points in order to define the precise representative character of O'Connor by mentioning the question of identity and, with it, that of individuality. One can deduce from O'Connor's work a shifting emotional ground. In terms of scene, language, types and themes, the underlying ground of his work is to be seen in the ideas of the Nation and the Church. These ideas, when translated into the day-by-day life of average people, result in a lack of development and fulfillment. The feeling of smallness of the narrator of "Guests of the Nation" is related to a discovery that the national idea, translated into a feeling for brotherhood, lies behind an action he must take which is, to him, perhaps as criminal as any action that would violate this feeling of brotherhood. The Invincibles are abandoned both by the representatives of the Church and the Nation. They are lonely, abandoned martyrs. The peace-time in the period after "The Troubles" shows the men aging before their time, that is, unfulfilled. There is no one type of attitude or of perspective which a writer needs to take in order to make of his art the expression and revelation of a full life-cycle of experience. One cannot arbitrarily state that a lack of positive identification with one or another force or tendency in a society will predetermine his becoming a good or a bad artist. And no one at all sensitive to literary art is likely to declare that Frank O'Connor is a bad artist. No Irish fiction writer since Joyce has come upon the Irish literary scene with more talent than O'Connor. But it remains, I think, that this shifting emotional background conditions the character of most of the stories printed in his *Bones of Contention, Crab Apple Jelly,* and *The Common Chord.*

Most of these stories have an anecdotal quality. The prejudices, the language, the feuds, the rigidities of Irish men and women are all worked into stories which often read like expanded anecdotes. Many of the tales are stories in the traditional sense. The elements underlying O'Connor's earlier writing are here washed over. In this respect, O'Connor has not developed in any degree compatible with his early promise. He has, rather, perfected a form of story-telling which leaves these elements in his work—and in Irish life—where they were—unresolved. His anecdotal stories have a quality of reality for he can create characters on paper, and he has mastered the conversational patterns of the types he draws so that their speech has a ring of reality. Humor and pathos are mingled in stories which depend for their effect on their local color, their quality of speech, and the sadly funny ignorance, prejudice and rigidity of the characters. Comedy, in the form of an anecdotal story, becomes a bridge of compromise between Nation and Church. On the one hand, the prejudices of the characters are often related to their religious attitudes, and to their puritanism; on the other hand, the priests of *Crab Apple Jelly* and *The Common Chord*—especially one Father Ring who appears in many of the stories—are humane and understanding, and they treat the laity with a certain paternal kindness which amounts to a form of benevolent manipulation.

The Common Chord of the latter title is sex. Sex, the power of instinct, is set in contrast to ignorance and puritanical attitudes. The stories deal with frustration, but mostly in a vein of comedy. The conventional attitudes which the characters have towards sex and love result in misunderstandings, in thwarted instincts, in various confusions. Instead of knowledge, the characters have recourse to additional superstitions, to miracles, and to Father Ring. Father Ring and the other priests have their own human problems, and they try to square human instincts with doctrine.

These stories are done most expertly. But they are all of a piece, and they are tales which cover up the basic problems and polarities that were rooted in O'Connor's early writing. Reading them, one cannot feel that here is an artist who is plunging forward to handle the antinomies in his own material, who is—as Joyce tried to do—seeking to create his own artistic structure out of these antinomies. In fact, if O'Connor were not so gifted, these tales would be stage-Irishman tales. They are very close to the stage-Irishman tradition. They have charm, local flair, and they embody many touches of comedic ignorance—qualities which are to be found in the stage-Irishman tradition. These should suggest how so often there is a compromise character to the prevailing notions of Irish charm. It serves the function of stratifying contradictions or antinomies. On the one hand, I can only admire O'Connor's gifts, and urge readers to familiarize themselves with his work; on the other hand, I feel, with each of his recent books, that there is a writer of first rate capacities who does not make the fullest use of his talents. And this is the story of all Irish writers except the greatest, like Joyce, Yeats, and Synge. O'Connor, perhaps the most gifted of contemporary Irish writers, represents these antinomies in contemporary Irish experience. His stories are tending, more and more, to become expert compromises of contradictions. And let me repeat, Irish charm is very frequently a compromise of this kind.

A Harvest of O'Faolain[1]

Sean O'Faolain is now fifty-seven. He has been with us for a long time. As a biographer he is not as widely recognized as he deserves to be, and, for instance, you rarely run into persons who have read his unforgettable biography, *Constance Markievicz.* I read it in Dublin almost nineteen years ago but to this day, it remains vivid and alive in my memory. And his work on Daniel O'Connell, *King of the Beggars,* contains some passages which I consider to be among the finest penned by an Irishman in the whole post-Joycean period of Irish literature.

Unlike so many of his contemporaries, he has remained in Ireland and continued to write. This is most difficult and Eire's literary men have been, almost all of them, wild geese. Not only economically, but socially and morally, the lot of the Irish writer who remains at home is a pretty hard one; it is easy for his thoughts and feelings to become distorted by anger and bitterness. This has not happened to O'Faolain. Besides the skill, the insight, the fine style which he brings to his work, you recognize on reading and re-reading him that his perspective is balanced. He has an eye for the comic as well as the sad, a good ear for Anglo-Irish speech, and the heart to feel with his characters.

The Finest Stories of Sean O'Faolain consist of thirty tales selected by the author. They range from stories written in his twenties to the most recent ones. He has refused to rewrite some of the earlier pieces— although they are studded with purple patches—because these reveal a part of what he was. A romantic feeling for the countryside and the atmosphere, dawn and twilight, the disillusionment which a sensitive Irishman felt after the Black and Tan war and "the troubles," the simple and often so amusing people of Ireland—these are among the ingredients of his work. Especially, it should be noted, O'Faolain writes of love with extraordinary taste and a grasp of the range of feelings which men and women possess for one another.

1. Reprinted from *The New Republic* 136 (17 June 1957): 19–20. The essay has also been reprinted in *James T. Farrell: Literary Essays, 1954–1974*, pp. 113–14.

Like Yeats, Sean O'Faolain improves with age. He is saturated with a sense of Ireland, but he is not parochial. He is a literary man of the world whose stories reveal the true dignity and the reality of some of his people. In this age of literary deadness and pretense, the re-publication of these stories of Sean O'Faolain takes on the character of a literary event. The word "finest" is not at all misplaced in the title of this book. These are some of the *finest* stories written in English during the last quarter century.

A Portrait of James Connolly[1]

I

The Irish national revolution can be viewed as a historical labora-
tory of the so-called national question. As the Irish rebelled, or threatened to rebel again and again during the nineteenth century, the
movement included elements from various classes and groups within the
country. To be sure, it is a commonplace to state that a national revolutionary movement comprises elements from more than one social class;
nonetheless, this commonplace must be stressed in any study of the
Irish national revolution. Just as there has been unity, there has also
been disunity. Differences within the Irish movement have often been
focused in terms of an opposition between the social question and the
political question, interpreting the latter to mean the central aim of
achieving national sovereignty or independence.

The Irish movement was energized by the Great French Revolution.
The United Irishmen, organized at the end of the eighteenth century,
were directly influenced by the men of the Great French Revolution.
Wolf Tone, a leader of that period, would serve as but one illustration
of this fact. John Mitchel, one of the strongest and bravest figures of
1848, was condemned as a felon and deported to the far Pacific. Even
though there was a strong conservatism and aristocratic feeling in his
nature, even though he defended the South against the North in the
American Civil War, he nevertheless showed a Jacobin streak. One
might say that Mitchel suggested both the tory socialist and the Jacobin.
Michael Davitt, one of the leaders of Parnell's party, continued the
tradition of these rebels. James Fintan Lalor, the hunchback, who was

---

1. Reprinted from a series of five essays published in *New International*: "The First Irish
Marxist: A Portrait of James Connolly," 13 (1947): 279–82; "Portrait of James Connolly
—II: Connolly as Nationalist and Internationalist," 14 (1948): 21–24; "Portrait of James
Connolly—III: Connolly's Democratic Views," 14 (1948): 40–41; "Portrait of James Connolly—IV: The Politics of Connolly's Catholicism," 14 (1948): 78–80; and "Portrait of
James Connolly—V: The Link Between Connolly's Catholicism and Marxism," 14 (1948):
120–23. The text of these essays has here been adapted mainly in accordance with Farrell's
manuscript galley-proof corrections [198], which were not incorporated in the *New International* version.

one of the most fiery and eloquent of all nineteenth-century rebels, based his thinking on the events of the Great French Revolution. And he was also encouraged by the revolutions of 1848 on the continent, as when he wrote:

> *Mankind will yet be masters of the earth.* The right of the people to make the laws—this produced the first great modern earthquake [the great French Revolution]. . . . The right of people to own the land—this will produce the next. Train your hands, and your sons' hands, gentlemen of the earth, for you and they will yet have to use them.[2]

Men such as Lalor and Davitt did not separate the social and the political question. Involved in the thinking of the major Irish rebels was an acceptance of the dignity of the individual which flows out of the traditional ideas of individualism. The Irish rebels were painfully aware of the degradation of the Irish people: they saw and knew the conditions of squalor and misery which were forced upon them. Mitchel saw the corpses of those who starved in the famine; he saw the wretched laden famine ships leaving for other lands. In Ireland, we can clearly see one of the psychological derivations of conditions of oppression and injustice. Poverty and a lack of sovereignty in a poor nation create attitudes of dependency. Except in rare moments of revolutionary momentum, the poorest sections of the masses of the people usually develop dependent attitudes. Robespierre, in one of his great speeches, declared that the Jacobins desired to create a nation in which men would rise "to the full stature of humanity." The poor usually fail to attain anything approximating that full stature. And the Irish rebels did not need to indulge in psychological theorizing in order to know about facts such as these. They grasped truths like these in their direct contacts with the Irish people. In this way, the notion of attaining manhood was linked with the idea of rebellion. In other words, rebellion offered them the road to manhood, not only for themselves, but also for the Irish people as a whole. On the one hand, they wanted to lead the Irish on the road to freedom; on the other hand, they saw the differences between themselves and the great masses of their fellow Irish. By rebellion, they were finding the way to the fullest possible attainment of their own manhood: feelings such as these served to link their personal experiences with their reading of Irish history. And those who saw most clearly realized that the attainment of their ends required consideration of the social, as well as of the political question.

---

2. From Lalor's "Faith of a Felon," as quoted in James Connolly, *Labour in Ireland* (Dublin: Maunsel & Co., 1917), p. 188.

At the present time, there are endless discussions of the question of personality and politics. Such discussions can often be interpreted as a consequence of the revolutionary defeats and failures of recent decades. A concept of personality was implied in the thinking of some of the outstanding Irish rebels of the nineteenth century. This is seen in the idea of the nation in Irish culture which was held by some of the nine-teenth-century Irish rebels. The Young Irelanders saw in culture—in poetry, balladry, literature—a means of whipping, lashing, encouraging the Irish into a feeling of pride and dignity in their own manhood.[3] Such a conception is unmistakable in the writings of Thomas Davis, or in the cultural writings of John Mitchel. A clear illustration is the introduction which Mitchel wrote to the poetry of James Clarence Mangan. Briefly, these men desired a nation of men, men in a qualitative sense of that word. Their desires motivated a trust in the potentialities of their fellow countrymen. And their trust was not confined to their ideas on culture, but was also integral in their political words and deeds. This trust underscored their lack of fear of violence and force. They tried to use all the means at their command to rouse the Irish people. When arrested, Lalor proudly flung the word, "felon" back into the faces of his jailers. After his arrest, and just prior to his deportation, John Mitchel refused to sign a statement urging his followers not to attempt his rescue from jail. The aim of national independence signified a nation of individuals with dignity; it envisaged an Ireland in which Irishmen would attain "the full stature of humanity." Samuel Johnson once remarked that "Patriotism is the last refuge of a scoundrel." This is often true, yet it is sometimes false. In nineteenth-century Ireland, patriotism was a first step on the road to manhood.

These comments should suggest aspects of the tradition which James Connolly represented in the Ireland of his day. The first Irish Marxist, he was the heir, the continuator and the expositor of this tradition. His real predecessors were those who did not sacrifice the social question for the political question; he fused both aspects of the

---

3. FARRELL'S NOTE: I am well aware that this statement can raise (all over again) questions concerning literature and propaganda. Inasmuch as I have dealt in detail with these questions in *A Note on Literary Criticism* and in other writings, I shall not go into them here where the discussion would raise side issues. It might be said, however, that men such as Mitchel and Thomas Davis revealed the best taste of their times. To criticize their taste, ex post facto, is merely to quarrel vainly with history and to raise sterile questions. The concept of the nation in Irish culture has remained to the present day, although this concept has gone through various permutations. But it should be added that taste does not flow directly out of concepts. The fact that Irish rebels such as John Mitchel had a political conception of culture in Ireland does not mean that they were crude in their reading habits.

Irish national tradition in his own works and in his own political life. He was an extraordinary figure during the early years of the twentieth century, not only in the Irish movement, but more broadly in the world movement for workers' emancipation. The intellectual fruits of his life are to be found in his work *Labour in Ireland.* This book is not only fundamental for a study of modern Irish history, it is also a contribution to the world library of socialist thought.

James Connolly has been the subject of a recent biography by R. M. Fox, an English socialist. Mr. Fox has lived in Ireland for years, and is widely read in the history and the literature of Ireland. Besides this recent book, *James Connolly: The Forerunner*, Fox has written other books on Ireland. His volume *Green Banners* is a story of Irish struggles, valuable for its assemblage of facts and material. His work *The Irish Citizen Army* is valuable for similar reasons, and, also, because it serves as a reminder of the significance of this organization, the first army of the working class in the twentieth century. It was written at the request of the organization of veterans of the Irish Citizen Army. Relatively few Englishmen are capable of writing objectively about Ireland and about the personalities of the Irish movement. Mr. Fox, like Raymond Postgate, author of an excellent biography of Robert Emmet, is something of an exception. He brings sympathy, energy, command of the facts, and knowledge of the history of the British and the European socialist movements to his work. At the same time, I feel it necessary to note that he sometimes succumbs to that parochialism which is fairly pervasive in Irish political thinking. (I would add parenthetically that there was no parochialism in Connolly.) His sympathy seems to fall over into an emotional identification with the Irish which, at times, is not devoid of localism and even sentimentality. And with this, his identification is part of the process whereby he establishes Irish nationalism as a criterion of judgment. Unlike Connolly, his biographer has not "fused" his socialist ideas with his adopted Irish nationalism.

However, it seems to me that there is an integral connection between Fox's virtues and his deficiencies. His writings can help to revive interest in the social side of the Irish tradition. He is retelling the story of the Irish struggle, refreshing memories concerning Connolly and the Irish Citizen Army, and emphasizing the best elements in the Irish tradition.

Fox's lucid account of the life of Connolly is based on the best sources. On the one hand, Fox offers paraphrases of Connolly's ideas, and gives full quotations from his writings; on the other hand, his recitation of the events in Connolly's life definitely conveys a sense of the man. Fox writes: "The story of the poor boy who becomes rich and successful has always made a strong appeal. But this is a story of far greater splendor—of a boy who did not become rich and yet his career remains an inspiration to all who strive for social justice."[4] It is the story of James Connolly. The son of poor parents, he was a self-educated worker. Forced emigration from Ireland was no hearsay tale for him. Both Connolly and his father could find work in England or Scotland, but not in Ireland, where, before their time, the English had seen to it that manufacturing could not exist. His own family story was but part of the general story of forced emigration from Ireland. He was born in a gloomy Irish cabin in 1870. His father was a farm laborer. The family had to leave Ireland for Scotland. There, he became a child laborer. At one time, he was placed on a box in the factory in order that he might appear to be taller than he was when the factory inspector came around. While still a youth, he worked at many jobs. He did work of the type which destroys the health and morale of men and women, let alone boys. He studied history, politics, literature, by candle light in an Irish cabin, or in a city tenement after harsh hours of work. He studied Marx, and his economic views were based on Marx, particularly on *Capital.* He became a Socialist in Scotland while still in his teens. But in his first period as a Socialist, he was quiet and did not thrust himself forward. He listened, observed, studied, learned what he could from older comrades before he came forth to assert and express his own views. When, in his youth, he did step forward, he became one of the leading Socialists in Glasgow. He married, worked as a Socialist, shared the hard life of the workers. In 1897, Connolly returned to Ireland to organize for Socialism. He lived there as did the exploited workers, and founded the Irish Republican Socialist Congress. As early as 1900, he participated in international socialist congresses, and at these meetings he generally supported the left wing. In Dublin, he played the role of an agitator, an organizer and an editor. He shared in the organization of the famous anti-British demonstrations in the year of the jubilee of Queen Victoria. In 1904, he came to America. Here, he worked at various jobs including that of an insurance agent, and he participated in the activities of the American labor and socialist movements. He was associated with Daniel De Leon, with the Industrial Workers of the World, and later, with the Socialist Party in the time of Eugene V. Debs. He had political disagreements with De Leon and these were exacerbated because he was a practicing Catholic. His experiences in America were of prime importance in his later career. Here, he saw, at first hand, the capitalism in an

---

4. R. M. Fox, *James Connolly: The Forerunner* (Tralee: Kerryman Press, 1946), p. 16.

advanced country. This helped him to see the problems of Ireland more clearly than could many of his contemporaries. Here also his association with the IWW showed lasting influences. His own conceptions of industrial unionism, as well as of strike tactics and agitational methods, were all influenced by the Wobblies.

Connolly returned to Ireland in 1910 and became an organizer in Belfast for the Irish Transport Workers Union, playing a major role in the organization and the development of the Irish Labor movement in the North of Ireland. He became associated with Jim Larkin, and went to Dublin to participate in the leadership of the Dublin transport strike. He helped to organize the Irish Citizen Army, led it in the Easter Rebellion, was wounded during the fighting, and was one of the leaders who was executed. He was carried to his execution in a chair because of his wounds. When his wife visited him for the last time, he tried to comfort her. Telling her not to cry, he added: "Hasn't it been a full life? And isn't this a good end?" On learning that his son had been in jail, his face lit up, and he remarked: "He was in the fight. . . . He has had a good start in life, hasn't he?"[5]

In most of the photographs of Connolly, he looks like an ordinary, almost an undistinguished, man. Judging from these pictures, he might be any Irish bar tender, small business man, craftsman. He was a simple, quiet man, careful, precise, thoughtful and determined. Capable in theory although self-taught, he was also highly practical. No Irish contemporary of his could match his qualities, his strategical understanding and his extremely clear sense of tactics. He studied with the most practical of aims: in order to learn how best to carry forward the Irish struggle. And, in turn, he saw the Irish struggle as part of the struggle of the workers all over the world. He studied the revolutions of the past in Ireland and on the continent in order to teach himself, and the Irish, how they might strike their own blows for freedom most effectively. In various articles, he tried to bring the experiences of other countries to the Irish. Democratic, both in theory and practice, he asked every member of the Irish Citizen Army if they wanted to go through with the fight they were going to make in the Easter Rebellion. They did.

A few personal anecdotes and stories about Connolly will perhaps best give a sense of the man. These are taken from Mr. Fox's book and from other sources. Connolly's daughter, Nora Connolly O'Brien, wrote a moving personal account of her father, *Portrait of a Rebel Father,* which well might be read in conjunction with Mr. Fox's biography. It is per-

---

5. Ibid., pp. 214–15.

sonal and intimate, and the emotions motivating it are truly beautiful. In *Portrait of a Rebel Father,* Nora Connolly O'Brien tells how once at Mass, the priest violently denounced Connolly in a sermon. Although Connolly was not mentioned, it was clear to him and to his daughter, and also to many others present, that he was the object of this attack. The daughter was disturbed and distressed; she wanted to squirm, to do something. But Connolly sat unruffled, listening with no sense of strain or agitation showing on his face. Afterwards, she asked him why he had not done anything, why he had not at least walked out of the church? He answered: "Well, Nora, because they lose their dignity, we don't have to lose ours."

In 1915, during the course of a strike on the Dublin quays, the police were harassing the strikers. Clerks had been forced to work as scabs. Connolly, on learning of the continued police treatment of the workers, declared that this would have to stop. He called out a squad of the Irish Citizen Army. They reported for duty wearing their dark green uniforms, and armed with rifles and bayonets. They marched to the picket line in formation; there, they marched along at the side of the pickets, informing the police that they had come to protect their striking class brothers. The pickets were no longer molested; the clerks inside fled. Soon after this incident the strike was settled.

Not long before the Easter Rebellion, the British sent the police out to raid rebel papers, and to confiscate copies of these and the equipment used in printing them. The police arrived at Liberty Hall, headquarters of the Irish Transport Workers, and, also, of the Irish Citizen Army. Connolly asked them if they had a warrant. They had none. He drew his revolver and declared that they would not be allowed to search the hall. When they returned with a warrant in order to search the premises for copies of nationalist papers, Connolly, revolver in hand, stood by the door leading into the room in which was printed the paper that he edited. He told the police that he would shoot the man who entered this room, insisting that the warrant did not apply to it. The police searched the rest of Liberty Hall, found no nationalist papers, and departed. Connolly's paper was, at that time, not suppressed. Following this raid, Connolly sent out orders for the mobilization of the members of the Irish Citizen Army. Irish workers downed their tools, left wagons in the streets and rushed to Liberty Hall. Some even swam the Liffey to get there. They reported in working clothes, rifles in hand.

Connolly was arrested during the labor battles of 1913. He went on a hunger strike, and was released from prison, weak from want of food. Once when he was lecturing in America, he was interviewed by a reporter. This journalist had questioned other Irishmen, and many had claimed that they were descended from the kings of Ireland. More generally, the journalist had a fixed notion that Irishmen always boasted of the grandeur of their country and of their own ancestry. He asked Connolly a question about his ancestors, and added that he wanted to know if they had owned estates or castles in the old country. Connolly answered: "I have no ancestors. My people were poor and obscure like the workers I am speaking to now."[6] Recalling his youth and his early readings, he once said: "I always remember the first time I sent . . . for a bundle of *Penny Readings* and how delighted I was when they came. . . . It was always so difficult for me to get to read as a boy that I thought it wonderful to receive a parcel like this."[7]

When he led the Irish Citizen Army out for the Easter Rebellion, he told the members that they would be given the post of honor: they would attack. And he also told them to keep their rifles because some of those (the Nationalists) with whom they were joining to fight, would not be willing to go as far as the workers must go: they might need their rifles again.

Connolly was a man of genuine simplicity and of deep humanity. No problem of the Irish workers was too small for him to give it his attention. No sacrifice was too great for him when his ideas were at stake. His writings were clear, simple, direct, and marked by flashes of genuine eloquence. *Labour in Irish History* and *The Re-Conquest of Ireland* were written over long periods of time under conditions of great difficulty. He had to work for his own living, and to carry on his practical political activities. He had none of the leisure of the trained scholar or the professional intellectual. The completion of these works was, in fact, a triumph of his own will, a revelation of his persistence and determination. And these books are, as Robert Lynd stated, "of infinite importance to Ireland."[8] Their importance is not solely to Ireland, but to the whole world.

II

Connolly was not only a brave and bold fighting man, he was also a bold and stimulating thinker. One of the reasons which helps to

---

6. Ibid., p. 58.
7. Ibid., p. 27.
8. Connolly, *Labour in Ireland*, p. xxvi.

explain why many American Marxists have often been rigid and schematic is that they have not sufficiently grasped the problems of capitalism from the standpoint of a backward country with an undeveloped economy, in contrast to those of an advanced country with a modern economy. Because of this, I think that Connolly should have an especial interest and significance for Americans. He was a Marxist who came from the depressed working class of a backward country, a nation which had not won national sovereignty.

Once we realize this fact, seeming contradictions in his work and his beliefs can be explained. Connolly, besides being a Marxist and a revolutionary leader who came from the working class, was also a nationalist and a believing Roman Catholic. He was born amidst conditions of life which feed discontent: the alternative to discontent in conditions such as those of his childhood is an attitude of submissiveness. Rebellion and discontent became for Connolly the road for the development of his own personality, his individuality.

He was but one of a mass oppressed by capitalism; at the same time, this mass bore most heavily the burden which was imposed as a result of English control of Ireland. As Connolly studied and matured, he came to see that a complicated series of burdens lay on the back of the common people of Ireland: there was more than one oppressor. He was able to understand with lucidity the complicated nature of the problems which were involved in the Irish problem.

Reading his work, or the accounts of his life, one is struck by the fact that there was little subjective blockage in Connolly's nature. He was direct and simple. He was capable of drawing clear and warranted correlations. He was able to measure actions, large and small, in terms of his ultimate aim—the aim of a democratic and socialist world. His own personal experiences and observations were drawn into his thought; and on the basis of these he was able to grasp facts from his studies with amazing lucidity and to arrive at firm theoretical conclusions.

There was considerable variety of experiences in his own life. He saw at first hand the conditions of life of workers in Ireland, in Scotland, in America. He was clearly aware of differences between Ireland and America. Even before he came to the United States he had studied economics by himself and had written about the differences in methods of agricultural production in Ireland and in the United States. Thus he wrote:

The agriculture of Ireland can no longer compete with the scientifically equipped farmers of America, therefore the only hope that now remains is to abandon competition altogether as a rule of life, to organize agriculture as a public service under the control of boards of management elected by the agricultural population (no longer composed of farmers and laborers, but of free citizens with equal responsibility and equal honor), and responsible to them and the nation at large, and with all the mechanical and scientific aids to agriculture the entire resources of the nation can place at their disposal. Let the produce of Irish soil go first to feed the Irish people, and after a sufficient store has been retained to insure of that being accomplished, let the surplus be exchanged with other countries in return for those manufactured goods Ireland needs but does not herself produce.

Thus we will abolish at one stroke the dread of foreign competition and render perfectly needless any attempt to create an industrial hell in Ireland under the specious pretext of "developing our resources."

Apply to manufacture the same social principle. Let the cooperative organization of the workers replace the war of the classes under capitalism and transform the capitalist himself from an irresponsible hunter after profit into a public servant, fulfilling a public function and under public control.[9]

And speaking along the same line, he discussed the proposal to create peasant proprietors instead of a landlord class. He wrote:

Have our advocates of peasant proprietary really considered the economic tendencies of the time, and the development of the mechanical arts in the agricultural world? The world is progressive, and peasant proprietary, which a hundred years ago might have been a boon, would now be powerless to save from ruin the agriculture of Ireland.[10]

The small farmers could no longer compete with the mammoth farms of America and Australia, and he continued by pointing out how the American farmer, with his thousands of acres and his machinery could outsell the Irish farmer in the English market.

Economic backwardness is a phenomenon which needs to be evaluated relativistically. It must be gauged from the standpoint of the world market. At the present time the phenomenon of backwardness is more complicated than it ever was in the past. Advanced countries such as England are being placed in a position that is at least remotely analogous to that of the Irish farmers in Connolly's time. British workers must work harder and get less than the American workers. This is a consequence of competition on the world market. It is to Connolly's merit that he grasped this fact and stated it simply and clearly in his very first years as a socialist.

Without the formal academic training of many economists, Con-

---

9. Quotation from Connolly's *Erin's Hope: The End and the Means* (1901) in Fox, *James Connolly: The Forerunner*, p. 231.
10. Ibid., p. 232.

nolly saw the relationship of the Irish problem to the problems of the world market. In simple language he was able to state the nature of the impact which the world market made on Ireland, on its farmers and also on its workers. His political nationalism was not turned into an excuse for "economic" nationalism. He wanted Irishmen to be free men, free and proud and dignified: he did not believe in the development of national resources in a backward country at the expense of the moral and social development of the people of that country.

In this sense he may be contrasted with Joseph Stalin. Connolly advocated democratic collectivization as a means of feeding the Irish people and of organizing Irish economy in a rational and just manner. Stalin's forced collectivization was diametrically opposite to that proposed by the young Connolly.[11] Connolly here had a very clear insight, one which should be carefully considered by those who have argued that he was too nationalistic to be a socialist. His nationalism was, in reality, consistent with his internationalism. And both were consistently developed not only in political but also in economic terms.[12]

---

11. FARRELL'S NOTE: As Manya Gordon demonstrates factually in her book *Workers Before and After Lenin* (New York: E. P. Dutton, 1941), the Russian people as a whole got less food after collectivization than they did before it. Collectivization provided Stalin with a labor supply needed for industrialization. The development of national resources was implicit in the implementation of the theory of "socialism in one country"; but all this, as we know, was done at the expense of the Russian people.

12. FARRELL'S NOTE: A good way of testing Connolly's clarity would be to contrast his ideas—such as those quoted above—with the ideas of the Irish Stalinist, Brian O'Neill, in *The War for the Land in Ireland*. Both here and in his book *Easter Week*, O'Neill pays tribute to Connolly.

Writing in the 1930s, O'Neill dealt with the world agrarian crisis, and he had no trouble demonstrating that the Irish farmer was the victim of the world market and produced at a grave disadvantage in competition because of the development of farming in advanced countries. Attempting to point the way out, O'Neill quoted the passage of Connolly which I have cited above. And the way out proposed by O'Neill is described as that taken by the Soviet Union, with planned economy and collectivized agriculture. As part of his proof O'Neill offered culled statistics from the various Soviet sources, but he did not compare and evaluate them. He may well have been sincere, but from the standpoint of the present it is clear that he depended on the usual bureaucratic generalities and abstractions. The Irish problem was treated as though it were the Russian problem: win a "third-period" revolution on paper and then Ireland could be modeled after the Soviet Union. Without any real relevance to his argument, O'Neill insisted that the increase in the number of tractors and harvesters in the United States from 1910 to 1930 should have permitted American agriculture to double its sowing. This did not happen; American agricultural production increased by only 13.5 percent during this period. Needless to say, I am not an economist or a statistician. But I can see the utter shabbiness of arguments of this kind.

I mention this fact because, when I originally read O'Neill's book in 1936, it fooled me. And the way that Stalinism fools persons untrained in economics and statistics can thus be suggested. Isolated statistics are used falsely. By a meaningless comparison of abstracted statistics, a false conception of production in the Soviet Union relative to the United States is indicated. We now know that the Irish workers and farmers, bad as was their lot, fared better than did the Russian workers and farmers during the period of forced

Connolly absorbed the democratic national tradition of Ireland. When he released the first issue of his paper, *The Workers Republic*, in Dublin on August 13, 1898, he stated:

> We are Socialists because we see in socialism not only the modern applica-
> tion of the social principle which underlay the Brehon laws of our ances-
> tors, but because we recognize in it the only principle by which the working
> class can in their turn emerge in the divinity of FREEMEN, with the right
> to live as men and not as mere profit-making machines for the service of
> others. *We are Republicans because we are Socialists,* and therefore enemies to all
> privileges; *and because we would have the Irish people complete masters of their own
> destinies, nationally and internationally, fully competent to work for their own salvation.* [13]

Spiritually or intellectually, he was a product of the great French Revolution, of the Irish tradition of rebellion, of the Marxist international movement, and also of the Catholic Church. And, as we have

---

collectivization. After the famine in Russia in the early 1930s, the Russian government was forced to make concessions: it permitted a certain portion of the agricultural product produced on collective farms to be sold directly on the market. Here is the way O'Neill described this: "The produce of farms is disposed of in two ways. It can be handed over entirely at a fixed price to the cooperative organizations, to be distributed by them to the consumers, or twenty percent can be sold direct (a method introduced in 1932 to induce the collectives to market more of their produce). The advantages of this latter modification are that larger supplies are available at lower prices due to the more direct path from the producer to the consumer, while the collectives are often able to receive more for their produce. Vegetables grown in the garden may also be sold direct to the consumer, but no middleman is permitted to step into the transaction." (Brian O'Neill, *The War for the Land in Ireland* [New York: International Publishers, 1933], p. 173.)

This last sentence is further suggestive. O'Neill introduced this reference to the middleman as an obvious appeal to prejudice and as a rationalization. In general, he gave no clear picture of Soviet agriculture; at the same time he stressed the chaos of capitalist agriculture. He threatened to outdistance American agricultural production with a mini-mum of percentages. And here is a sample of his general style and method of Stalinizing the tradition of Connolly: "By 1926 it could be said that agriculture had been saved [in the Soviet Union]. . . . But hand in hand with this development, there was not only an increased prosperity for small and middle farmers; the wealthiest peasants and the kulaks —the hated gombeen men of the village, who worked their farms by hired laborers and who were often, in addition, shopkeepers, money-lenders or publicans—had their posi-tion strengthened, with a corresponding hardening of their capitalist psychology. And while agriculture had been restored, it had not developed on the new social basis, in the sense that while in the towns the means of production were long since socialized, agricul-ture, in which the ownership of the land and the implements was not centralized, was relatively much more backward." (Ibid., pp. 171, 172.) The reader can learn about the real situation which was masked by this double talk by reading Manya Gordon's study cited above [n. 11].

A contrast between Connolly and O'Neill will show the difference between a real socialist and a Stalinized intellectual. In Connolly's heated passages, there is indignation, indignation over the condition of the Irish masses. Contrast this with the way that O'Neill uses phrases like gombeen men, money-lenders and publicans in order to create Irish enthusiasm for Stalinism, which drove the gombeen men out of Russia just as truly as St. Patrick drove the snakes out of Ireland. Also, Connolly studied conditions outside of Ireland in a critical spirit, and in order to draw a lesson from them; O'Neill merely applied Russian solutions to Irish conditions in a literal-minded manner.

13. Quoted in Fox, *James Connolly: The Forerunner,* p. 46.

noted, he himself lived the hard life of the workers. He arrived at his ideas by patient and methodical study. And the aim of his thought and activity was to work for genuine freedom. Once when a lady was disturbed by a speech he had delivered, he answered her remarks by declaring: "Revolution is my business." His total life experience led him forward to revolutionary action. He saw this action as taking place in Ireland. But he linked it with the idea of an international struggle for socialism and democracy.

When away from Ireland he participated in the socialist movement in Scotland and in America. When the First World War broke out, he called for action not only in Ireland but elsewhere. He saluted Karl Liebknecht. And when there was a false rumor that Liebknecht had died, he wrote:

> We cannot draw upon the future for a draft to pay our present duties. There is no moratorium to postpone the payment of the debt the Socialists owe to the cause; it can only be paid now. Paid it may well be in martyrdom. . . . If our German comrade, Liebknecht, has paid the price, perhaps the others may yet nerve themselves for that sacrifice. . . . All hail, then, to our continental comrade, who, in a world of imperial and financial brigands and cowardly trimmers and compromisers, showed mankind that men still know how to die for the holiest of all causes—the sanctity of the human soul, the practical brotherhood of the human race.[14]

Connolly worked on *Labour in Irish History* for many years. During this period he was also engaged in many other activities, editing, lecturing, organizing, leading strikes, participating in anti-British demonstrations, traveling from Ireland to America and back to Ireland, and at the same time earning a modest living for himself and his family. This work, along with *The Re-Conquest of Ireland,* offers an economic and social history of Ireland. Connolly claimed that capitalism was a foreign importation brought to Ireland by the English. With capitalism, feudalism was also introduced into Ireland. The life of the Gaelic clans, where property was owned by the clans, was in consequence broken up. In clan life a rudimentary form of democracy had been practiced. Then he traced the course of the development of capitalism in Ireland, a subject nation. He related this development to the successive struggles for national independence. These struggles he evaluated and interpreted from a socialist standpoint. Early in *Labour in Irish History,* he quoted, as a premise, the following passage from Marx:

---

14. Ibid., p. 239.

That in every historical epoch the prevailing method of economic production and exchange, and the social organization necessarily following from it, forms the basis upon which alone can be explained the political and intellectual history of that epoch.[15]

He traces the alterations in the prevailing method of production in Ireland through feudalism to capitalism, and he describes the class character of every movement which struggled for Irish freedom. The tradition of social struggle in the Irish national movement is here outlined step by step, generalized, evaluated and in this way ordered in terms of a coherent analysis and doctrine. The lesson which he persistently draws from the analysis of Irish struggle is that the social question is inseparable from the political question.

He reveals that one of the factors involved in the failure of Irish rebellion is the fact that there was always more than one class. This lesson is presented in his first chapter, and it is then illustrated by a series of lucid analyses which are concerned with every important movement for liberation in Irish history. He wrote:

During the last hundred years every generation in Ireland has witnessed an attempted rebellion against English rule. Every such conspiracy or rebellion had drawn the majority of its adherents from the lower orders in town and country, yet under the inspiration of a few middle class doctrinaires the social question has been rigorously excluded from the field of action to be covered by the rebellion if successful; in hopes that by each exclusion it would be possible to conciliate the upper class and enlist them in the struggle for freedom. . . . The result has been in nearly every case the same. The workers, though furnishing the greatest proportion of recruits to the ranks of the revolutionists, and consequently of victims to the prison and the scaffold, could not be imbued *en masse* with the revolutionary fire necessary to seriously imperil a dominion rooted for 700 years in the heart of their country. They were all anxious enough for freedom, but realizing the enormous odds against them, and being explicitly told by their leaders that they *must not expect any change in their conditions of social subjection, even if successful,* they as a body shrank from the contest, and left only the purest minded and most chivalrous of their class to face the odds and glut the vengeance of the tyrant—a warning to those in all countries who neglect the vital truth that successful revolutions are not the product of our brains, but of ripe material conditions.[16]

Connolly's conclusion to his study affirms the view that labor must take the lead in the liberation of Ireland. It must be the most forward, the most daring champion of both national liberation and social justice

---

15. Connolly, *Labour in Ireland,* p. 15.
16. Ibid., pp. 6–7.

in Ireland; it must assemble all discontented Irishmen around it. This is the road to the re-conquest of Ireland. Thus:

> As we have again and again pointed out, the Irish question is a social question, the whole age-long fight of the Irish people against their oppressors resolves itself in the last analysis into a fight for the mastery of the means of life, the sources of production, in Ireland. Who would own and control the land? The people or the invaders?[17]

Here in Connolly's view was "the bottom question of Irish politics." But:

> It is undeniable that for two hundred years at least all Irish political movements ignored this fact, and were conducted by men who did not look below the political surface. These men to arouse the passions of the people invoked the memory of social wrongs, such as evictions and famines, but for these wrongs proposed only political remedies, such as changes in taxation or transferences of the seat of government (class rule) from one country to another. . . . The revolutionists of the past were wiser, the Irish Socialists are wiser today. In their movement the North and South will again clasp hands, again it will be demonstrated, as in '98, that the pressure of a common exploitation can make enthusiastic rebels out of a Protestant working class, earnest champions of civil and religious liberty out of Catholics, and out of both a united social democracy.[18]

Connolly's basic lines of thought were continued from *Labour in Irish History* to *The Re-Conquest of Ireland*. The first sentence of the foreword to this volume expresses its guiding thought:

> The underlying idea of this work is that the labor movement of Ireland must set itself the re-conquest of Ireland as its final aim, that their re-conquest involves taking possession of the entire country, all its powers and wealth—production and all its natural resources, and organizing these on a co-operative basis for the good of all.[19]

Following a historical account of the conquest of Ireland, Connolly describes the conditions of life of the Irish masses in the early twentieth century, in Dublin and Belfast; he discusses problems and questions of democracy and of political morale and of morality, quotes statistics and otherwise reveals in a voice of eloquent and passionate indignation the moral and physical consequences of exploitation; he deals with the problems of education, describes the position and fate of women, and analyzes the value and the possibility of the cooperative movement. His

---

17. Ibid., p. 214.
18. Ibid., pp. 215–16.
19. Ibid., p. 219.

book embodies vision and idealism, and at the same time no detail concerning the misery and wretchedness of the masses is too small for his attention. At one point in the book, he states: "For the only true prophets are they who carve out the future which they announce."[20]

Connolly here announced a future for Ireland. This ideal future—a socialist commonwealth—was the standard by which he measured the Irish present, and it was the basis of his political faith. In action, he sought to lead Ireland toward the realization of that ideal; in his writing, he sought to implant this faith and this ideal in the minds of Irishmen. He wrote:

> A people are not to be judged by the performance of their great men, nor to be estimated spiritually by the intellectual conquests of their geniuses. A truer standard by which the spiritual and mental measurement of a people can be taken in modern times is by that picture drawn of itself by itself when it, at the ballot-box, surrenders the care of its collective destiny into the hands of its elected representatives.
>
> The question whether such elected persons have or have not the power to realize the desires of their constituents scarcely enters into the matter. It is not by its power to realize high ideals a people will and must be judged, but by the standard of the ideals themselves.[21]

This quotation furnishes a suggestive insight into the thought of Connolly. His thinking was both practical and visionary; it gave energy and direction to a fighting faith and a concept of a free future.

III

Writing about Dublin in the early twentieth century in *The Reconquest of Ireland,* James Connolly declared:

> It is, indeed, strange that the people of a nation which has known indomitable determination in its struggle for possession of the mere machinery of government should exhibit so little capacity to breathe a civic soul into such portions of the machinery as they had already brought under their control.[22]

This quotation is but one of many which could be taken from Connolly's writings in order to suggest the thoroughgoing character of

---

20. Ibid.
21. Ibid., p. 251.
22. Ibid., p. 249.

his democratic views. It was Connolly, the Socialist, who explained and developed democratic views perhaps more fully than any Irish political figure of his time. A working-class and trade-union leader, Connolly brought democratic ideas of leadership and democratic conceptions of a rank and file into the Irish rebellion.

The difference between the Fenian Brotherhood of the nineteenth century and the Irish Citizen Army would indicate this. The former was organized along the lines of a secret society, and the reins of control were centered in the leadership. When the Fenians were ready to strike a blow the leadership hesitated in making a decision; the Fenians missed their opportunity and disappeared from history.[23]

We have already noted that before the Irish Citizen Army went through with the Easter Rebellion, Connolly gave every member an opportunity to decide on whether to go along in the struggle or drop out. The Irish Citizen Army, despite its democracy, disappeared from history as did the Fenians. But it left an addition to the legacy of the Fenians and to the entire tradition of the Irish national rebellion—a legacy of democracy in thought and practice.

At the present time many socialists think of democracy mainly in relationship to a democratic party organization and to the ideal of developing a democratic internal life in left party organizations and movements. This is important. But democratic socialist thinking should require a broader interest, and at the same time it should dictate a concern with those small practical details of organizing life which are now viewed in a routine manner, if not with outright cynicism. Socialism should sponsor ideas of a genuine civic consciousness which is preached but not practiced in our own time. Connolly's remarks in the above quotation reveal his own sense of civic consciousness—of municipal patriotism, if one will.

At the beginning of this essay, I spoke of the recurrent division in the history of the Irish national revolution, a division on the question: Does the political or the social question come first? Connolly, as we know, belonged to the tradition of Irish rebels who stressed the social question. But his stress was not made merely in large and broad terms. He drew conclusions from his social position which he applied in small matters as well as in large ones. His ideas on civic consciousness derived from his social views. They were expressions of his socialist position.

Connolly valued all rights and liberties too sincerely to want to see

---

23. FARRELL'S NOTE: See *Recollections of an Irish Rebel: The Fenian Movement,* by John Devoy (New York: C. P. Young Co., 1929) for an account of the Fenians, their internal life, and their organizational character.

them wasted. He observed that after the Irish had gained democratic rights in municipal affairs, they did not use these rights; they demonstrated a lack of civic consciousness. Wanting national sovereignty, they were badly utilizing the voting rights which they had already gained. And Connolly's discussion and criticism here served as a means for an illuminating socialist discussion of democracy.

Connolly, let me repeat, was most thoroughgoing in his democratic thoughts and ideas. Thus, in writing of "the function of public bodies as a governing factor in Irish municipal politics," Connolly emphasized that these functions of public bodies should be seen and used not merely as offensive political weapons to be won from an enemy, but also as "effective tools to be used in the upbuilding of a healthier social edifice in which to give effect to the needs of the citizens for associative aids to their individual development and culture." It is a commonplace to remind readers that Marx's real starting point was the ideal of a society which would permit the fullest and freest development of the human personality. Such an ideal was central in the mind of James Connolly. He would use every democratic gain as a means of contributing toward the development and culture of the Irish people. All political action was a means to be used in creating a freer society in which the individual could live and develop in dignity. During the First World War he wrote:

> We believe that in times of peace we should work along the lines of peace to strengthen the nation, and we believe that whatever strengthens and elevates the working class strengthens the nation.
> But we also believe that in times of war we should act as in war. We despise, entirely loathe and despise, all the mouthings and mouthers about war who infest Ireland in times of peace, just as we despise and loathe all the cantings about caution and restraint to which the same people treat us in times of war.[24]

Connolly did not see violence as an end, nor did he love violence as some rebel spirits seem to love it. Likewise, he did not see power as an end in itself. He visioned a nation, a society, a world in which men and women, living with dignity, would be healthier than they are, better fed, better educated, more cooperative.

This vision was neither Utopian nor millennial. He would not compromise with the principles on which this vision, this ultimate aim, was based. But he would not, at the same time, scorn any immediate rights and advantages that could be gained. Immediate democratic gains were

---

24. Quoted in Fox, *James Connolly: The Forerunner*, p. 242.

means toward greater gains; and they could also become tools for trying to lift the cultural level of the people immediately. In times of peace, he did not scorn means of peace in order to talk of weapons of war which he did not yet possess.

Thus, ideas of civic consciousness and municipal patriotism were no mere platitudes to him. They were integral in his broader social and human attitudes which embodied a clear conception of social responsibility. Thus he wrote that "We require in Ireland to grasp the fact that the act of voting at the ballot box is the one act in which we get the opportunity to give expression to the soul of the race. . . . The ballot box is the vehicle of expression of our social consciousness."

Like almost all, if not all, great revolutionaries, Connolly was an educator. And he saw in the practices of democracy a means of educating the people. In effect, his political teaching on democracy served as a way of preparing the people for the exercise of power. Just as he studied revolutions of the past and wrote articles on these in order to teach Irish workingmen how to prepare for the rising which came in 1916, so at an earlier period he tried to teach the Irish masses how to exercise democratic rights, how to use these rights in order to provide for and improve the conditions of their own welfare.

He knew too well the price of liberty to be cynical about any liberties which had already been won. Thus, he wrote in *The Re-Conquest of Ireland:*

> Assuredly it was within the realm of probability that a people suffering under the smart of intolerable conditions caused by a misuse of political power and social privilege should at the first opportunity set itself to the task of sweeping away such conditions by a public-spirited use of their newly-acquired control of municipal powers.[25]

But such did not happen when the Irish gained democratic rights.

> If today the cities and towns of Ireland are a reproach to the land and a glaring evidence of the incapacity of the municipal rulers of the country, the responsibility for the failure lies largely with those who in the past had control of the political education of the Irish masses and failed to prepare them for the intelligent exercise of those public powers for which they were taught to clamor.[26]

And need we emphasize that observations of such a character lead to the basic conclusion which Connolly repeated over and over again—labor must take the lead in the Irish struggle.

---

25. Connolly, *Labour in Ireland,* pp. 252–53.
26. Ibid., p. 253.

In April, 1916, shortly before the Easter Rebellion, he declared: "The cause of Labor is the cause of Ireland, the cause of Ireland is the cause of labor."[27] And that cause was one to bring dignity into human life. The general welfare, the dignity of man, this was the cause of socialism. It was at the same time the cause of democracy. The democratic tradition of the French Revolution, which was inherited by predecessors of Connolly, Tone, Emmet, the Young Irelanders of '48, Lalor and Davitt, was absorbed by Connolly.

And no matter what aspect of Connolly's social and political thinking we take, we see how it was always admirably consistent. However, his was not the formal consistency of a sectarian who disdains all struggles for immediate gains on the ground that such gains will not necessarily mean socialism; nor was it the consistency of a critical theoretician who was never forced to act, to take decisions involving the greatest risks. It was the consistency of a dedicated and devoted man who had committed himself to go the long, hard and dangerous road that is demanded of all who want men really to be free.

At the same time we can see, in Connolly's consistency, his love of the people. Connolly's indignation always flared when he learned of injustice, of indignities heaped on the people. And his was an indignation different in quality from that of some contemporary Marxists whose greatest anger seems to come when they discover a theoretical error in the writings of an adversary. Unlike Connolly's, theirs is an indignation of self-love. It has contributed toward poisoning the streams of modern socialist thought. Connolly's consistency is a consistency based on love, on a realization of common identity between himself and the workers whom he led. It is this feeling of common identity which further motivates his conception of democracy.

IV

The historic experiences of Ireland as a subject and exploited nation can be described as the other and non-progressive side of the rise of English capitalism and the Industrial Revolution.

If we look at England, without in any way minimizing the horrors of the new industrialism, we can see the advances made with the rise

---

27. Quoted in Fox, *James Connolly: The Forerunner*, p. 219.

of capitalism. There was an enormous economic development and, in addition, there were real political gains of a democratic character. England became one of the most democratic countries in the world.

But if we look at Ireland, it is much harder to see these advances. Here was a nation invaded and despoiled by foreigners. Its industry was smashed. Its people were driven off the land and out of the country. Its clan system was broken up. The faith of its fathers was ruthlessly abused by the despoiling invaders who were also the professors of an antagonistic religious creed.

Consider these facts—which are but roughly and hastily generalized here but which were vivid, concrete and intimate to generations of the Irish—and it should not be difficult to understand how and why Catholic Irishmen would not see the progressive side of the Reformation. That liberty of conscience which has historically been so influenced by the rise of Protestantism had to be defended and fought for by Catholics. In their own country, Irish Catholics lost their citizenship. They were exiles in their own country, and in fact it can be said that here are the historic roots of that melancholy sense of alienation which is to be found, even to this day, in so many Irish and even in Irish-Americans who are far removed in space and time from remote and oppressed Catholic Irish ancestors.

Sean O'Faolain, in his biography of Daniel O'Connell, *King of the Beggars,* writes of Catholic relief bills prior to the rise of O'Connell as a political leader: "After 1771 an Irishman might lease a bog for a brief period, if it was a mile from a town . . . and if the lessee guaranteed to reclaim at least half of his bogland within twenty-one years." And after 1782, as O'Faolain also wrote:

> A Catholic, i.e., one of the people was suddenly acknowledged as a species of citizen, if a very inferior species of citizen; so inferior that our historians of Dublin under the Georges have been unable to find a single detail about the people, and all we can gather about them is to be inferred from the contemporary theatre in which they begin to appear as the faithful, if rather foolish, servant . . . every office was closed to the native—unless he apostatized—the army, the law, and the civil service—though he could become a doctor in private practice, or open an apothecary's shop. Not until 1793 . . . could a native Irishman enter the army. . . . But he could take neither hand, act, nor part in the government of his country. . . . He walked with the word Pariah branded on his forehead.[28]

One could add many details concerning the persecution of Catholics, including the clergy, and the ways in which religious persecution

---

28. Sean O'Faolain, *King of the Beggars* (London: Thomas Nelson, 1938), pp. 54–55.

was linked with national and social oppression. Connolly himself, in *Labour in Irish History,* wrote:

> War, religion, race, language, political reform, patriotism—apart from whatever intrinsic merits they may possess—all serve in the hands of the possessing class as counter-irritants, whose function is to avert the catastrophe of social revolution by engendering heat in such parts of the body politic as are farthest removed from the seat of economic inquiry.[29]

England is noted in the history books for having perfected the technique of divide-and-rule in modern times. The policy of ruling an oppressed nation or race by dividing it was worked out, as it were, in the terrible empirical-historical situation of Britain's seven-century rule of Ireland.

The Irish were, then, beggared and oppressed for a long period. The horrible conditions of life in Ireland in the eighteenth century were revealed in Swift's masterpiece of irony and sarcasm, *A Modest Proposal for Preventing the Children of the Poor People in Ireland from Becoming a Burden on their Parents or Country, and for Making them Beneficial to the Public.* This began:

> It is a melancholy Object to those, who walk through this great Town [Dublin], or travel in the Country, when they see the *Streets,* the *Roads,* and *Cabbin-Doors,* crowded with *Beggars* of the female Sex, followed by three, four or six Children, *all in Rags,* and importuning every Passenger for an Alms. These *Mothers* instead of being able to work for their honest livelihood, are forced to employ all their time in Strolling, to beg Sustenance for their *helpless Infants,* who, as they grow up, either turn *Thieves* for want of work, or leave their *dear native country* to fight *for the Pretender in Spain,* or else sell themselves to the *Barbadoes.* [30]

Swift proposed to find "a fair, cheap and easy method of making these Children sound and useful Members of the common-wealth." And he found a way whereby these children could be used to "contribute to the Feeding and partly to the Clothing of many Thousands." Calculating that there were about 120,000 children of the poor born annually, Dean Swift pointed out that this number could not all support themselves by agricultural and handicraft work or by thievery. Thus the children, when they reach the age of one, would become "a most delicious, nourishing, and wholesome Food, whether *Stewed, Roasted, Baked,* or *Boyled,* and . . . it will equally serve in a *Fricassie, or a Ragoust. . . .*" One hundred thousand of these children could be so disposed of, and since as food they would be dear, they would be "very *proper for Landlords,* who,

---

29. Connolly, *Labour in Ireland,* pp. 5–6.
30. *Swift: Gulliver's Travels and Selected Writings,* ed. John Hayward (New York: Random House, 1934), p. 512.

as they have already devoured most of the Parents, seem to have the best Title to the children."[31]

This enterprise would be profitable all around, it would even give the mothers a profit, and Swift also suggested that "Those who are most *thrifty . . .* may flay the Carcass; the Skin of which, artificially dressed, will make admirable *Gloves for Ladies,* and *Summer Boots for fine Gentlemen."* Swift, with his melancholy and savage genius, revealed the essential features of the Irish problem. Ireland was despoiled as a cognate part of the capitalist advance of England. Swift's sarcasm draws this out with a genius that has been, to my mind, unmatched in centuries.

At the same time that we consider this long historic oppression, it is necessary to remember that even in national oppression there were class differences. Connolly pointed this out. He noted that the poor Protestants as well as the poor Catholics were oppressed and exploited in Ireland, and he declared, in *Labour in Irish History,* that the Penal Laws against the Irish

> did indeed make the life of propertied Catholics more insecure than would otherwise have been the case; but to the vast mass of the population the misery and hardship entailed by the working out of economic laws were fraught with infinitely more suffering than it was at any time within the power of the Penal Laws to inflict. As a matter of fact, the effect of the latter code in impoverishing wealthy Catholics has been much overrated. The class interests which at all times unite the propertied section of the community operated, to a large extent, to render impossible the application of the power of persecution to its full legal limits. Rich Catholics were quietly tolerated, and generally received from the rich Protestants an amount of respect and forbearance which the latter would not at any time extend to their Protestant tenantry or work-people.[32]

In 1763, a bill was even introduced "to give greater facilities to Protestants wishing to borrow money from" Catholic money lenders. Though this bill was defeated, Connolly suggested that its mere "introduction serves to show how little the Penal Laws (against Catholics) had operated to prevent the accumulation of wealth by the Catholic propertied classes."

Connolly's historical thesis was, as R. M. Fox has indicated, "that England was the exponent of the feudal-capitalist system in Ireland." The *peculiarities* in Irish history are not to be found only in the modern period. They are to be found in Ireland's long history, and most especially during these seven centuries of English oppression. Let me repeat,

---

31. Farrell's Note: Swift also argued that this reform plan would have the added advantage of "lessening the Number of Papists among us."
32. Connolly, *Labour in Ireland,* pp. 20–21.

then, that Ireland under English rule reveals the cost, the other side of progress.[33]

In this context, Connolly observed that "one of" the "Slave birth-marks" in Ireland was "a belief in the capitalist system of society: the Irishman frees himself from such a mark of slavery when he realizes that truth that the capitalist system is the most foreign thing in Ireland."[34]

In Ireland, then, the role of the Church was different from that which it played on the continent. There it was bound up with the feudal system and was a rich landowner in its own right. Involved in the bourgeoisie's attack on the feudal aristocracy was its attack on the Church. The ideology of feudalism is penetrated through and through with that of Catholic thinkers. Not only on the planes of politics and economics, but also on that of ideology, the Church was attacked. In France the desire of the peasantry for land and for freedom from many remaining feudal restrictions over-weighed (in many parts of the country) their loyalty to the Church.

Briefly, the Church was not bound up with the system of oppression in Ireland as it was in feudal Europe. Even though Connolly did observe that propertied Catholics in the eighteenth century did not suffer as did the poor, it does remain true that they were discriminated against. In addition, the alleviation of the operation of the Penal Laws, in the case of the rich Catholics, was not a matter of law. The Irish were penalized by the foreign invader and ruler because of their religion. Catholicism and nationalism became bound together in the minds of many Irishmen. The consciousness of individual Irishmen was not divisible into compartments so that Catholicism would be fitted into one compartment while hatred of an oppressor and desires for freedom would be placed in another. To be Irish and to be Catholic were, in effect, synonymous.

For an Irishman under these conditions to be free meant to escape from penalization because of his religion as well as his nationality. The logic of this attitude runs through the entire O'Connell movement in the nineteenth century. In fact, Daniel O'Connell is often referred to as the Great Emancipator. The victory of Catholic Emancipation in 1829 and 1830 was a signal step forward in the Irish struggle; and yet, as Connolly observed and as is well known, it was achieved at a time of

---

33. FARRELL'S NOTE: In *Capital*, vol. 1, Marx has many illuminating observations on Ireland, and these tend to give substantiation to this generalization of mine. Cf. *Capital*, 1:767–83. *The Correspondence of Marx and Engels* also contains interesting comments and observations about Ireland.

34. Connolly, *Labour in Ireland*, p. xxxiv.

marked miseries and destitution. Connolly, in fact, described the period between 1830 and 1848 in Ireland as "A Chapter of Horrors." And he wrote about the tithes imposed on the peasantry by the clergy of the Episcopal and Catholic Churches as follows:

> The fact that this was in conformity with the practice of the Catholic Church in countries where it was dominant did not, of course, make this more palatable to the Catholic peasantry of Ireland, who continually saw a part of their crops seized upon and sold to maintain a clergy whose ministrations they never attended and whose religion they detested.[35]

When the discontent of the peasants flared in rebellion, "The Episcopalian clergymen called on the aid of the law, and, escorted by police and military, seized the produce of the poor tenants and carried them off to be sold at auction." And what aid did the peasants get during the period of rebellious struggles which were carried on under the leadership of secret societies? Connolly's answer to this question reads as follows:

> The politicians gave neither help nor countenance to the fight, and save for the advocacy of one small Dublin newspaper, conducted by a small but brilliant band of young Protestant writers, no journal in all Ireland championed their cause. For the Catholic clergy it is enough to say that while this tithe war was being waged they were almost universally silent about that "grevious sin of secret conspiracy" upon which they are usually so eloquent. We would not dare say that they recognized that as the secret societies were doing their work against a rival priesthood, it was better to be sparing in their denunciations for the time being; perhaps this is not the explanation, but at all events it is noteworthy that as soon as the tithe war was won all the old stock invectives against every kind of extra-constitutional action were immediately renewed.[36]

With Emancipation, the ground was cut from under O'Connell's feet. As O'Faolain, his biographer, says, he "could not form a solid block of Irish votes, an Irish Party, immediately after Emancipation, as Parnell did later." The Emancipation Act was, in reality, only a partial emancipation. And it only tended to open up some eyes more clearly to the social question. The Young Irelanders of '48 and James Fintan Lalor opposed O'Connell and O'Connellism. Connolly, in *Labour in Irish History*, justifies their criticism of and opposition to O'Connell. They, and Connolly later, moved in the direction of social emancipation. They— and Connolly after them—were advocates of extra-constitutional action, of rebellion.

---

35. Ibid., p. 146.
36. Ibid., p. 148.

The foregoing should reveal that Catholicism is not a separate question in Ireland. In fact, *religion is never a separate question,* divorced from all of the political questions and struggles of a period.

O'Faolain quotes Balzac's remark about Daniel O'Connell: "he incarnated a whole people." And then O'Faolain also pointed out how O'Connell, a Tory, frightened by the French Revolution, became a "Radical." He goes on to say that O'Connell

> toppled on the brink of Atheism. He recovered as a Deist. He ended not quite as a Catholic, but as an Irish Catholic, which among Irish intellectuals is so often little more than two words for one. I doubt if there were more than one or two Irish patriots who did not run a similar course in relation to religion—Tone, Emmet, Lord Edward, Davis, Mitchel, Parnell, Stephens and most of the Fenians, Collins, Clarke, Connolly, almost all wavering in a typically ambiguous way barely stopping short on the edge of complete revolt from orthodoxy.[37]

Rebellion in Ireland was not rebellion against orthodoxy. It was national rebellion. In some instances it was purely national, in others it was both national and social. In the case of James Connolly, he was both nationalist and socialist.

Leftists have criticized him as a nationalist whose socialism was either impure or else abandoned in his last days. Sean O'Casey's first writing was a pamphlet, *The Irish Citizen Army,* in which he declared that Connolly died not for socialism but for nationalism. To discuss Connolly in such terms is to become formal, abstract; it results in the posing of formal questions which can only lead us away from insight. The foregoing parts of this work have offered more than sufficient evidence on the character of Connolly's socialist views. Abstract purists usually see the politics of a man as though they were completely separated from that man.

Just as they fail to see Connolly's nationalism as bound up with his socialism, so do they see his socialism as in flagrant contradiction with his belief in Catholicism. But his works, and the accounts of his life with which I am familiar, would reveal no such glaring contradictions. Connolly as much as O'Connell, or as much as any other Irish patriot or rebel, can be called the incarnation of a people—to the degree that any one man can be so characterized. His writings show to what degree the Irish tradition was fused in his ideas. He studied this tradition and evaluated it, made distinctions, and consciously made choices. At the same time his emotions, his consciousness was molded out of the life

---

37. O'Faolain, *King of the Beggars,* pp. 40, 74–75.

of Ireland. His personal religious beliefs were deeply felt and genuine. To assume that he pretended to a belief he didn't hold is really to slander the memory of a great and honest man.

V

R. M. Fox in his biography *James Connolly: The Forerunner* (which has led me to write this essay), remarks:

> He [Connolly] was a man of great individuality, combining an acceptance of the Marxian view of economics and of history—as a record of social struggles—with the Catholic outlook which emphasized the value of the human soul. Connolly is not by any means the first man to realize the revolutionary implications of Christianity. If a man is simply a bubble of gas, a product of chemical action, he may be used as a machine or as cannon fodder without any question of the degradation of humanity. But once admit his possession of a soul and the case against human degradation becomes infinitely stronger.[38]

Here it is clear that Fox is seeking to explain the fact that Connolly was both a Marxist and a Catholic. And while this explanation is, in a sense, true to the spirit of Connolly, it is, I think, unnecessary.

The revolutionary implications of Christianity need to be seen historically. The Christian idea of the immortality of the soul—even though it be the soul of a slave—was, in the humane sense, an advance over the ideas of the pagan world. The concept and the practice of charity, the ideas of love and of brotherhood of Christ and of the early Christians—these also should be seen as attitudes which signified moral progress.

But even so, we shouldn't regard the pagan world and pagan ideas in a monolithic sense. It is a well-known fact that the Greeks laid the basis for western civilization. Also, prior to the rise of Christianity, the ideas of the Greek materialists had already been exhausted, and the main streams of Greek thought had been given their course by Socrates, Aristotle and Plato. Lange, the nineteenth-century scholar, in his *History of Materialism*, points out that when the great progressive ideas of an age wear out, become exhausted, insight and observations are then linked up with regressive ideas, so that inasmuch as human beings do constantly have good insights, they tend to believe that these are *neces-*

---

38. Fox, *James Connolly: The Forerunner*, p. 131.

sarily related to regressive ideas, if these regressive ideas are the dominant ones of an age.

Lange here was criticizing Socrates, Plato and Aristotle; he defended the early Greek materialists. One of his arguments was that materialism had produced a high conception of morality. This is true for all ages. Philosophical materialism—as distinguished from the crude materialism of money-grubbing—has given voice to the most noble moral sentiments and ideals, and it stands in no need of apologizing before the bar of anti-materialist criticisms. Many examples could here be cited, but I shall merely refer to the nobility of expression of Lucretius.

At the same time that we realize this fact, we need also to see that Christianity and its contributions to western civilization cannot be taken merely on the level of philosophical discussion and criticism, as the anti-materialists so often tend to take it when they attack materialists. Socially, Christianity made a major contribution to civilization. It advanced a broader idea of the dignity of man. This relates to the positive side of Christian ethics. The negative side is to be seen in the doctrine of Christian meekness.

Christianity cannot, then, be seen as a unified and strictly logical and intimately consistent body of ideas. And our consideration of Christianity here is not a philosophical one. The above remarks have been made merely in order to try to clarify issues.

Just as Christianity registered an ethical advance for mankind, so did the philosophy of political democracy. The best of Christian ethics was absorbed by democracy. There is a direct connection between the idea of the equality of the soul of man and the ideas of such great democrats as Thomas Jefferson. Thus: "We hold these truths to be self-evident; that all men are created equal; that they are endowed by their creator with certain inalienable rights; and among these rights are life, liberty and the pursuit of happiness."

At the same time, we should observe that mankind has advanced in the realm of ideas much more than it has in the realm of overt action. In all ages, we can observe that, on the one hand, there is a wide and frightening difference between the ethical conceptions of conduct of the noblest thinkers of the age, and, on the other, the gross realities of day-to-day living. The entire history of civilized mankind is a history of exploitation, slavery, cruelty, war and injustice.

I have quoted from Swift's *Modest Proposal* concerning conditions in Ireland in the seventeenth century, and I have, mainly with references from Connolly's own writings, given additional quotations which indicate the injustices from which the Irish people have suffered. Readers of this essay will be sufficiently familiar with the story of the injustices in advanced capitalist countries, in the past and in the present, so that

I need not document these facts here. Suffice it for me to point, in modern America, the freest and the richest country in the world, to the phenomenon of Jim Crow, of lynchings in the South, and of the slums of all of our major cities.

At the present time, various Christian and especially Catholic thinkers deal with the phenomenon of modern injustice, cruelty and slavery from the standpoint of Christian moral precepts. They argue on this basis that inhumanity in capitalist countries flows from the principle of bourgeois liberalism, and that the inhumanity of Stalinism[39] flows from the principles of socialism as a continuation of bourgeois liberalism. Later on, I shall have more to say on this point. Here I shall only suggest to the Christian critics of liberalism, socialism and materialism that they consider the history of men in society since the advent of Christianity. I shall offer merely passing reminders to them.

On the opening page of the first volume of Henry Charles Lea's great scholarly work, *A History of the Inquisition of the Middle Ages,* we can read:

History records no such triumph of intellect over brute strength as that which, in an age of turmoil and battle [the twelfth century and the early thirteenth], was wrested from the fierce warriors of the time by priests who had no material force at their command, and whose power was based alone on the souls and consciences of men. Over soul and conscience this empire was complete. No Christian could hope for salvation who was not in all things an obedient son of the Church, and who was not ready to take up arms in its defense; and, in a time when faith was a determining fact of conduct, this belief created a spiritual despotism which placed all things within reach of him who could wield it.[40]

And Lea also writes of the priest:

---

39. FARRELL'S NOTE: In passing let me observe that Stalinism has even abrogated those rights which man had in feudal society. Morally it represents a backward swing of history which goes beyond the abrogation of the rights of man attained through the rise of political democracy and bourgeois liberalism.

40. FARRELL'S NOTE: It is my opinion that Aquinas' conception of God can be correlated with spiritual despotism: "God is not only His own essence . . . but also His own being. . . . God is the first efficient cause. . . . There can be nothing caused in God, since He is the first cause. . . . God is absolute form, or rather absolute Being. . . . God is His own existence." These and many other sentences could be culled from Aquinas to show that God, as conceived by this scholarly saint, is completely and totally independent of man and of all the laws of matter. He is utterly sufficient unto Himself, a principle above all principles. God, demonstrated as a self-evident existence and proved by the principles of Aristotelian logic, is so above humanity that I would consider Him here to be unapproachable. Face to face with God as He is verbalized in the cold pages of Aquinas, humanity becomes totally dependent. I would suggest that the interested reader compare Aquinas on God with Augustine, who was a poet and an artist as well as a theologian. The conception of God as a logical principle, in my opinion, offers the best possible source for, and rationalization of, spiritual despotism.

Not only did the humblest priest wield a supernatural power which marked him as one elevated above the common level of humanity, but his person and possessions were alike inviolable. . . . The man who entered the service of the Church was no longer a citizen. He owed no allegiance superior to that assumed in his ordination.[41]

Here we can see some of the historical factors which served as a basis for the Inquisition. And Lea shows that the development of the Inquisition "was . . . a natural—one may almost say an inevitable—evolution of the forces at work in the thirteenth century. . . ." Lea documents statements such as these with the most minute detail. He shows that the Inquisition was a development of the social struggles of the times. The punishment of heretics, the burnings at the stake, the tortures, all of this was part of a complicated historical evolution in the process by which Rome emerged triumphant over local interests. Writing of the rise of the mendicant orders—one of which was founded by the great and lovable St. Francis—he concludes that even though their work was not lost "they soon sank to the level of the social order around them."[42] This social order was marked by cruelty, pitilessness, misery. Heresies, called forth by the wretchedness of the poor and by their desire to find the early Christ, were mercilessly crushed. Out of such social conditions, the Inquisition was founded.

The life of mankind goes on, as it were, on both the material and the moral level. The written history of mankind reveals to us, in a confused way, the growth of moral ideas which are, however, constantly contradicted by actual practice. Moral realities and moral statements do not harmonize. And yet moral and ethical ideas do have their influence. They have given even a sense of dignity to slaves, to the poor and ignorant. The story of the growth of moral ideas is as elevating as the story of their repudiation and betrayal is in practice odious and frightening.

The continuity in ideas and ethical conceptions in our society is one which stands in the background of Connolly. From Christianity he absorbed its moral values, and in his mind there was no apparent contradiction between his Catholicism and his socialism. This is, I think, an important point to keep in mind if we study his life.

In the previous parts of this essay, I have indicated that there were circumstances in the history of Ireland which easily led Irishmen to see the Reformation differently than did European Continentals. On the

---

41. Henry Charles Lea, *A History of the Inquisition of the Middle Ages,* 3 vols. (New York: Harper, 1888), 1:2.

42. Ibid., 1:304.

European continent, the Reformation was a major revolutionary development leading to the breaking of the chains of spiritual despotism. Early voices of the Reformation, such as Martin Luther, were spiritually revolutionary and socially conservative. The Reformation was part of the complex historical development which saw the rise of capitalism.

As Tawney says in *Religion and the Rise of Capitalism,* "The storm and fury of the Puritan revolution has been followed by a dazzling outburst of economic enterprise. . . ."[43] This economic enterprise, with all the suffering entailed, led men a step nearer to that emancipation of which they still dream and from which they are still so far away. But Ireland, as we have already noted, was part of the underside of this development. As Fox states, the Reformation was to Connolly "the capitalist idea appearing in the religious field." He quotes Connolly:

> As capitalism teaches that the social salvation of man depends solely upon his own individual efforts, so Protestantism, echoing it, taught that the spiritual salvation of man depends upon his own individual appeal to God.[44]

Fox further remarks on this conclusion of Connolly's that capitalism is the parent, the Reformation is the child, and that it is irrational to condemn only the child.

In Connolly's mind, ideas of the dignity of the individual and of community were linked together. "We are all members of one another," he declared in *The Reconquest of Ireland.* And in his conclusion to this same book he declared:

> The objective aimed at is to establish in the mind of the men and women of Ireland, the necessity of giving effective expression, politically and socially, to the right of the community (all) to control for the good of all, the industrial activities of each, and to endow such activities with the necessary means.[45]

Here is one of the ways in which Catholicism was tied in with his thinking. He linked up ideas of community and conceptions of the dignity of the individual. The link, historically, in the chain of political and moral ideas in Connolly's mind was political democracy.[46] This is important. He absorbed, largely through his Irish predecessors like Lalor

---

43. R. H. Tawney, *Religion and the Rise of Capitalism* (New York: Harcourt, Brace, 1926), p. 197.
44. Fox, *James Connolly: The Forerunner,* p. 133.
45. Connolly, *Labour in Ireland,* p. 333.
46. FARRELL'S NOTE: Connolly also wrote in *The Reconquest of Ireland,* "As Democracy enters Bureaucracy takes flight."

and others as well as from Marx, the political ideas of the Great French Revolution.

He did this as an Irishman. The differences in the historical experiences of the Irish and of the English and the continental Europeans here tell in the whole outline of Connolly's ideas. To him, individualism was moral and it was also political—political democracy. As a moral doctrine, it found its source in his feelings and beliefs as a simple Catholic. He believed in the equality of souls. The ideas of community flow into the ideas of the nation. The struggle for a free Ireland was, for Connolly, the idea of a free Irish community. Among the Irish, the race is often seen as a family. The Irish nation, the Irish community, the Irish as a family, these ideas touch on one another.[47]

Connolly's ideas about the Irish nation and his views on democracy are similar to the view of the nation as the republic of virtue held by the earlier French revolutionaries, particularly the Jacobins. In the Abbé Sieyes' pamphlet—*The Third Estate—What Is It?*—which was so influential in the Great French Revolution, the author's emphasis was on the legal and political arguments which would justify and show the rights of the third estate to constitute itself the nation. In their thinking, Jacobins like Robespierre and Saint-Just went a step further than this. They envisioned the nation not only in terms of popular will and sovereignty but also in terms of the individuals who would be the members of the nation.

In their thinking, one finds an austerity suggestive of Protestantism. And the dignity of man, to them, was not associated with Catholic thinking. Reason and republicanism provided them with their basic premises. To them, the foreign foe was outside the country. The enemies within were the aristocrats. This suggests a difference in the outline of their political ideas as compared with the outline of political ideas in the mind of Connolly, who was, in a sense, one of their heirs.

Speaking of religion and theocracy in his *Esprit de la Révolution*, Saint-Just expressed the opinion that if Christ were reborn in Spain—in the time of the French Revolution—he would be crucified again by the priests, on the ground that he was a factious man who, under the signs

---

47. FARRELL'S NOTE: An interesting illustration of this is to be seen in Frank O'Connor's great short story "Guests of the Nation." This story, told in the first person, recounts how members of the IRA, during the Black and Tan struggle, hold two Limeys as hostages. They become fond of the Limeys, who, in turn, regard these Irish boys as friends. Then the Irish lads are ordered to execute their prisoners. The human sentiments of the narrator are wrenched as a result of the execution. Heretofore he had felt that "disunion between brothers seemed to me an awful crime." These are the words with which he translated national spirit into personal emotion. This feeling was, however, shaken by the execution of these English guests of the nation.

of charity and modesty, meditated the ruin of church and state. He argued that a reign of virtue, patience and poverty would be a danger to monarchy, and also that the Christian churches had lived most purely in countries that had become republican. He thought that the people of Spain—a Catholic country—would be the last to conquer their liberty, and he contrasted Spain with England where the hand of the priests did not lie heavy on the people as it did in Spain. Historically, of course, Saint-Just is a predecessor of Connolly. But he serves as a good concrete illustration, nonetheless, to suggest more clearly the historical features of Connolly's own thought.

France was the cradle of modern liberty in Europe. The progressive features of national ideas, of ideas of the nation, come from France. The French Revolution would inevitably have influenced the Irish, as it did, and its political features and ideas would be absorbed by the Irish. The Irish did not pay a price for the French Revolution; they did for the earlier English Revolution—the price of the Cromwellian invasion of Ireland. From France, the Irish could get ideas of the politics of liberty; from England, they got the economics of capitalism. Along with the latter came the Puritan invader with gun and cannon.

A man as deeply sincere as Connolly, a self-educated Irish working lad, a man devoted to the struggle of his own people like Connolly, most obviously would not see the Reformation as a Continental would see it. The so-called peculiarities in historical developments register not only in social and economic relationships, but also in the outlines of the thought of men and in their feelings. Connolly's own thought was one such register of the peculiarities of Irish history.

R. M. Fox quotes an article of Connolly's in which he replied to a priest, Father MacEarlen, who had criticized socialist thought. In this reply, Connolly wrote:

> I admit unquestioningly the obligation resting upon the Holy See to recognize the *de facto* Government and the *de facto* social order in any given country or age. But side by side with, part and parcel of, that admission, and not to be divorced from it, I insist upon the right of the individual Catholic to disregard that obligation and to be a reformer of, or a rebel and reformist against, the Government which the Holy See is compelled by its international position to recognize.
>
> Without this right, Catholicity would be synonymous with the blackest reaction and opposition to all reforms. As an example Ireland is illuminating. For the greater part of seven centuries, the *de facto* Government of Ireland has been a foreign Government imposed on the country by force, and maintained by the same means. The Holy See was compelled by its position to recognize that government, but the holiest and deepest feelings of the Catholics of Ireland were in rebellion against that government, and,

in every generation, the scaffold and the prison and the martyr's grave have been filled in Ireland with devout subjects of the Holy See, but with unrelenting enemies of the *de facto* government of Ireland. The firm distinction in the minds of Irish Catholics between the *duties* of the Holy See and the *rights* of the individual Catholic has been a necessary and saving element in keeping Ireland Catholic, and he, by whatever name he calls himself or to whatever order he belongs who would seek to destroy that distinction, or make acquiescence in the political obligations of the Papacy, a cardinal article of Catholic faith, is an enemy of the faith and the liberties of our people.[48]

And also in the same article, he declared:

As individual Catholics, we claim it as our right, nay, as our duty to refuse allegiance to any power or social system whose authority to rule over us we believe to be grounded upon injustice.[49]

Connolly then fused in his thought Christian and democratic ideas of the past. He was not, however, fighting the battles of the past, but those of his own present. As he indicated, he considered these to be battles against injustice. He believed in economic justice, and he wrote: "Socialism is neither Protestant nor Catholic, Christian nor Freethinker, Buddhist, Mohammedan, nor Jew; it is only human."[50] It was his idea of what was human, of human dignity, which was central in all of his thinking.

---

48. Fox, *James Connolly: The Forerunner*, pp. 135–36.
49. Ibid., p. 135.
50. Ibid., p. 132.

Lest We Forget: Jim Larkin, Irish Labor Leader[1]

I

Jim Larkin died in Dublin on January 30, 1947, at the age of 69. Along with his associate, James Connolly, he was one of the outstanding leaders of the Irish working class in the early years of this century. He and Connolly played major roles in the organization and development of the Irish trade union movement. He reached a great peak of his career in the great Dublin transport strike of 1913 and in the lockout which followed it.[2] Thousands of Irish workers lived in misery and squalor, scarcely different from the conditions of life of the workers during the time of Marx and Engels. Larkin was intimately associated with the militant struggles to better the workers' lot. With the aid of his inspiration and example they lifted their heads, and they set out to act like men rather than slaves. Under his leadership, the militant Irish Transport and General Workers' Union became a menace to the Dublin employers. The year 1913 was a period of labor unrest all over Europe. In Dublin there were at least thirty strikes from January to August, 1913. The climax of labor militancy and unrest was reached in August 1913.

William Martin Murphy, head of the Dublin employers group, and the bitterest enemy of Jim Larkin, informed dispatch workers of *The Irish Independent* that they must choose between Larkin, "the strike organizer," and their jobs. A similar ultimatum was given to the tramway workers. During Horse Show Week in August—the time when the biggest social events of Dublin are held—the tramway workers went out on strike. The employers began a war of extermination against the unions, and against Larkin. The most bloody and bitter class warfare in the history of modern Ireland broke out. Connolly came down from Belfast to

---

1. Reprinted from *Thought* 13 (27 May 1961): 9–10, 18. The essay had appeared in slightly different form as "Jim Larkin, Irish Revolutionist: Fighter for Freedom and Socialism," *New International* 13 (March 1947): 86–89. The present version incorporates some manuscript revisions by Farrell in 1961 which did not appear in the *Thought* version; see "Lest We Forget: Jim Larkin, Irish Labor Leader" (1961) [372].

2. FARRELL'S NOTE: I have drawn on R. M. Fox's *James Connolly—The Forerunner* (Tralee: Kerryman Press, 1946), for some of the facts cited here.

participate in the leadership of the strike. On August 29 a big mass meeting was held—in Dublin. Larkin was one of the speakers. He burned a proclamation which forbade a meeting, planned for the coming Sunday, and at which he was to speak. He talked, and he sang to the workers. He declared that if Carson in the North could organize volunteers, then also, Irish workers could organize their own army for self-defense. This was one of the first public calls for the organization of a workers' army in Ireland. During the strike, the Irish Citizens' Army was organized by Connolly, Larkin and others. Jim Larkin was the first leader of this organization, the first army of the working class in the twentieth century. In this same speech Larkin also promised that if force were used against labor, labor would reply by force. He declared that if he were alive on the following Sunday, he would speak, regardless of the police order prohibiting a meeting.

Larkin hid out at the home of the Countess Markievicz. She reserved a room at the best hotel in Dublin for her "country cousin" who was, presumably, a parson. This hotel was owned by William Martin Murphy. On Sunday, August 31, the workers and their wives poured into O'Connell Street, then, I believe, named Sackville Street. A large force of Peelers was on hand. Larkin, disguised and wearing a false moustache, passed through the police lines unnoticed. Suddenly and dramatically, he appeared at one of the windows of the hotel, and pulling off his false moustache, he began to speak. The Peelers charged the workers with batons. There were at least five hundred casualties in Dublin. This day has been commemorated as Bloody Sunday in modern Irish history.

Larkin was arrested but soon released. Murphy and the other employers took the offensive against the workers. The Federated Employers issued a document in which they demanded that the employees of 404 firms sign. It read:

> I hereby undertake to carry out all instructions given to me by or on behalf of my employers and, further, I agree to immediately resign my membership of the Irish Transport and General Workers Union (if a member), and I further undertake that I will not join or in any way support this union.

The Irish workers refused to sign this document. Many who were unaffiliated with the union, and who were not even interested in the union, came to the defense of the union. The Great Dublin Lockout began. William Martin Murphy and other Dublin employers set out deliberately and cynically to starve about a hundred thousand workers with their wives and children into submission. And they called this lockout "The Larkin Conspiracy." Thirty-seven Dublin unions supported Larkin. The heroism of the Dublin workers and their wives during this lockout constitutes one of the noblest chapters in the story of the labor movement anywhere in the world during this present century. Half-starved, without funds, they held out for eight months. They asserted their manhood and their womanhood at a terrible personal cost. They pawned everything they owned for food. They stood on the streets and the corners of Dublin, pasty-faced, hungry, miserable, wretched and shivering. They waited day after day for a settlement. But the employers remained adamant. When representatives of the British labor unions attempted to negotiate a settlement, the employers broke off negotiations. Similarly, the efforts of the Archbishop were in vain. But the Dublin workers stood hard and firm. Those workers who joined the Irish Citizens Army, at this time, marched and drilled on half-starved stomachs, and with broomsticks and hurley sticks. The literary men of Ireland rallied to the support of the workers. Meetings were held in England, and both Connolly and Larkin appealed to British labor for aid. They secured help from British labor in the form of food ships, but the sympathetic strikes which they wanted and needed didn't materialize. Only sympathetic strikes in England could have secured the victory of the Irish workers. Larkin campaigned up and down England in the interest of the strikers. His speeches were acidulous and violent, but justice was on his side. In December 1913, a Special Trade Union Congress was called in England in order to deal with the demands that the British workers come to the support of their class brothers by strikes and/or by a blockade of Dublin. The officials of the British trade unions turned this Congress into an effort to defeat Jim Larkin. Smarting under the lash of his tongue, speaker after speaker rose and denounced him as a disruptionist. He replied with equal fire. He rose to answer the attacks on him, and began: "Mr. Chairman, and human beings." He delivered a scorching speech. At one point, there was a shout from the floor. "You said we were human beings."

"Yes, but you don't give much evidence of it," Larkin answered.

James Connolly also spoke. He declared that the conference was called to help Dublin. He said: "Remember the workers of Dublin have been locked out for months. They are hungry and desperate."

A hostile delegate jeered at Connolly, telling him that he should have thought of all this before the Dublin workers had been driven to such a plight. Connolly answered by declaring: "If you think we are ready to withdraw a single word of criticism of your inaction, you are wrong. We will raise this at the proper time and place. We want you to concentrate on helping Dublin." He stood with Larkin.

The workers lost; they were driven back to their jobs by hunger.

They were laughed at, scorned. But the victory of the employers was not complete. The union was not broken. However, the Irish workers of that time never fully recovered from the effects of this struggle. The story of the Easter Rebellion in 1916 might have been much different, but for this defeat.

Larkin came to America in 1914. He was associated with The Industrial Workers of the World. He was active in strikes in America, and he was one of the founders of the American Communist Party. Along with Ben Gitlow, he was sentenced to Ossining prison in New York State on charges of criminal syndicalism. He was subsequently pardoned by the late Governor Al Smith, and was deported to Ireland. He returned to Ireland about 1924. After that time, he did not play the same role as he had in his younger days. He could not regain control of Liberty Hall and of the Transport Workers Union. The Irish union movement had slid into the same pattern as that of the British. Larkin was a great agitator. But he was not the type of leader to be at the head of a movement in retreat or in stabilization. He was still feared and hated in Dublin, and I am sure that when he drew his last breath, he was, equally, the object of fear and hatred. He was head of some unions, among them clerks, butchers, abbatoir and hospital workers.

II

I saw Jim Larkin in Dublin in August of 1938. At that time he was sixty-two or sixty-three. Jim was a broad-shouldered giant. When I first went to his union headquarters, the building was being remodeled. Inside of it there were stone pillars. Work was going on. As I entered, I saw a huge gray-haired man in a spotted unkempt blue suit, swinging a sledge hammer. It was Jim. He used the sledge hammer with more force and power than many a younger man could.

He was very cordial and hospitable. He wanted to know what he could do for me, what he could show me. It has often been remarked that Dublin is a whispering gallery. It is. Jim knew that I was in Dublin. He knew something about me. He knew that I was an anti-Stalinist, and we had only talked for a few moments when he called me a Trotskyist. Subsequently he introduced me to his son: he told him that he wanted to introduce his friend, Farrell, but that he should beware of him because he was a Trotskyist. He expressed disappointment that I had not come to see him sooner. He offered to take me around and show me various features of Dublin. We left his office, and entered his car. He asked me if I wanted to see the monument to the Invincibles. (The Invincibles were a group of Irish terrorists, mainly working men, active during the time of Parnell. They assassinated a British official, and most of them died on the gallows, isolated and scorned. Their memory is held sacred by some Irish patriots.) Jim's chauffeur drove us out to Phoenix Park. I imagined that I was going to see a statue, but this did seem passingly curious. The idea that there would be a monument commemorating the Invincibles in Dublin didn't make sense. We stopped in Phoenix Park, just opposite the Archbishop's palace. This had, in the eyes of Parnell, been the headquarters of the British rulers of Ireland. We got out. Jim walked along a path, looking down at the grass. I was bewildered. Jim became nervous, and he stared on the ground with some concern. Then he pointed. There it was. I saw a little hole where grass had been torn up. A cross had been scratched in the earth with a stick. I gathered that many Dubliners did not know of this act commemorating the Invincibles. Jim's boys always went out to Phoenix Park, and marked this cross in the earth. No matter how often grass was planted over it, it was torn up. The cross was marked in the earth.

He drove me around Dublin, and out to Howth, the sight of the famous gun-running episode in 1914. His home was near Howth. We went there, and Jim cooked lunch, scrambling eggs and frying bacon. He talked continuously, incessantly. His conversation was chaotic, rambling. Flashes of the Jim Larkin of his earlier days would constantly enliven this old man's talk. He would suddenly burst out in sudden indignations and denunciations, describing his adversaries and his enemies as "twisters." This was the splendid style of his past. Jim seemed bitter and disillusioned. He had stood for the Dail, and he had not been elected. He felt that he had been let down by the Irish workers. He said that they didn't remember their own. He was interested in housing. He drove me about and showed me the new houses that were being built in the slums of Dublin. I had wandered the streets of these slums fairly frequently during my stay in Dublin, and I had visited some of the rotting old houses, and had talked with those who lived in them. They were beaten and cowed people.[3] Jim spoke at length of the new houses, of his hopes that they would do some good. He showed me various ones which were in the process of being built. He knew that these would not

---

3. FARRELL'S NOTE: In my story "A Summer Morning in Dublin in 1938," *When Boyhood Dreams Come True* (New York: Vanguard Press, 1946), pp. 164–73, I have tried to describe the conditions of life in the slums of Dublin. These suggest the conditions of life for the workers of Dublin in the days when Larkin and Connolly led them in great strikes.

at all be adequate, but he was very proud of them. I also met him at a hospital where members of his union worked. He was having difficulties, and he spoke of those with whom he was dealing as "his lunatics." He described the hospital as a lunatic asylum. There was some trouble concerning a girl. It seemed that she was having a child out of wedlock, and an effort had been made to discharge her. Jim prevented it. He had mingled humor, argument, threat and castigation in his successful defense of the girl. He introduced me to various people at the hospital, but always in the same way. "I want you to meet my friend, Farrell. He has written great psychological novels, but you dare not read them for fear of losing your immortal soul." (He had not, of course, then read my books.)

As we walked around, Jim was recognized by almost every one we saw. Now and then, he would nudge me, and he would tell me to look at some one. He would make some remark such as, "Now, there's a twister." And he would launch forth. And then, he would ramble on. He said that he had never smoked nor drank, and he attributed his health and strength to this. He, at one minute, lamented the condition of Ireland, and the next, he spoke hopefully, with pride. I spoke of the Moscow trials. He didn't commit himself, other than to say: "The trouble with Trotsky is that he doesn't know how to work with anyone." This criticism was often and justly made of Larkin himself. He spoke warmly of Bukharin, and remarked that he had told Bukharin once that Trotsky was unable to work with any one. This was just about the substance of what he had to say of international affairs or politics.

He spoke of the Corporation of Dublin with irony. He liked to needle the city officials. In fact, he didn't fancy the Corporation at all. Jim was a Catholic, and he was proud that Ireland had a Christian civilization. The world needed (he said) a Christian civilization, based on the sanctity of the family. He spoke with pride of his own family life. He had almost no respect for the literary men and the Abbey crowd in 1938. He asked me about some of those whom I had seen, and when I mentioned them, he was sharp and ironical. Of the IRA (Irish Republican Army), he was somewhat ironical, also, but he seemed to have admired them. But he remarked that they had done little for labor. At the hospital, we ran into a doctor who had been one of the IRA diehards in the days of "the Troubles." I had met him and some of his old comrades-in-arms. I observed that he and this doctor greeted one another coolly.

When Jim took me to the abbatoir, he explained the work there in detail. In fact, he described it with some pride. An air gun was used to kill the sheep. It permitted humane slaughter, and this was what struck

Jim. With all of his fire, his wild angers and indignations, his bitter struggles, he was warmhearted, sentimental, hurt by cruelties to others.

The last time I saw him, we spent a number of hours together. We went to his sister's home in Dublin. No one was home. He scrambled eggs and made tea for our meal. He wanted to give me some of the James Connolly papers. Many of his books and papers were kept at his sister's house. After eating, Jim spent an hour looking for papers of Connolly and for some Irish books. One of them was *The Labour Leader,* a play by Daniel Corkery. Jim was the model for the hero of this play. His books were in dusty cabinets along the floor. He bent down on his knees, and grumbling and muttering to himself, he kept pulling out books and spreading them all over the floor. Nothing was in order. He found everything but what he wanted to find. He flung out piles of books. One's throat became dry and one almost choked because of the dust in the room. And Jim kept looking, wondering where he had put Connolly's papers, and where he had put the Corkery play, and some plays of Boyle which he also wanted to give me. This seemed to go on endlessly. Finally, he grunted with pleasure. He had found the books. He gave them to me to take back to America. But he couldn't find Connolly's papers.

When we shook hands in farewell, he told me that he would always like to hear from me. He said:

"Write to me, Jim Larkin, Dublin. Everybody knows me."

Jim Larkin became a legendary figure in his own lifetime. Stories and anecdotes about him are endless. Many of them are true. At Ossining, he was popular with both the guards and the prisoners. One of the stories about Jim at Ossining was told to me by a class war prisoner who served time at a later date. Most of the guards (called hackies) were Irish. On St. Patrick's Day, they asked Jim to make a speech, and he got up on a table. Jim's speech began: "St. Patrick drove the snakes out of Ireland. They all came to America and they became hackies and warders . . . ." This was the beginning and the end of Jim's St. Patrick's Day speech in Ossining.

An anecdote told of him in Dublin may or may not be true. But it suggests the contradictions in his character. Jim was once on the way to an important meeting. He noticed a bird trapped in some telephone wires. He was moved by the plight of the bird, and he became indignant with the Corporation. He telephoned immediately, said that it was Jim Larkin speaking, and that a bird was trapped in some electric wires, and that it might be electrocuted unless it were quickly rescued. He demanded that men be dispatched immediately to save the bird. Jim kept calling back, demanding, expressing indignation, threatening. He waited on the spot until men did come and saved the bird. In the meantime, his important meeting was delayed.

Another anecdote concerns the time when he returned from America. He went to Liberty Hall, and ensconced himself. He had been leader of the Irish Transport Workers Union. He was back. He took over. His adversary, O'Brien, went to court. During the court case, Jim had a quarrel with his lawyer. He fired him and then appealed for a delay. The court ruled against Jim remarking that it was not responsible for the defendant's difficulties with his solicitor. Jim declared that he would defend himself. And he did. He put his adversary on the stand and asked all kinds of questions. He was very dramatic, and his gestures were magnificent. He would point a wagging and accusing forefinger at his adversary and ask him, with a glint in his eyes, if it were or were not true that the defendant had been guilty of peculations when he was in (let us say) the milk wagon drivers union? This went on for several days. There was a fine and a very appreciative gallery. But Jim lost his case.

Michael Gold used to tell a story about Jim in America. A unity meeting was called among various of the Irish in New York. Jim brought Michael Gold to the meeting. (I might add that he was very fond of Gold, and called him Mickey. While he spoke sharply concerning many of those whom he'd known in America, he talked most warmly of Mike Gold.) Jim started to deliver his "unity" speech. As he got warmed up he began pointing around the room, telling those in the audience that so-and-so who was sitting in this or that place was a "twister," and a double-crosser, and not to be trusted, telling someone else what Jim Larkin thought of him, and that this went on until the unity meeting agreed on one proposition: it was a good idea to have a riot. Heads were cracked, blows exchanged, chairs broken. Thus ended the unity meeting at which Jim spoke.

In one of his flaming speeches during his stormiest days in Dublin, he bared his chest to the Peelers, and challenged them to shoot him, then and there.

Stories and anecdotes about Jim could be recounted almost endlessly. The ones which I have given are typical.

Larkin was almost the polar opposite of his associate, James Connolly. Connolly was precise, methodical. He thought and planned ceaselessly. He tried to take everything into account in advance. He studied the revolutions of the past in order to draw lessons which he might apply in the Irish struggles which he anticipated. He had deep indignations, but he was usually controlled. Larkin was emotional, impetuous, violent, extravagant. In his speeches and in his actions, he was an improviser. He did not stop to reason or to plan. He spoke with a rapid flow, with sweeping gestures. His speeches were filled with hyperbole, with castigation, with acidity, with sentimentality, and with rousing appeals. In one speech he declaimed that it was his divine mission to preach subversion and discontent to the working classes. This more than suggests his style. He was brave to the point of foolhardiness, and he was self-sacrificing. Again and again, he was ready and willing to give up his life and to be a martyr of the working class. In his great days as an organizer and an agitator, he lived a life of danger. He flung challenges into the teeth of the police of the British Crown. He flung bold and insolent challenges into the face of Martin Murphy and the other employers of Dublin. He gave his services to the struggle for the emancipation of the working class of the world: at the same time, he refused to appear on the same platform with an American Socialist of international repute because this man was divorced! In a period when the most depressed sections of the Irish working class were militant, he was peculiarly fitted to play the role of agitator. His ability to lash their enemies, and to rouse and stir them, enabled him to appeal to their manhood, to the will to freedom which slept within their hearts. He added his own daring example to the appeal of his words. And when he led these workers in strikes he was adamant, uncompromising, and in the forefront where danger lurked. His bravery and daring were as extravagant as his foibles. But in a period of letdown, of retreat, of the sodden rule of the middle classes and the clergymen in Ireland, he was like a lost child. In the slums of Dublin after "the Troubles," he could not repeat what he had done in this same area in the early days of this century. This was apparent when I saw him in Dublin in 1938. He was embittered.

Now this man is no more. When Larkin's associate, the wounded Connolly, was carried in a chair to face the guns of his executioners, he was asked if he wished to say a prayer. He answered: "I will say a prayer for all brave men who do their duty." We, who do not pray, might alter this fine statement. We will pay our last respects to all such brave men. And Jim Larkin was such a brave man. He was a brave soldier of the working class. He was a great agitator. He gave his spirit, and the best years of his life in their service. Karl Marx spoke of the great heart of the proletariat in his pamphlet on the Civil War in France. Jim Larkin came from this great heart. One bows one's head in memory of this brave Irish labor leader.

A Summer Morning in Dublin in 1938[1]

It was a muggy morning, warmer than usual for Dublin. The sky was overcast, and the sidewalks were drying after a brief rain. We drove west of Grafton Street on the south bank of the Liffey and stopped before a ruined Georgian house. The street was one of those typical streets of the Dublin slums, wide and treeless and dusty. Dirty slum kids were playing and shouting all over the street. Near by was a row of new model houses that were being completed as part of the slum-clearance program. The block was composed about half of new houses that had not been occupied and half of old and dilapidated Georgian houses. The building we entered was perhaps the worst in the block. The hallway was filthy. Ragged little Irish children looked at us, silent but with curious eyes. My friend knocked at the first door on the left. A slatternly middle-aged housewife, with her hair uncombed, peeked out through a half-opened door. Recognizing my friend as a doctor who was often in the slums, she admitted us.

Since he last had been to this house, there had been a change of tenants. The family that had occupied this room before had moved. It had been a family of nine, and they had lived in this one room. A plague of diphtheria had struck them. The doctor had been called too late. When he had arrived, a two-year-old child was dead in one corner and a five-year-old girl lay dead in another. A boy of eight lay dying in the bed in which six slept. The boy had since died. The other children had been saved, however. The mother, a Dublin widow, the doctor informed me, was a hard and tough woman, brutalized by her years in the slums. But for once she had broken down. Then this family had moved. In its place was a family of seven. The room was wide and square-shaped, cluttered with household goods; a fire was going in the fireplace. There was a desk in a corner, and odds and ends of clothing were hung about

---

1. Reprinted from Farrell's collection of stories *When Boyhood Dreams Come True* (New York: Vanguard Press, 1946), pp. 164–73. The story had appeared earlier in *Western Socialist* 12 (June 1945): 67–69.

the walls and by the large bed. On the mantlepiece over the fireplace were cheap porcelain figures. There was a small table in the center of the room, close to the bed, on which there were crumbs of bread and a piece of cheese. The walls were lined with large, framed holy pictures, one of the Sacred Heart, another of the Holy Family, others of saints, of Mary, and of Christ. The woman smiled at us perfunctorily. She had bad teeth, and there was a gap where two were missing in the front of her mouth. She told us how many were living there, and then she added.

"And, sir, himself is not working."

"How do you live?"

"Himself gets a pound a week at the Labor Exchange."

"What rent do you pay?"

"Sure, the agent comes around every week and collects three shillings."

"Who owns this house?"

"Sir, and that nobody does," she said.

She padded about the room on her bare feet. Her youngest child was about a year and a half; he looked up at us, dirty-faced, from the slivery board floor near the fireplace. A toothless grandmother watched us closely and played with her straggling hair.

"Sir, there is no owner," the grandmother said.

"Well, how do they collect rent?"

"The agent, Mr. Longford, does be collecting it every week for Murphy and Johnson."

"Why do you pay it?"

"Sure, and he's here every week collecting three shillings a week from all of us," the mother said.

"And nobody owns it?"

"They do be waiting for to condemn it and tear the building down," the grandmother said.

"Then what will you do?"

"We're waitin' for one of the new houses but, sure, we can't be going outside of the city in one of the new places for, sure, how can we be affording it with himself drawing only a pound a week at the Labor Exchange."

They continued talking about their conditions. The husband had been out of work for a year, and they had been living on his dole. The building was to be demolished, but the real-estate company continued collecting its rent. The two oldest boys slept on the floor. One of them was fourteen, and they were hoping he would find work now and that would help them. They wanted one of the new houses under construction, but they feared they could not afford to move. If the father found work, the carfare from a suburb, where many of the model houses were going up, would eat up too much of the income, what with all the mouths they had to feed.

When we left this apartment, there was a small collection of neighbors waiting for us. Several of the women bowed. They were all shabby, and most of them were dirty. An old woman importuned us.

"Do you want us to look at your apartment?" the doctor asked.

"Doctor, come. Look at what an old woman has to live in. It isn't fit for a human being. I don't be knowing but when the roof is to be on me head in me cottage out back. I moved me bed down to the first floor. Doctor, the roof was on me head," she said.

She led us past the stairway in the musty and odorous hall and out to a stone cottage in the back court, built on the model of many of the country cottages in Ireland. Inside, it was sparsely furnished, and the wall was lined with holy pictures; I looked at a large one of the Sacred Heart. In a small alcove off the room there was an unmade bed with dirty sheets and a heavy blanket.

"There's me bed now, Doctor. It was fallin' on me, Doctor."

"Did you tell the real-estate people?"

"That I did, and the man told me that he could do nothing for me. The house is condemned," she said.

"Why don't you refuse to pay rent?"

"And the man is here every week, every week, and he takes me three shillings. Come upstairs, Doctor, and, I ask you, is it fit for a human being to be living in?"

She led us up the stairway to the second floor. It was a large, bare room, and there was plaster all over the floor.

"Look, Doctor," she said, going to a corner where she pointed a long and gnarled index finger at the ceiling. The plaster had fallen, and the roof was beginning to collapse.

"It's the same all over the room. Sure, when it rained, I was pelted and I didn't know but when I went to me bed but that I would be finding meself awake with the roof on the top of me," she said.

"How long have you been living here?"

"Twenty years," she said.

"And what does the agent say when you show him these conditions?"

"Sure, and he says what can he do and he only coming for the rent. I pay him three shillings a week. I ask you, Doctor, is this for a human being to be living in? Sure, and it was pelting me with rain, and look, all over, the roof is falling on me old shoulders," she said.

The old woman, like the woman of the family we had just visited,

was inured and stupefied in this kind of life. She, like the grandmother
and the mother in the front apartment, was patient in her hopelessness.
Week after week she had given out three shillings, money mainly ob-
tained by begging in the better sections of Dublin, and in the meantime
the house in which she lived had begun to fall down on top of her. She
was still patiently waiting—for what?

Outside her cottage was the one toilet, which served the families in
the seven one-room apartments in the building as well as herself; opposite it was a small pump, the only source of water for all this little
community. We looked at the toilet. Flies buzzed about it, and the odor
of human defecation was unbearable. The plumbing facilities were very
old; the seat was dirty; the stone flooring was muddy with dirt, urine,
and human excrement. We went back to the house.

A thin, pale woman was waiting for us.

"Doctor, have you seen the place upstairs front yet?"

"No, who's there?"

"Mrs. O'Malley. She has six, and, sure, Doctor, it's aloive with
insects. There's every variety of insect life known to be found in her
place, and, sure, Doctor, it's aloive with them. It's aloive with them, and
the cockroaches. And, Doctor, we would all be eaten by the rats only
for our cats," she said.

"You don't have them here?"

"And don't we all have cockroaches?"

"And rats?"

"If it weren't for the cats, I don't know what we'd be doing. But,
Doctor, you look upstairs and see Mrs. O'Malley's. Doctor, it's aloive
with every variety of insect life known. Bluebottles and every variety.
Sure, Doctor, and isn't Mrs. O'Malley's house like a museum of insect
life," she said.

We left this apartment and the building. We drove away, crossing
O'Connell bridge and going east on the north bank of the Liffey. We
stopped at a building opposite a large waste space where there were old
bricks and much refuse.

The house was similar to the other one we had visited. It was old
and run down. In the hallway, the plaster was cracking. There were
women and children crowded about us in the hallway just as there had
been in the other place. We knocked on a door at the entranceway and
were admitted.

The mother of the house was a woman of about forty. The doctor
had told me something of the history of this family. The father had had
consumption and had been in a sanitarium. He had been released. He
had returned home. A baby had been born infected, and it had died. A

young boy had died of consumption. The father had died. Now there were five in the family, three children, the mother, and an adopted daughter of eighteen who had already started to whore. The barefooted mother wore a ragged dress and a dirty apron. She looked at us meekly. The girl was plump and plain-faced. The doctor asked the mother how everyone was. She said that she was not feeling any too well herself and pointed to the adopted daughter, remarking that the girl had been away for a few days and had spit blood. And the young boy, Tommy, was not feeling any too well, either. He was coughing badly these days, and, as she talked, she herself was racked with coughing. I looked around the house. The differences in these one-room apartments in the Dublin slums are minor. All are fairly large rooms, but they seem smaller because so much is crowded into them: one or two beds, a table, sometimes a desk, all the family possessions, and the inevitable framed holy pictures. This one was no different. The large bed was the same bed in which two of the children and the father had died.

"Haven't you tried to get out of here?"

"That I did. And here, I have the letter they sent me," the mother said.

She dug among papers in a corner and fished out a letter to show us. The letter stated that her application for one of the new homes being built had been received and filed under the heading of families of five living in one room. That was all. She was patiently waiting. She stood patiently before us.

"How do you live in here?"

"Sure, and we do. One of the boys sleeps here on the floor, and, you know, it isn't good for him, him with the coughs coming on him, and it is cold in here," she said.

"And the rest of you sleep in the bed?"

"Yes, sir. Himself died in that bed," she said.

Her story went on in the same vein as the other stories. The little boy had a flushed face and coughed in a crouplike manner. The girl coughed. The mother coughed again. It seemed fairly plain that the entire family was eaten with consumption and that its fate would be that of the father.

We were no sooner outside than a thin woman was asking us to see her place at the top. We climbed two flights of rickety stairs and entered a rectangular room. A boy of fifteen sat on a box by the fire, smoking a cigarette; he was shoeless and wore stockings with big holes in them. The mother picked up a baby and held it. There were the holy pictures, the clothes on hooks on the wall, the musty odors, the dirt. There were tea bowls, a hunk of bread, and a small slab of cheese on the table.

"Doctor, it's coming down on us. Look there. The roof is coming through," she said, pointing to a portion of the ceiling where the plaster had broken. We looked and saw that it was breaking and that it was no protection from the inevitable and regular Dublin rains.

"Doctor, will you look at him?" the mother said, pointing to a boy.

"What happened to him?"

"He was playing over across the street, and a wall fell on him. Sure, we thought he would be dead or never have the use of his limbs again. The man came around and gave me ten pounds for not going into the court," she said.

"Why didn't you go to court?"

"The man came and gave me ten pounds for not going into the court," she said.

She looked at the boy.

"Show the doctor."

He took down his trousers, and we could see where he was healing after an operation. The bones in his thigh had been split but were now knitting. The doctor said that he was all right, but that the boy should come to see him.

"Can't you do anything, all of you not pay rent and make them do something for you?"

"Sure, the man comes around every week and collects three shillings off us, and, Doctor, I ask you, is this a place fit to live in? Doctor, we can't eat, what with the torment of the flies, and then cockroaches are always on top of us. And when we do be eating, sure, and doesn't the plaster be falling into our tea? I ask you, Doctor, is this a place to live in?"

Again, the same hopeless story. After we left, we went downstairs, and a small, spiritless man in a shabby blue suit asked us to look at his apartment. It was on the first floor, to the left of the entrance, and it was smaller than the others we had seen. There was a fire going, a table in the corner, a bed on one side, and a small cot on the other. The wife was thin and worn, with sallow and unhealthy skin. She wore a red shawl and held an undernourished infant in her arms, the baby looking quiet, curious, dirty-faced at us.

"How many of you live here?"

"Eleven of us. Six of us sleep in this bed, three in the cot, and my two oldest boys sleep on the floor," the man said in a quiet, gentle voice.

"Are you working?"

"Yes, sir."

"Where?"

"Down at the docks."

"What do you earn?"

"Three pounds a week. One of the boys, my oldest, is working now and brings in a pound. And the girl here," he said, pointing to a thin girl of about seventeen, "she was working until things got slack."

"How long have you lived here?"

"Twenty-four years, sir."

"Have you applied for one of the new houses?"

"Yes, sir, but there doesn't seem to be any room for us."

"You pay rent?"

"Three shillings a week, sir."

The doctor looked at the baby and asked the mother to bring it to see him. The baby was quiet; its face was pallid and its color unhealthy.

"Where was it born?"

She pointed to the large bed in which six of the family slept.

"There, on Christmas Eve. It's eight months old, sir."

The man showed us the window.

"Sir, in winter, it doesn't keep out the cold, and the two boys sleep there on the floor, but it is not good for them," he said.

They faced us patiently.

What was there to say to them? Patiently, for years, the woman, like so many of her Dublin sisters, had been breeding like an animal. Patiently, the man had been working for years for a few pounds a week. There they were. I realized that they were only one family of the ninety thousands in the Dublin slums. Here these people were, in the wide streets, in the crumbling old Georgian houses, living in filth. Here was disease and undernourishment, rickets and filth. Here new generations were being spawned.

We left. I walked about later in these districts. Wide drab streets. Unkempt women, dirty, playing children, patient little men on corners. There is a lace curtain in every window, and there are shrines and holy pictures in every house. There is a public house on most corners throughout the section. Here these people have lived like their fathers and forefathers and their forefathers before them. Ireland has risen again and again. The Ascendancy crowd has left Ireland. The Sinn Feiners have come into power. The newspapers are full of the work and future of the new Ireland, the commemoration of the Revolution, and still these ninety thousands live in the Dublin slums. On a summer morning in Dublin one can walk north of the Liffey and there are the ancient Georgian houses, the lace curtains in the windows, the toothless old grandmothers with their black shawls, the mothers worn out and beginning to lose their teeth at the age of thirty, the ragged, pasty-faced children, the little girls of six, seven, ten, wheeling unwashed infants in creaky baby carriages. And if one goes inside these houses, one sees the filthy toilets, the little pump serving all with water, the dirty and slivery floors, the crowded rooms with the unmade musty beds, the holy pictures and saintly statues, the flies and tea bowls and cheese and hunks of bread, and one hears these people talk patiently of how they live, one sees them patiently living, patiently waiting with all of the blessed meekness of the poor.

I went back and wandered through these same sections again and again while I was in Dublin that summer. I thought of these people, and of poverty in Paris and London from which I had come, of poverty back in Chicago, in New York, of the world ringed with cities in which people live like this, and have lived like this for generations. New deals, new Irelands, these have and will come and go, and these people and their children and their children's children will go on living and suffering like this until they, they and all of their brothers, rise up in their own might and take their destiny in their own hands. Now it is almost seven years since that summer morning in Dublin when my doctor friend and I visited these people.

The thoughts that I had on that morning in Dublin, the thoughts that I had going back to that section, these return to me. These people will rot in meekness until they rise up and fight. This is the real fight, the only fight for humanity.

Selected Letters
and Diary Notes

(30 July—11 December 1938)

To Felix Kolodziej[1]

30 July 1938
Dublin, Ireland

Dear Felix:

Well here it comes straight from the ould sod. And as you will note I enclose a clipping which can only silence all of your arguments for once and for all and for ever. Incidentally, after reading the enclosed clipping, would you mail it to James Henle, Vanguard Press, and thanks.[2]

I picked up still more books here including one on the forged diaries of [Roger] Casement, and a biography of James Connolly by his daughter.[3]

My impressions of Ireland are, as yet, superficial, and must be considered as such. Next week, Hortense[4] and I are making a bit of a tour, going to Galway, Killarney, and Cork, which will keep us out of Dublin for about five days, and then, perhaps I shall have more solid impressions. At all events, Ireland is a backward country, a kind of outpost of civilization, and it carries with it all that that entails. The principal characteristic, naturally, of a backward country is, and must be, a lack of organization of life. Some of the Irish boast of this, and of their lack of a sense of time, and lack of slavery to the clock. They tend

---

1. Farrell had known Felix Kolodziej during his days at the University of Chicago. See Edgar M. Branch's "American Writer in the Twenties: James T. Farrell and the University of Chicago," *American Book Collector* 11 (Summer 1961): 28.

2. The clipping (not extant) seems to have been evidence in Farrell's facetious running argument with Kolodziej concerning the Irish and the Poles.

3. William J. Maloney, *The Forged Casement Diaries* (Dublin: The Talbot Press, 1936) and Nora Connolly O'Brien, *Portrait of a Rebel Father* (Dublin: The Talbot Press, 1935).

4. Hortense Alden (later married to Farrell) had traveled with Farrell from New York, preceded him from Paris to Dublin by a week, and later left for New York again a week earlier than Farrell.

almost to create a dichotomy: civilization or the clock. Actually, of course, the concept of time is one of the precious intellectual achievements of civilized man, and the invention of time in no way means that there is a necessary loss of either charm or of civilization. It is when there is no sense of time that one is the slave of time, and not when there is a sense of time. It is when there is no sense of time and no consequent organization of the life of a society that more time is taken in paying attention to the mundane necessities and common activities by which life proceeds. It takes longer to do everything—get clothes pressed, buy articles, etc.—when there is no sense of time. But then, Irishmen do not think with acute logic, and there are sad wounds between their conceptions of cause and effect. Modern science, of course, has not made severe and important inroads here in God's country. Ireland impresses me as a nation whose national aspirations were defeated in the period of the rise of nationalism, of capitalism, of nations, and of the fight for colonial position and imperialist hegemony. It did not develop a large bourgeoisie, and with that a machine industry, and it has remained an agricultural country. Its own efforts were always thwarted, and it was poor, and in consequence many of the best spirits were drained from the country while others languished in British jails, died for high treason, wore themselves out trying to do something in this sorry old isle.

In many ways, the people are warm and lovely, most cordial, friendly, and hospitable. Everywhere we have gone, we have been received with most touching hospitality.

The slums of Dublin are very drab, and the people are very poor. There are children everywhere. They sprout like mushrooms. You see women, dirty, ill clad, semi-toothless, with crowds of kids, and a pregnant belly. The poor women get worn out early with this life, and you see it in their faces, their loss of figures. You see further—despite the reputed Irish colleens—few good looking girls on the streets of Dublin. There is a large unemployment roll, and men stand on the quais by the Liffey, on corners, all over, all day, and they just stand, that is all.

Practically no trains run on Sundays here. Dublin—Hortense tells me because she arrived here on Sunday—is like a coffin, and the town is closed up tight. The pubs close at five or five-thirty. On weekdays they close at ten. The town closes up early, and there is little to do, and we can't read after that, because we have only one light, and that is far away up at the top of the high ceiling, and there you are.

Ireland is very much what I expected it to be. It does not surprise me in any sense. The people are the main interest, and they are very charming. I have never met with such hospitality in my life as that here.

Your old friends Mrs. O'Flaherty, Lizz O'Neill, and that Connerty one[5] —they are all to be seen on almost every corner. You could take Lizz, plant her down here, and it would seem, in a week, as if she had been here all of her life.

I'll write again soon. As ever, and Hortense sends her best.

To Meyer Schapiro[6]

30 July 1938
Dublin Ireland

Dear Meyer:

Ireland is something to see. It is a backward country, and its national aspirations have been defeated in the period of the rise of the modern nation. It is, in the south, predominantly agricultural. Life here is organized as it should be expected to be in a backward country. The trains do not run on time and all the rest of it. And now that freedom, or relative freedom, has been gotten from England, it is in the hands of the gombeen men and the reverend clerics. Its economic situation is pretty hopeless, and it has been engaged in a long tariff war with England.

The Irish themselves are most charming and lovable, and sometimes fantastic. I have never met a more warm and hospitable people. We call up someone, and immediately are invited over for tea or to have a drink, and they will talk all night with you.

The writers are insular and have little contact with intellectual currents outside of Ireland. It is an outpost of western civilization. It is little interested in anything beyond this green isle. Its intellectuals are little interested in what goes on beyond the bordering seas. The government is trying to force Gaelic into the position of being a national language. And of course it is preposterous. Gaelic can never be used outside of the island, and it cannot be substituted for English as the language by which life is carried on in the island. And it is compulsory in the schools. The whole business is a bit fantastic and ridiculous. Gaelic became a shibboleth in the national revolution because English is the language of the English, and the old myths and Gaelic culture

---

5. Mary O'Flaherty, Lizz O'Neill, and Mrs. Connerty are all characters from Farrell's O'Neill/O'Flaherty novels. Lizz O'Neill was modeled after Farrell's mother.

6. Farrell carried on an extensive and interesting correspondence with Columbia University art historian Meyer Schapiro, growing out of their mutual opposition to Stalinism in the 1930s but ranging widely over the decades into varied areas of art and literature as well as politics.

were used as arguments of Irish greatness. It became part of the warp and woof of the nationalist movement, and it is a shibboleth now just as socialist words are in Mexico, where there was a national revolution also.

Ireland makes me think of Mexico. Both have bitter histories and are frightfully poor. But in Mexico progressive streams of ideas have currency and here not. Mexico is in a much more progressive period than Ireland and more has been done there to limit the power of the Church.

Puritanism runs high here. It is a fantastic country to say the least. The Irish are deficient in certain sensory capacities. What they do with food is something that resides among the mysteries. Their public statues are beyond imagining. The city of Dublin is an eyesore, except for a few government buildings, some fine old Georgian houses, and Trinity College. However, Dublin was built by the English. The Irish are not a city-dwelling and city-building nation. They are agricultural, and they were in the old days a war-like race of tribes. Much [words missing[7]] -cably urbanized as I am will come under the heading of Marx's phrase, "the idiocy of rural life."

Next week we are going to make a bit of a tour, going to Athlone, my grandmother's territory, Galway, if possible the Aran Isles, Killarney, Cork, and back to Dublin for the festival of the Abbey players.

The Abbey Theatre has gone down a bit, and it is an authors' theatre run by authors and largely in authors' interest rather than that of actors. The acting is not up to what it ought to be to say the least. In many instances, they behave on the stage, and they behave with charm, and make great efforts to realize a play. What saves them is a fine repertory of good plays, that and almost that alone.

We looked up some of the literary people. Peader O'Donnell[8] is an old IRA fighter. He is one of those who fought. I am told that Ireland is as full of those who have been in jail as America is of descendants of the Mayflower pilgrims—that is since the "troubles," as they call them. O'Donnell has written at least one lovely novel of the Aran Islanders, *The Way It Is with Them*. And he is now Stalinist. When I said that the war business had gone too far and there was no stopping it, he said I was an old gray beard and that hadn't I ever attended international

---

7. These letters are printed here from Farrell's carbon copies, many of which were damaged when, while they were still kept in Farrell's own apartment, a fire broke out in 1946.

8. Peader O'Donnell had worked in the IRA from 1920 until 1934, also producing numerous novels during and after this period.

congresses of writers. He now works in rural areas with some international peasant organization, issuing bulletins etc. from Amsterdam, which is undoubtedly Stalinist.

O'Faolain[9] is softened up by nature so that he needs not even be softened up by the English to fit the pattern of the English man of letters. He is a fine talent but a minor one, and his mind is completely a literary one and rimmed in intellectual clichés. He writes literary criticism as if he were describing Irish mists.

Gogarty[10] is the reputed wit and a good minor poet. We went to see him but his daughter and Hortense were there and he was not bawdy. If not fascist, he is pre-fascist. He is frightfully anti-semitic, calls de Valera[11] a Jew whom we should have kept in the Bronx—perhaps along with Trotsky—and declares that already England is too red.

The Irish men of letters who are not completely insularized are touched with the English literary life and get softened up by English periodicals and writings. It makes of Irish literature—perhaps the most consistently good literary tradition of our times—a strange sort of growth. I think that it is a kind of parallel development to German philosophy. When German national aspirations were in the slough, Germany developed its philosophy, which became a kind of compensation. The same with Irish literature, with its dependence upon the old Gaelic myths, the mists and fairies and [words missing] Deirdre and Cuchulain. This side of it to [words missing] me an affectation. Then further along, realism developed, and it has been best in Joyce and O'Casey. Coming here, one understands Joyce's rejection of Ireland. There is a killing insularity here.

French chauvinism was never more funny than when the king visited Paris.[12] The French papers just patted themselves on the back. What a fine thing it was for France to entertain the King of England so wonderfully. Look at what hosts the French are. The military display, it is the most powerful in all history. The order of the French *foule* has

---

9. Sean O'Faolain had reviewed *Studs Lonigan* in 1936 by quoting Henry James on an Arnold Bennett novel: " 'a monument not to an idea, a pursued and captured meaning, or in short to anything whatever. . . .' " O'Faolain went on to characterize Farrell's book as "a typical monument to nothing; 840 pages of it. . . ." (untitled review, *Ireland Today* I [July 1936]: 70).

10. Oliver St. John Gogarty had lived for a few months of 1904 with Joyce in the old Sandycove tower south of Dublin, was later a protégé of Yeats, and was anthologized by Yeats in his *Oxford Book of Modern Verse*.

11. Eamon de Valera had taken part in the Easter Day Rebellion of 1916, became leader of the Sinn Fein Party, and later was elected president of a revolutionary Irish republic. After the Black and Tan war and the Civil War, de Valera became head of the Irish Free State in 1932. In 1937 he introduced the fully independent constitution of Ireland. He had visited the United States in 1919.

12. The British King George VI had visited Paris 19–20 July 1938, a demonstration of Anglo-French solidarity in defense, while Farrell was still in Paris.

been unparalleled. Etc. The papers in both England and France described it as a mission of peace, a service to peace.

In England the war-like spirit increases, evidently because of the speed at which the rearmament program is being carried on. It is all a den of thieves. France sells about 750,000 tons of iron ore a month to Germany. Germany sells machine tools needed for England's rearmament. Trade between Russia and both Germany and Italy is brisk. Same as before, with everything signed, set, and sealed.

A newspaper man from Spain told me that Caballero[13] had been arrested once leaving Valencia and then released. That the C[ommunist] P[arty] has licked everybody who opposed it. That the CP wouldn't let the anarchists onto the Aragon front, divided them up in other outfits, left raw and inexperienced but devoted troops on that front, and that these cracked with Franco's big push. The English attitude is stiffening on Spain, and the French frontier is being opened up again.

Anyway I'll write again soon and Hortense and I send our best to both of you. As ever,

Jim

To James Henle[14]

31 July 1938
Dublin, Ireland

Dear Jim:

We planned to go to Glendalough today. The bus was supposed to leave at 11 o'clock. We went down to the quai. There was no bus. About 11:30 a sign was put up stating that the bus would leave at 12:30. We went away and after hunting found a hotel where we could get a cup of coffee. We came back a little after twelve and there was a new sign up. No tours today. We took a walk and passed again a little after one, and there was still a new sign saying that a bus would leave for Glendalough at 2:30. The Gaels just have no sense of how to organize something. They can certainly make true a boast which some of them make—that they are not victims of the timepiece.

Dublin on a Sunday is something to get you down. The town is closed up and much like a coffin. In the morning, hardly anything is

---

13. Francisco Largo Caballero, a Spanish labor leader and politician, had been Socialist Premier of the Spanish Republic with the support of the Spanish Communist Party in 1936–37. Thereafter Largo and the Communists were enemies.
14. James Henle was Farrell's publisher at Vanguard Press.

open but the churches. We went by the Pro-Cathedral, and honest to God, there was a large line outside of people waiting to get in. Just like a queue before a London theatre. Well over two hundred people waiting, too. In fact, there were three lines, not one.

Dublin finally simmers down to the pubs. In the public houses you can soon talk to anyone, and soon after you have begun with the weather, someone is insisting on paying for your drinks. The Irish have no hesitancy to talk to strangers and get down to business. Yesterday, one Irishman we met in a pub told us that the Irish are descended from the Egyptians. We met an old Dublin man who is off his nut, cute and quaint. It was his seventy-fourth birthday and it was the anniversary of the day that his darlin' darlin' wife died, and he couldn't drown his sorrow in whiskey even. And soon he was whispering to me about the buggering of little boys and the raping of eight-year-old girls, and the awfulness of the Folies Bergeres. He had wonderful gestures, sweeping ones which an actor could acquire only after years of practice, I feel. But there is a curious life in the pubs. We waited in one to catch a bus and kept getting different directions on the time of the bus, the place it left from, and all that; and in addition I learned why America is in a bad way —it is Roosevelt, and the capitalists are against him, and only the ignorant are for him, and you should have seen my informant. And you run into arguments that seem to have come right out of an O'Casey play. Two old harps were having a go at one another, and one was telling the other that he was only a bloody Englishman. The other one said [words missing] man as anyone. The first harp was saying why must "we be divided." The second harp was saying that the world was going mad. The first harp said why didn't the second harp do something about it. The second harp said why should he, he was only tellin' him what it seemed like to his way of thinking. The first harp was saying we're going to give England what she gave us in the past. The second harp said the world was full of bloody madmen. The first harp said he was an Irishman and the second harp was a bloody Englishman. The second harp said that the world was full of madmen. The first harp said that there was nothing new in history and that the things that were happening now had all happened before. The second harp said well whether they were new or not, the world was bloody well full of madmen and the human race was destroying itself. The first harp asked the second harp why didn't he do something. The second harp said he didn't see why he should, and he was only telling him what it seemed like to his way of thinking. The first harp said all he was doing was telling him according to his way of thinking, and that he knew the second harp's way of thinking to a "t." The second harp suggested that he would buy whiskeys, and on the treat they went on for a further go at each other, and said the same things. They each just had something to say according to their way of thinking, that is all.

One nowhere can see the profusion of children one does here. I am sure that the Dublin medicos must be conducting scientific experiments to try and shorten the length of pregnancy to six months so that the women can have more. Again and again, you will see Dublin women, pretty worn out, some with many teeth missing, and a family of five trailing around with them, one baby in arms. And today in the slums —perhaps the dreariest slums in the whole world—they all have their Sunday suits on. The children are all dressed up and the men are in their Sunday suits, and they look a little as if they are strangers to their Sunday best. And they have to wait until two-thirty for the pubs to open. Here on Sunday practically nothing is open and in competition with the Holy Ghost, and the Holy Ghost reigns supreme. An Irish girl told Hortense that some there are who only go to church on Sunday and think that they are doing enough and that that can last them for the whole week! On Sunday, they come home from the churches in droves. And the streets are quiet. And they do not wear rubber heels. You hear the steady echo of footbeats on the stones, and it comes as a surprise in the quiet atmosphere.

The Irish papers are funny. The news consists of men stealing cows, fights in court rooms after a conviction, efforts to convict people of political conniving when the juries won't agree, will cases, more cases of political connivance. And feature articles to the glory of old Erin. One streamer announcing an article featured in a paper: IRISH KINGS AMONG BOXERS.

In Cork there has not been a mayor for two years because they can't elect one, the city council being split, and no one can get a majority. There is going to be another effort to elect a mayor on the 20th of September.

As for the food here you cannot believe it. The Irish put it through some strange process and boil it all into a state of rarefied indigestibility, and then you eat it. Somehow the matter of living is not of much importance to the Gael. He cares much less about his food than he does about his Guinness. Let him have his drinks and the food can be anything, and who cares. Food is as unimportant as time. O'Faolain told us a story of how when he came back from America he tried to buy a car. He went around and the fellow told him to come back at four. He went back and the fellow talked to him for three hours, and not one word about the car he wanted to buy could he get in edgewise.

On the street, we saw a little old lady talking to a biddy, and suddenly she makes a long and magnificent bow and says—"To your majesty!" For all the world it could have been your friend, Mrs. O'Flaherty. And in a pub near the slums a biddy came in. Her daughter went over to England with her man when there was a strike here. But her daughter couldn't stand it in England, even though her man was doing well. Her daughter couldn't stand the food! The cooking was too bad! You know, we Irish, we like things on full, plenty of beef and cabbage on the table. So her daughter is back here where she can get good food and have beef and cabbage on the table and plenty of it.

The clan of Farrell is quite enormous. We see the name on all kinds of establishments, even a hairdresser. I tell you there are plenty of Farrells here. Sure and didn't I always say that the Farrell came from kings of Ireland. If Lizz was here she would go into every place named Farrell and tell the Farrells their family history. There is no place in the world where Lizz would fit more than in Ireland. It is a divine disharmony in the entire universe that she was born and has lived all of her life in Chicago. She is a little bit of Ireland out of place, that is all, and she could settle down here and in a week it would be as if she had been a Dublin woman all of her born days. Indeed it would.

And further about Dublin—you know the Celt has gone to battle for many causes and on many occasions. But never in his history has the Celt ever gone forth to battle for the freedom of the bathtub. That is excluded.

Of course there is no need of newspapers here. The Irishman cares little what happens outside the boundaries of this isle. And for other news, well everybody knows it. If someone does not know something about a Dublin man, that Dublin man goes to a pub, starts talking, and soon he tells that something that is unknown. There is no bashfulness on that score. You go to a pub, sit down, tell your nearest neighbor that it is bad weather. And then you pitch in. "I'm from Donegal," or "I'm a Galway man," and on it goes. "And so you're an American. I have eight cousins over there, and I have an aunt that lives on Ninth Street in Brooklyn. Ah, if ever I go to America, I'll never be wantin' for a night's lodgings." Even in the poorest pub after a few minutes, some old harp is wanting to buy the drinks, and pointing to Guinness and saying, "Now that's a real drink."

Frank O'Connor, author of *The Saint and Mary Kate,* is the latest scandal. He is one of the directors of the Abbey Theatre and is one of a group advancing the notion that there should be no professional actors. If you have a Connemara character, go to the hills and *get* a Connemara character. Well, he got in an English gal to play a lady on this plan—she was no actress—and she runs off with him to Wexford and there he is condemning his soul to everlasting fire by living in sin with her. And he is reputed to be afraid to show his face in Dublin. He is supposed to lecture at the Abbey Festival, and there is rife speculation as to whether or not he will return. It is a live issue, it appears.

Ah, but 'tis a strange race, indeed it is. And a strange country. I'll write again soon. Our love to everyone.

As ever,

To Meyer Schapiro

6 August 1938
Dublin, Ireland

Dear Meyer:

When I returned to Dublin today, after a hasty circular trip about Ireland, I received your letter of July 19th, which we were both very glad to receive. I note what you said of Kafka. I am extremely anxious to read him and am going to do so when I return. I am also interested in what you think of Joyce on rereading him. Recently I was thinking that it is now sixteen years since Joyce completed *Ulysses,* and in that period he has devoted himself to making a private noise. That is what I consider his *Work in Progress.* [15] I have heard a victrola record of Joyce reading one section, "Anna Livia Plurabelle." It sounds almost as if it had meaning, and creates a melancholy mood. But by and large it is meaningless to me, and is a signal of a man of genius with colossal egotism. Wilson tried to defend it in *Axel's Castle* as being a record of the dream and sleeping life of man.[16] But that is, to me, indefensible. It has no meaning in that respect. Joyce is compounding a language all his own, and the pattern is beyond the dream and sleeping life of man. There is much stunt stuff in it—thunder represented by joining together the words for thunder in sixteen or twenty-six languages. It is a kind of rejection of all our art, and all our standards, methods, conceptions of art at the present. But then, I swing with a remark of Dewey's in *Art as Experience.* Dewey says that the only demand you can make of an artist is that his product be communicable in some sense to someone, or words to that effect.[17] And Joyce's is, I fear, not. The stunt stuff here is too strong for my taste. However, I should be very interested to know

---

15. This was to be titled *Finnegans Wake.*
16. *Axel's Castle,* pp. 225–36.
17. John Dewey, *Art as Experience* (New York: Capricorn Books, 1958), pp. 104–5.

your impressions of Joyce's other works on rereading. Joyce rejected Ireland completely, and clings to it in all of his emotional life. Rejecting Ireland is different from rejecting, say, America. The latter does not make a great deal of sense. Ireland is a country where nationalism runs perhaps higher than anywhere else in the world. Ireland was defeated in its struggle for nationhood for years. It persistently fought. Shaemas O'Sheel has two lines in a poem on the Gael:

> *They went forth to battle*
> *And they always lost* (or fell—I forget which word).[18]

Ireland has a strong emotional meaning in the consciousness of the Irishman, and this is more active than is America in the consciousness of the American. A favorite subject of discussion in the Irish novel or play is Ireland. Joyce throws Ireland in its own face, and calls it something like a dishrag at the end of *A Portrait of the Artist as a Young Man,* and declares through Stephen Dedalus that he goes forth to create the consciousness of the world in the smithy of his soul. And Joyce is forever Irish. I am told that he follows life in Dublin from Paris with a sort of microscopic intensity, asking about landmarks, buildings, if they changed, even reading the death notices in the Dublin papers. And his portrait of Dubliners in *Ulysses* is, I feel, wonderfully exact. When one is here, one gains an added sense of what Joyce meant in his rejection. There is something more international in Joyce than in his fellow Irish writers. Ireland is extremely insular. Foreign influences do and have come into the life of this island, but they get twisted up in local peculiarities. For instance, the ideas of the French Revolution had their strong influence here. But it remains a kind of outpost in our civilization, with a life that is almost characteristically parochial, and this was too much for Joyce. I think that Joyce is a genius, but if one starts asking who is a greater writer, Joyce or Dostoevski, one wouldn't hand the palm to Joyce. Dostoevski went on writing in a more intense and active sense, was more bothered, more concerned with coming to grips with the tendencies of his day that were agitating people's minds. It is true that Dostoevski was against everything progressive coming into Russia from western Europe, but he was fighting these things, dealing with them, and these tendencies became part of the warp and woof of Dostoevski's consciousness. The same thing has not continued in Joyce, it seems. But here I am speaking of Joyce as a phenomenon and not

---

18. "They went forth to battle but they always fell" is actually the first line and title of the poem; see Shaemas O'Sheel, *Jealous of Dead Leaves* (New York: Boni & Liveright, 1928), p. 12.

discussing his great books, and I think that *Dubliners, A Portrait of the Artist as a Young Man,* and *Ulysses* are all great books. Also, have you ever read his play *Exiles?* It is Ibsenish, and discusses the relationships of a man and a woman and modern marriage in a way far outside the boundaries of parochial Ireland.

I find Ireland most interesting. The Irish people are lovable and charming and at times fantastic. They have no sense of time the way we have. The man from County Kerry says to you that such and such a distance is a mile and a bit, and the bit is more than the mile. That is suggestive of the Irishman's sense and orientation on time and distance. He refuses to be rushed, and often it seems that he has refused to be rushed even in his revolutions. The south is an agricultural country. The southern Irish have not built cities, and their cities are not interesting the way other cities often are. There is not much architecture except archaeological remains, and in Dublin, Trinity, a few other buildings, and fine old Georgian houses, but too many of them. And of course, the Irish tend a bit to leave cleaning up the cities to the hand of God rather than of man. Which means the rain keeps the cities from accumulating more dirt. Scenically the country is in many places lovely, the coast line of hills around Galway, Connemara, and County Clare, and the lakes of Killarney. Nothing has been done, and they are set in hills and amidst greenness and lavish verdurousness, growing thick, and rank, tangled together, no artifice or human art changing them. Even the ruins of old churches and monasteries are left with hardly a touch of restoration. When we were there it was an over-clouded day, without a ripple on the waters, and with clouds hanging over the tops of some of the hills.

During the time of the increase of population all over the world, population decreased steadily in Ireland. Today one authority states that only twenty-five percent of this fertile island is cultivated, and the green lands, which could yield so much more, lie idle and are used largely for cattle grazing. And again and again the best spirits in the nation were drained off in emigration, and more were executed by Downing Street. Ireland is a classic example of the British policy of divide and rule. After the bloody Black and Tan war, England signed the Free State Treaty, giving self-government to twenty-six counties, and retaining six in Great Britain. She knew that she could thus transfer her troubles to Ireland, and dodge out of them all and out of moral opprobrium from all over the world by pointing—see the Irish are always fighting among themselves, and now look at them. In other words, she knew that the treaty would split the Irish Republican forces, as it did in the Civil War or what they call "the troubles" here. There has been a consistent and, at times, conscious demoralization of Ireland by England for centuries, and the results are shown in the state of the nation today—divided, with much fertile land left to the weeds and the cattle, with a parochialism of outlook, and many other ills. One out of three still emigrate. De Valera is trying to encourage local production, but this is a hard task. For one thing, given the tempo of life here, that kind of skill, timing, and efficiency which, for instance, the American workman possesses is lacking, and that is not learned or developed over night. For another, industrialization costs great quantities of money, and it means, even when it is achieved, competing in world markets with nations containing greater mineral and technological resources. And the division of the country leaves a rural south and an industrial north, and this splits the economy, erects tariff barriers, etc. And also, Ireland has been engaged in a long economic war with England that has driven prices way up. It is more expensive, I fear, to live here than it is in America. Food stuffs are as high and higher.

The Irish seem to have little sense of the possibilities of visual enjoyment. They have little sense of using color to make color a value in life. In dress, wallpapering, etc. it is all dull and dreary. This is also partly a Victorian influence. The pace and character of life here, in fact, retains something of a Victorian character.

The English conquest caused religious division. The Church became tied up in the nationalist revolutionary movement. In France the bourgeois revolution was internal, and the Church was defending its feudal privileges and property rights. In Russia, the same. Anti-clericalism, although it has flourished time and again, has here never had that kind of background. The Church too was dispossessed. Part of the Irish struggle was for freedom of worship, and priests, at times, were hunted in the hills. The Church furthermore has been in-between in the struggles and troubles, always against any real revolutionary push, playing both ends against the middle. The Irish made an admirable and tenacious struggle to retain their own integrity of societal life, and in doing that, the Catholicity of the Irish was strengthened at a time when the Church was losing ground in many parts of the world. The Church thus remains very strong here today. However, politically the Church has often taken lickings, lickings in the sense that their counsel has gone to the winds and the Fenians, the United Irishmen, the revolutionists of 1916 went ahead. James Connolly was the first Irish Marxist, and a genuine revolutionary internationalist. And yet he remained a good Catholic, went to mass often, and died after receiving the last sacraments. Once, his daughter tells in her book, *Portrait of a Rebel Father*, Connolly was in church at mass, and the priest gave a sermon denouncing Connolly to the parish, looking at him, and there was a steady turning of heads and fixing of eyes on him. Afterwards, his daughter was incensed. Connolly told her if others lost their heads, they shouldn't. The Irish Nationalists thought that men like Connolly and Larkin were too socialistic, and the Socialists thought that they were too nationalistic. Nationalism and religion have become intertwined here in a curious way. The Irishman, by and large, has little interest in the outside world except that he wants to emigrate to where things are better. And of course he is interested in Vatican news. American news in the Irish papers largely consists of news about Irish in America and Irish-Americans. There is more news of cows being stolen, political connivance and the like than there is of international events.

However, I fear that I could go on at too great length concerning Ireland, and I'll have to postpone more. . . .[19]

We are going to attend the Abbey Theatre Festival here starting next week and I shall try to find time to write you about it. Have you ever read much of Irish literature, and the Irish literary renaissance? It is an extremely interesting movement, and perhaps the most consistently good literary tradition, containing the steadiest output of good works, of any tradition in recent years. For forty years now, it has produced more than a respectable stream of good writing, included in which are great works by Joyce, O'Casey, Synge, and Yeats.

I can order you a Rosmer book.[20] It is worth getting. I'll do that and you can pay me when I return. Did you get the Einstein and Wilson books. Hortense joins me in sending our best to you and Lillian.

As ever,

Diary Note

Saturday
6 August 1938
Dublin, Ireland

O'Flaherty is a name from around Galway and the Aran Isles. Farrell seems to be a midland or a Dublin name. In Cork I found O'Keefe a number of times, and suspect that it is a Cork name. The Irish names

---

19. Here is omitted a lengthy digression on matters unrelated to Ireland.

20. Alfred Rosmer's book was *L'Assassinat Politique et l'U.R.S.S.* (Paris: Les Humbles, 1938), a discussion of Stalinist killings of political refugees from the Soviet Union.

are nearly always an O' or a Mac, but often the O' has gone in time, either here, or in America, more frequently in America.

The Aran Islanders say, "We don't *house* our cattle in winter." For lots, Irish often say, "any amount." I.e., "We get *any amount* of fruits from America."

An Englishman on the bus from Killarney to Cork. His first comment on Ireland: "They could clean it up a bit." He feels that it is not in the temperament of the Irish to become a progressive, industrial nation. But they are charming all the same, he added.

O'Faolain said that Cork was like a French provincial town. The only substantial I found for such a claim is narrow winding side streets.

Off Grafton Street, there is a Carmelite Church, and a shrine of the Little Flower.[21] There seems to be some Carmelite success here in the Little Flower adoration. In fact, in this very room there is a large statue of the saint.

Driving from Killarney to Cork, I noticed very few automobiles on the road. A number of little carts. And livestock. The technique of driving in Ireland is not so much avoiding fellow automobiles as avoiding livestock. Also bicycles.

Many Irish girls apparently wear shorts, and it is not frowned on.

When a clergyman got on the boat to go to the Aran Isles, an Irishman, middle class on vacation, said to a friend, "Look at him. He walks on as if he owned the boat."

An Englishman from the midlands coming over from Holyhead with me called a bicycle a push bike, and a motorcycle a motor bike.

FIR—Gentlemen or Men.

MNA—Women or Ladies.

Diary Note

Monday
8 August 1938
Dublin, Ireland

We met a man who is a housing investigator named Murphy in Byrne's bar yesterday. He believes that everybody will be speaking Gaelic in fifty years. He is a very nice and friendly fellow, but highly

---

21. Farrell's high school education had been by Carmelite priests in Chicago; cf. Introduction, above, pp. 5–6.

"nationalistic." Also, we met a French maître d'hotel who works at the Hibernian, and who likes London better than Paris, and is, for all practical purposes, a Frenchman who became an Englishman. He said he did not like American cooking and cited, as an example, Americans who ask for steaks stuffed with oysters. Neither Hortense nor I ever heard of this as an American dish. The maître d'hotel had the earmarks of his occupation in his consciousness, his views on Ireland, and on the goodness of England for Ireland, etc.

Took a walk in slums by the Liffey. Sometimes the dirt and filth in Ireland seem overpowering. Many of the children were dirty, almost filthy. There were two tots in a buggy who were especially so, almost turning one's stomach as one got a passing look at them.

Higgins[22] agrees with Hortense that Gaelic sounds like Russian.

It is difficult to find anyone here who will say a good word for a Corkonian. Usually it is said that the people of Cork are too "clannish."

Malone's lecture[23] today was largely anecdotal, and he ran past his time and had to condense facts at the end, because he had been so anecdotal. He even talked about seats and why he did not like seats to be too comfortable, because then the audience would fall asleep. He did present certain facts, more or less familiar, concerning the founding of the Abbey. The audience of the early Abbey was not bourgeois Dublin. Many of those who came were artisans. Also, a little later, the audience was largely civil servants, and it still is, Lennox Robinson[24] said. He, Robinson, then added that young Sinn Feiners such as Kevin O'Higgins and Blythe[25] went to the Abbey week after week in their student days. Malone told a story of the audience when a Conal O'Riordan play was put on. A piper played a tune. The air was that of "The British Grenadiers." The audience raised hell, but the piper played it to the end. Then, W. B. Yeats went to the front of the stage and explained that it was an old Irish air, and the audience was in humiliation and ready to slink out of the theatre.

Malone said afterwards that the article in *The Leader* on the Abbey is the article of a disgruntled actor. Whatever it be on this side, its point

---

22. F. R. Higgins was a poet, another protégé of Yeats, involved in all sorts of literary enterprises and squabbles in Dublin in the 1930s. Farrell and his wife talked with Higgins at the reception before the Abbey Festival on 6 August.

23. Andrew Malone, drama critic for the *Irish Times,* Farrell met at the Abbey reception; subsequently Malone gave the festival's opening lecture.

24. Lennox Robinson was an Abbey director/dramatist during the 1920s and 1930s.

25. Kevin O'Higgins, an early republican who had served as Minister of Justice in the Cosgrave Free State government, was assassinated in 1927 by dissident republicans. Ernest Blythe, a Gaelic enthusiast, survived his work as Minister of Finance under Cosgrave to become Managing Director of the Abbey years later in 1941.

about the Abbey being an authors' theatre is one that is well taken and makes seemingly sound sense.

Diary Note

Tuesday
9 August 1938
Dublin, Ireland

The Abbey Festival opened last night with productions of *Kathleen ni Houlihan* and *The Playboy of the Western World. Kathleen ni Houlihan* impressed me as being undramatic, a one-acter which is better read than seen. In part, this impression was created—or at least strengthened—by Eileen Crowe. Playing the part of Kathleen, she crowed. Almost literally, she crowed. The play is, also, a propagandistic play for Ireland, and it mixes symbolism and realism. It has historic importance in the history of Irish literature in the sense that it was one of the first to introduce the use of dialect and of simple speech. It is, however, not a play which inheres in the sense that a truly dramatic play inheres. A few odds and ends to make a situation, and then the entry of Kathleen. *The Playboy of the Western World* is of course gorgeous on re-seeing. Its sheer wonderfulness of language is, in itself, worth the seeing. The production was better than in America, largely because Ria Mooney was better in the part of Pegeen Mike than she was in America. Shields[26] was charming and extremely alive on the stage.

Frank O'Connor lectured this morning. There has been much gossip concerning him. Only last night, I spoke to Andrew Malone. Malone answered my question—Was O'Connor at the play?—by saying that he was in London with a woman, and wouldn't be back, wouldn't probably ever return. I asked him was that necessary. At first, he indicated that it wasn't, and that O'Connor was taking it over-seriously. Then he said that it was. He said that in England there are nine commandments, while here there is only one. Anyway, the gossip is overdone. O'Connor did show up, and did lecture. He had the girl with him. She is Welsh and more spirited and prettier than most of the wives here, and O'Connor seems to be happy. He introduces her as a Miss and not as a Mrs. and makes no bones about the two of them having a place together in Wexford. It is an introduction to the killing gossip of Dublin.

---

26. Arthur Shields was one of the leading actors at the Abbey in the 1920s and 1930s.

O'Connor impressed me as having more character than the other writers whom I have met here. He is a thin fellow, with graying hair, a thin face, great charm, and an easy manner. His lecture was sincere but muddled. He spoke of the source of literature being in folk myths and religion. This is, in a sense, true. He said that Yeats, Synge, and Lady Gregory had all realized this, and that they had gone back to these sources to gain purity. He said that they were against the middle class. But he did not calculate and think out and check more sources, and in not doing this his lecture became, to me, all muddled up. I pointed out to him afterwards that one aspect of *The Playboy* is the growth in self-consciousness of Christy Mahon. The kind of self-consciousness which Christy develops is not a simple folk self-consciousness, but one which is a development in the world following the rise of capitalism and of the bourgeoisie. In a sense, this is part of the bones of the time in which Synge wrote, and Synge had some of these bones. O'Connor attacked "naturalism" and "knowingness" in literature, but he did not make clear what he meant by these. Also, he attacked "representation." But it was not all clear to me. He criticized the second act of *The Playboy* on the ground that it introduces an element of French farce when Pegeen Mike is given the stage. He said that it destroyed the purity of the myth which Synge was using as his main theme, and that the main characters are Mahon and his father. I think that he is wrong. Pegeen Mike and the girls bring out the change in Christy. Further, it refutes O'Connor's own interpretation of the going back to simple and pure sources of literature. O'Connor inclined too much to accept the views of Yeats, Lady Gregory, and Synge at face value. Further, it occurred to me that this movement was one which was more than purely Irish. There was a going back to the people, a discovery of the peasantry, a growing indication of the peasantry and the rural elements having a voice and a political meaning in the world, etc. There was the Narodnik movement[27] and the phenomenon of Tolstoy and others in Russia. There was Gauguin. There was, in America, populism. Etc. This all was part of an intellectual, artistic, and political climate stretching beyond boundaries.

Talking with O'Connor and O'Faolain this afternoon, I learned that the Church here has a squealer service on priests and checks up on them. O'Connor says that Hayes,[28] one of the present directors of the Abbey, had a flare-up with Connolly. He heard Connolly give a lecture on street

---

27. The Narodniks were a populist revolutionary movement under the Czars.

28. Dr. Richard Hayes, a Dublin physician, was appointed government representative to the Abbey directorate in 1934. He became a full director in 1939. See Peter Kavanagh, *The Story of The Abbey Theatre* (New York: Devin-Adair, 1950), pp. 161 and 180.

fighting. Hayes asked Connolly what would happen if the British used their big guns. Connolly is reputed to have answered that any of those who were afraid to die could leave the hall. He says that Hayes never talks of Connolly much because of this instance. It is true that the British did use big guns, and that this, evidently, turned to naught much of Connolly's plans and his efforts to train the Citizen Army. Hayes was a Volunteer.

The Dublin bourgeoisie, according to O'Faolain, is not coagulating, and there is to be a fight for the people between it and the artists.

O'Faolain says that Macnamara[29] reneged on a censorship issue involving O'Casey and was kicked off the Abbey board of directors. Neither O'Connor nor O'Faolain respects Macnamara much.

Diary Note

Wednesday
10 August 1938
Dublin, Ireland

I had quite forgotten Synge's *The Well of the Saints.* Seeing it last evening was a wonderful experience. The production was the best of any I have seen so far here at the Abbey. Cyril Cusack playing Martin Doul was particularly good. He is their best actor. Yesterday, Frank O'Connor criticized *The Well of the Saints* on the grounds that Synge's invocation of heavenly properties in producing the miracle was too much machinery for the little result gotten, and that the result in dramatic terms did not justify such an invocation. But Frank O'Connor is just not a good critic. He is a composition, critically, of illogical and apparently shifting whims, and of a few simple notions of stage technique, stagecraft and the like. He just misses the point here concerning *The Well of the Saints.*

It is a fable, a fable which becomes the *raison d'être* for the revelation of a most mordant irony. The play is one of the bitterest and most beautiful of modern plays. The manner in which the characters lash one another with their tongues, the character of Martin Doul's vision, language and the like after his sight is restored to him, this is wonderful insight and fantasy combined, and it becomes the occasion for Synge's truly mordant irony. And then toward the end of the play, when Martin Doul and his wife are coming together again, they talk of old age, and their vanity takes on a new character. They begin to sing the glories of

---

29. Brinsley Macnamara left the Abbey company in 1912 to devote his time to writing. He produced several novels, and plays for the Abbey, through the 1930s.

old age, she of the wonderful hair she will have, he of the fine beard that he is going to be growing. Humanity isn't lost in this mordant irony, because Synge makes these two blind old beggars very human. It is little touches like this which give the play so much added humanity.

The play is very simple, so simple as to carry such points as it does. For it is a bitter criticism of many aspects of life. It is also anti-clerical. It is clear that Synge was strongly anti-clerical.

Riders to the Sea is Synge's finest play, wonderful in its quietness and simplicity. And the production of it last night was completely ruined by Eileen Crowe. She sang all her lines in the most dreadful manner until she had Hortense and me almost writhing in our seats. It is pure insanity and nothing less to give that woman parts in these plays, and something should be done to prevent her from ruining more plays in the festival and in the regular Abbey season. She would probably have been laughed off Broadway doing what she did, singing her lines, making them ridiculously melodramatic, taking the simple words of the mother's grief which Synge wrote and distorting them.

Lennox Robinson always stands too jollily in the lobbies as if taking bows and being a local figure. He is beginning to impress me as being too much of a small town celebrity for my taste.

Fontamara was banned in Ireland two days ago.

Finished reading *The Forged Casement Diaries*. The book is frightening in that it reveals what a powerful machine, a government, can do to a man when it wants to "get" him. And what is a man against such a machine?

Started reading Peader O'Donnell's *The Islanders*. Simple and charming so far. Also bought Macnamara's *The Valley of the Squinting Windows* last night to read.

Incomplete news of the Russo-Japanese incident in the papers still, and it is very disquieting. One wishes that both sides would contribute four mines and blow up the damn hill in the wastes over which they are fighting. But it is not just a hill in the wastes that is causing this latest war scare. In fact, it is not a war scare. It is a small war, a battle.

To James Henle

14 August 1938
Dublin, Ireland

Dear Jim:

Several times in letters you have mentioned the present status of liberty in Ireland. I am beginning to think that to a great extent, this status has something to do with the fate of Connolly and the Citizen Army in the Easter Uprising. The Irish Citizen Army was a workers' militia formed after the defeat of the workers in the great Dublin transport strike. Labor was militant in Ireland before the war, and Larkin was sometimes almost tying the employers in knots. When he went to America, Connolly continued with Larkin's work. After the defeat of the Rising, the economic question concerning classes here got sidetracked, and the revolutionary movement became national. Many of the nationalist leaders were purely bourgeois revolutionaries, and in some cases they were anti-labor. Griffith[30] is the best example here. After the Black and Tan war, it was this wing which came to the fore. There was a further split, and the poorer elements in some instances at least were with the die-hards. What we get today is a bourgeois state. It is poor, and it is trying to encourage its native bourgeois. There is an effort to stimulate home manufacture, and this effort is protected behind a tariff wall to keep prices up. The English bourgeois is engaged in an economic fight with the Irish bourgeois. The movement to free Ireland became a movement to beget an Ireland of the gombeen men and the priests. We are in a period of world-wide reaction, and we see one reflection of it here in this island. Nationalism here became abnormally strong owing to the age-long struggle with England. A kind of Thermidor developed here, and there we are. If we don't look at it in this way, we have to explain it in terms of the crazy Irish, local peculiarities, and the like, and I don't think that such are good working hypotheses for approaching a socio-politico-economic setup.

The phenomenon of ignorance is not an accidental one. When ignorance is put in the saddle, and when there is a consistent attempt to keep it there, there is a reason. Max Stirner writes in *The Ego and Its Own* that when an error persists in an age, some few profit from that error while many suffer from it. I am paraphrasing. The exact quotation is used in one of my stories in *Guillotine Party,* the one about the law student in the Studs Lonigan neighborhood.[31] This fantastic Gaelic revival here, where they even try to teach Euclid and Cicero in Gaelic—it is part of the theory of the Irish nation and nationhood which is the ideological foundation stone of Irish nationalism. We note that it is fantastic. But the gombeen [words missing] while voting for politicians who keep it in, still count their pennies in shillings, and they still use the interna-

---

30. Arthur Griffith, founder of the Sinn Fein Party, had once sought the creation of a dual monarchy of England and Ireland, like that of Austria-Hungary.

31. "All Things Are Nothing to Me," in *The Short Stories of James T. Farrell* (New York: Vanguard Press, 1937), p. 271.

tional language sign of the dough in their calculations. And when they translate works into Gaelic, give Gaelic readings in school, you'll find them teaching all about Cuchulain, but not Connolly's *Labour in Irish History*. Lenin somewhere wrote that if mathematics involved the interests of men, mathematics would not have undergone the surprising and astounding development which it has. And problems and issues here always get confused in some side alley. The Gaelic revival is an almost classic political detour, and it remains that whether it be conscious or not. Furthermore, there would be no Gaelic revival here if Saint Patrick had not driven the snakes out of Oireland and if the Gaels had not been Christianized.

But I'll write again soon. My love to everyone. As ever,

Jim

To Felix Kolodziej

24 August 1938
Dublin, Ireland

Dear Felix:

I shall be returning to the United States by the same boat which carries this letter. I am glad and sorry to be departing. Were I able to remain here six months, I should learn a great deal and produce, besides many articles, at least a whole book of Irish short stories. But then, that is that. My style has been cramped since Hortense left because I suffered from an attack of indigestion. Evidently, it was largely "the charm of Irish cooking." Now my last days are crowded. Just when one is ready to leave a country, one feels that one is beginning to learn something of it. And one feels that one is able to judge the people a bit better, to learn how to get better information and the like. Ireland, it must be remembered, is a difficult country in which to gain objective facts. Sometimes, to get objective facts is like pulling teeth, and the teeth do not come out easily. The outside world of course has many curious notions concerning the Celt in these green sections of God's famous globe. One of them is that the Irishman is such a sentimental creature. There is much less sentimentality in him than people think. Often, the Irishman is hard, and often he is very vindictive. The truth of the matter seems to me to be that the Irishman has never really been completely civilized. One side of his nature is pretty mean and vindictive. That side refers to the Celt unhappy and neurotic. And particularly because of Mother Church, neuroticism, like infanticide and the abandonment of illegitimate babies, is a constant here. Another of the psychological effects of the Church seems to me to be this. The Celt after all believes that he is going to go on living and that in the future life, it will not be Ireland, but something even better. This is part, I believe, of the Celt's inefficiency and his take-it-or-leave-it attitude, his easy-goingness and casualness concerning time and order in the arrangement of the business of permitting life to go on in these green isles. Sure and don't let it bother you, he says often for many questions of detail, order, efficiency, questions concerning the on-going of the process of society here. This is a particularly dull period in Ireland too. Ireland is now in the aftermath of one of those periods when Ireland rises as she has been doing so often in her history. And in the aftermath of dullness, the gombeen men are getting rich and the people get poorer and poorer. The labor movement is dull and in the hands of the bureaucracy, and there you are. I have collected a goodly small library on the Celt and I shall, from time to time, send on parts of it to you.

I was taken to some places in the Dublin slums today, and I have never seen the like of it. Not that you cannot find its match in [words missing] lumpen proletariat. In one place, a building which should be condemned—I believe that it is waiting for condemnation—there are, if I remember correctly, seven families living in one house, this one. There is a filthy outside toilet for the families, and there is one little water tap, also outside. In one room, there is a family of seven living. Of course, the place is dirty and filthy. In another, a woman lost three children from consumption, and six are left. In another house, crumbling, the ceilings have been fortified with boards. An old woman lives in a stone cottage in an inside court. The roof is falling through on her, and she had to move her bed down from the second to the first floor. We—I was with a doctor—were in one place, a room of say fifteen by twenty feet or thereabouts—and one family of eleven living in it. The oldest boys sleep on the floor. This family has lived in the same place for twenty-four years. The man is a dock worker. His oldest daughter, a girl of sixteen or seventeen, worked. But times are slack and she is laid off. An oldest boy of nineteen works and gets two pounds a week. The youngest child is eight months old, and undernourished. The people were very patient. The man seemed gentle and patient and explained that they had lived in this one place for twenty-four years. On the top floor, a family of seven. The ceiling is falling in on them. Rain leaks through. Some of the boys sleep on the floor. The place is "aloive with insects." So it goes. These people are charged three to three and six shillings a week for rent by rack-renters. Another family. The husband died in the large bed in the corner of the room. Consumption. A child lost by consumption. Four children and an adopted daughter left. All with consumption. The adopted daughter, a girl of about eighteen who has just begun her career of whoring. Women rendered very hard, some of them real biddies in all this filth and dirt and disease, crumbling buildings, falling plaster, decaying ceilings held up with long boards. And in all of the houses, the walls lined with holy pictures, a profusion of Mary and the Sacred Heart. I spent, Felix, a summer morning in Dublin this morning.

I shall write you from the boat or shortly after my return.

As ever,
Jimmy

Diary Note

Saturday
27 August 1938
On board *S.S. Manhattan*

I got off in good order. Cobh was pretty much of what Hortense warned me it would be. Except that I was not so bored. I walked about the town. I watched the kids playing about the boats in the waters inside the piers. I watched the townspeople fishing for mackerel after supper. During August, when the waters are calm, mackerel come into the harbor in schools and schools. It is easy watching them. They dove and darted about, pursuing minnows. There must have been literally thousands upon thousands of minnows. At times they would be so thick, fleeing the mackerel, that the water down below me would be black with them. After August the mackerel go out. Also, if it gets rough, they vanish. The mackerel, seen as they shot through the waters like submarines, were beautiful.

Cobh with its boats and harbor, is a wonderful place for kids.

The harbor [words missing] off in the direction of the [words missing] struck me. I do not think that I have ever seen so many colors on the water. About a hundred or two hundred yards out, there was a current, and the surface of the flowing water was a broken, deep, almost black blue. Inside this, it was calm and there were circles and patches pinked by the dying sunset. Out farther there were blues—Monet colors —pure blues. And off the green of the land, in varying shades, the greyishness of the buildings. And green here and there on the water.

Today was a dead day for me on board. I had to get up at three o'clock in the morning, and I only had brief naps in the morning and the afternoon. And a sour stomach. Very infrequently a pain. I hope my trouble is not coming back.

The crowd here looks to me to be exceedingly dull and bourgeois. But I haven't talked much. Except to a young student named Avery Hand, Jr. who eats with me. He is interested in archaeology and was in Ireland for that purpose. He said that Ireland is very rich in archaeological remains. He is inclined to be pro-German. Possibly he is even pro-Hitler. At all events, he said that Germany would not start a war unless Czechoslovakia did something to her. On my remarking what in hell would Czechoslovakia do to Germany, he did revise himself to the extent of saying that Germany might provoke Czechoslovakia into doing something. He is anti-Semite. He remarked that the boat was loaded with long-nosed kikes. He is a junior at the University of Pennsylvania. Obviously his folks have money. He travels quite a bit.

My roommate is a German doctor. I believe that he is Jewish. He is allowed a fortnight in U.S. His fare and hotel bills are paid, and he is allowed only $4 a day cash.

There was quite a bit of fog this morning. I finished Peader O'Donnell's novel *The Knife* to-day on ship. I am not sure what I think of it. Peader is not a novelist of character. It is a story of the Irish revolution. The novel contains some extremely interesting points, [words missing] of the life of IRA prisoners in Free State jails.

At Cobh, the waitress in the hotel, a nice looking but a bit cowy faced and dumpy, bow-legged girl, was quite lively. Every other word out of her mouth, almost, was "Hell." She remarked to me that someone was saying that the end of the world is coming. She said maybe it was.

Cork kids say "daid" for dead.

I am going to try to get back to reading French now on this trip.

To Leon Trotsky

11 December 1938
New York City

Leon Trotsky
Coyoacan
Mexico D.F.

My Dear Leon Trotsky:

We were both very pleased to receive your note. Hortense, jokingly, says that it must all be a Stalinist plot. While she is not disinterested in politics, she is, in no sense, a political person. However, she is no bitter foe. And in her own profession, the theatre, she must pay a price for her attitudes and the stand that she has taken. Stalinist influence is permeating the American theatre, and Hortense is automatically excluded from even being considered for roles in plays by certain managements because of this fact.

Concerning "the mysteries of my style,"[32] you may be amused to know that one Communist Party functionary described it, once in *The Daily Worker*, as "Trotskyite." And one of the most current criticisms of my writing in Stalinist sources is that "the rationale of Trotskyism" has given a basis for his "despair," and through that means he is degenerating.

This summer I was in Ireland, and I saw Jim Larkin. All men have weaknesses, but all men are not the victims of their weaknesses. Jim Larkin is a victim of his own weaknesses, and his own temperament. Now, he is embittered and envenomed. He feels that the Irish working class has sold him out. He was not returned in the last elections for the Dail, and he ran in a working class district. He defended the trials, but thought that Bukharin could not be interested. But Larkin's formal attitudes do not have much meaning. He is untheoretical and unstable intellectually. He is always a direct actionist, and his direct actionism takes whatever turn that his impulses lead him toward. In the midst, for instance, of a severe fight, he might be walking down the street and see a sparrow trapped in some electric wires where it might die. He will become incensed, and will telephone important members of the government and demand that they have men sent down to release the sparrow immediately, and then this will loom more important than the fight in which he is engaged. He is very garrulous, human and humane, witty, vindictive, vituperative, and he is Irish. At times, he is almost like an embittered version of the stage Irishman. In Ireland, there has never been much theory, and in consequence, never been many men with a rounded view of the reasons why Ireland was struggling. Before the war, the Irish labor movement was very militant and well toward the forefront of the European labor movement. It was defeated in the great Dublin transport strike of 1913, and out of this crushing defeat, the

---

32. In earlier correspondence, Trotsky had used this phrase referring to baseball terminology used in *A World I Never Made*, a copy of which Farrell had sent him. Farrell had first met Trotsky in Mexico at the inquiry of the Dewey Commission into the Moscow trials. See "Dewey in Mexico," in *Reflections at Fifty and Other Essays* (New York: Vanguard Press, 1954), pp. 97–123; and "A Memoir of Trotsky," *University of Kansas City Review* 23 (1957): 293–98. In his reply to this letter of 11 December, Trotsky encouraged Farrell to publish his views on Ireland.

Irish Citizen Army was formed. Larkin left for America, and Larkin says that one of the last things that he said to Connolly was not to go into the National movement, not to join the Irish Volunteers, which was the armed force of the nationalist movement. Connolly did go into the Easter Rebellion, and there is the disputed question as to whether or not he made a mistake. Sean O'Casey, the Irish playwright, in a pamphlet he wrote on the Irish Citizen Army, declares baldly that James Connolly died not for Irish socialism but for Irish nationalism. Others maintain that Connolly could not have remained out of the rising. At all events, the Irish Citizen Army was decimated, and crushed by the Easter Rebellion. There were no leaders left to carry on the social side of Connolly's doctrines. The entire movement was swept along in a frenzied rise of Irish patriotism and Irish nationalism. Sinn Fein was in complete control of the movement. The leaders of Sinn Fein had only the most vague notions of what they wanted—an Irish Ireland speaking Gaelic, developing its own Irish culture, free of the British crown, and some were not even fighting them for freedom from the crown. In 1921, when the treaty was negotiated in England, there was this same unclarity. Following the treaty, there was the split in the Irish ranks. The record of that split is most saddening to read. It was not a split on real issues. There were two or three documents with different wordings, and they all meant much the same thing. Instead of discussing social programs, they discussed Ireland, and they insulted one another. Out of this split the bitter civil war developed, and the comrades in arms of yesterday assassinated one another. The treatment which the Free State government meted out to its former comrades matches almost that which Stalin has meted out. The bravest fighters of the Irish Republican Army were taken out and placed up against a wall and butchered without any formality. And now, after all the trouble, the Irish people have changed masters, and a new Irish bourgeoisie is developing and coagulating, and the politicians of Sinn Fein are aligned with them and the Church, with reaction rampant, poverty to match even that of Mexico, progressive ideas almost completely shut out, a wall of silence keeping out the best Irish tradition—that of Fintan Lalor, Davitt, and Connolly, and poor Ireland is in a hell of a state. Larkin returned in the early twenties. After defeat, the Irish labor movement needed someone to lead it who could remould a defeated class. Larkin was a great and courageous agitator, but not a leader of a defeated army, and he could not work with any one. Gradually, he lost influence, and now he is old and embittered. Of course, Catholicism plays a strong role in Ireland, and Larkin is a Catholic and talks of the virtues of the Christian home. And suddenly out of his garrulous talk, a flash of his old fire comes through. Perhaps you are riding through the Dublin slums with him, and suddenly, seeing the poor in their filth, standing in front of the filthy buildings in which they are forced to live like animals, and a strong denunciation comes, and there is something of the Jim Larkin who defied the British Army, and at whose words the poor of Dublin came out into the streets in thousands, and flung themselves against the might of Britain and that of the Irish bourgeoisie. Human beings are social products, and Larkin is a product of the Irish movement. The principal instrument of the Irish revolutionaries was always terrorism and direct action, and when Larkin was unable to function with these methods on the wave of a rising and militant movement, he was lost, and the labor bureaucrats outmaneuvered and outsmarted him. When he returned to Ireland from an American jail, he got his following together, and marched on the quarters of the union he had formerly led. He took the building, but later lost it in the law courts, and he is no longer the leader of the transport workers. He has union following, and among his strongest support is that of the butchers and hospital workers.

He showed me something in Ireland that few people in Dublin know about. In the Parnell days, a terrorist organization, composed almost exclusively of Dublin workingmen was formed and named the Invincibles. The Invincibles committed the famous Phoenix Park murders in front of the vice-regal lodge, and were denounced by the Church, by Parnell, and by almost the entire Irish nation. There are no monuments in Ireland to the Invincibles. They died in isolation, some of them defiant to the end in their utter isolation. At the spot across from the vice-regal lodge in Phoenix Park, where the murders were committed, there is a patch of earth alongside of the park walk. No matter how often grass is planted over this spot the grass is torn up by the roots, and this spot of earth is left, and always, there is a cross marked into the dirt in commemoration of the Invincibles. Every week, someone—principally, I believe, one of Larkin's boys—goes there and marks that cross. This has been going on for a long time.

In Larkin, there is something of that characteristic of defiant defeat that runs through so much of Irish history, and with it, never any *real* investigation of causes. But even up to today, he remains the only figure of commanding proportions in the Irish labor movement. The rest is pretty nearly all bureaucracy, tied to the tail of nationalism, enfolded in the cassock robes of the priestcraft, seeing the problems of Irish labor as an Irish question. Ireland is having something of an industrial boom. Certain sections of the Irish working class, the most advanced trade unions—which have been in existence some time—these are better paid than corresponding trade unions in England. But the country is partitioned between an industrial north and an agricultural south. In the south, de Valera is engaged in a program of industrialization. The Irish market is small, and that means that monopolies must be parcelled out to various groups or persons. When these monopolies get going, there will be resultant crises, because they will be able to supply the Irish market with a few months work and production. Also, the new factories are being spread over the country—a program of decentralization—and in many instances, factories are being set up in agricultural areas where there is no trade union strength. It is necessary to further industrialization in Ireland to have, as a consequence, sweat shop conditions. There is a small labor aristocracy and even this lives badly. And below it, poverty that reduces thousands upon thousands to live like animals in the most dire, miserable, and inhuman poverty. I saw some of this poverty. One family of eleven living in one room. The family has lived in this same room for twenty-four years. The building is crumbling, walls falling, ceiling caving in, roof decaying. The oldest in the family is nineteen, the youngest is an undernourished infant of eight months. Six sleep in one bed, three in another, two on the floor. The infant was born last Christmas eve in the bed where six sleep. The role of the Church is important. The Church tells the Irish that they are going to live for ever and be happier in heaven, and this engenders patience. There is a mystic fascination with death in Ireland. In all the homes of the poor, the walls are lined with holy pictures, those of the Sacred Heart predominating. The poor live in utter patience. They have lived in this patience ever since the heyday of Jim Larkin. In those days, at his word, they thronged the streets and threatened the power of England, and of the Irish and Anglo-Irish bourgeoisie. But no more. However, with the industrialization program, there is likely to be some enlargement of the Irish working class, and the economic factors of proletarianization, plus the resulting effects of factory work and familiarity with machines is likely to cause some changes in the consciousness of Irishmen. Familiarity with machines is likely to rub off some of the superstition, and the economic conditions will pose their problems to the Irish workers. There is possibly going to be a change in Ireland because of these factors, and some of the eternal sleep and mud-crusted ignorance is likely to go. But being an agricultural country, a poor country, a country ridden by superstition, it now sleeps, and there is a lot of talk about Ireland, and little is done about Ireland, and a characteristic attitude is sure and what is the bother. Ireland is no longer merely a victim of England, but of world economy now. Irish nationalism correspondingly has altered from being a progressive movement to a reactionary movement. Fascism could easily triumph in Ireland were fascism vitally necessary to the new rulers of Holy Ireland.

The Irish Republican Army is split into factions, some demanding emphasis on a social program, others on a national program. Stalinists are in the former group, but Stalinism is very weak in Ireland, practically inconsequential. It amounts to a few pensionaries. Ireland does not need Stalinism. It has Rome. Rome handles these problems with the necessary efficiency. Rome confuses the struggles, poses the false questions, sidetracks protests as Stalinism now does in advanced countries.

As a kind of compensation, Ireland a defeated nation has developed a fine modern literature, just as Germany, defeated and still un-unified at an earlier period, developed German philosophy. But the moral terrorism in the name of the Church and the Nation, and the parochial character of the life and of intellect in Ireland might choke the literature now. So backward is Ireland that even the American motion pictures have a progressive influence in the sense that they make the youth restless, that they produce freer and less strained relationships between the sexes, and that they give a sense of a social life of more advanced countries that is not permitted because of the state of economy in Ireland. Ireland impresses me as being somewhat parallel to Mexico, except that in Mexico there are progressive strains in the country, and in Ireland these are weak and morally terrorized. In part, this is undoubtedly because of Ireland's lack of mineral resources and wealth, the backwardness and sleep of its labor movement, and the role of the Church. In Ireland, the Church was not the feudal landholder. Behind the scenes, the Church always fought against the Irish people, and spoke for law and order. But at one time, the Church itself was oppressed. The Church and the people became entangled in the consciousness of the Irish, and the religion question befogged the social and economic one. In Mexico, Spain, France, and Russia, the Church was more openly a part of a feudal or pseudo-feudal system. The peasants became anti-clerical because they wanted land. This did not happen in Ireland. In consequence, anti-clericalism did not take the same form. Anti-clericalism amounts to jokes at the priesthood, dislike of the arch-bishops, and so forth. In earlier days, it was stronger, particularly among the Fenians. But it never took the real form it took in France, Spain, etc. And so the Church has great power in Ireland today. In the most real, vivid, and immediate sense it gives opium to the people.

Poor Ireland! She is one of the costs demanded by history in the growth of what we familiarly call our civilization. There is an old Gaelic poem with the lines—They went forth to battle And they always fell. And today, after having fallen so many times, Ireland is a poor island on the outpost of European civilization, with all its heroic struggles leaving it, after partial victory, poverty-stricken, backward, wallowing in superstition and ignorance.

My favorite Irish anecdote is the following. The last castle in Ireland to fall to Cromwell's army was Castleross on the lakes of Killarney. At that time, the castle was held by the O'Donoghue. For several months, the British could not take the castle. The Irish infantry was more lightly clad than the British, and would always lead the better armored and more heavily clad British down into the bogs where their armed superiority became a handicap, and then the Irish would cut them to pieces. There was an old Gaelic prophecy that Castleross would never fall to a foreign foe until it was attacked by water. There was a proviso in this prophecy. For the lakes of Killarney empty into Dingle Bay, where the water is so shallow that foreign men of war from the sea cannot enter it. The British general heard of this prophecy. He went to Dingle Bay and built flat-bottomed boats and floated them up the lakes of Killarney. He fired one cannon shot at Castleross. And the O'Donoghue, thinking that the prophecy had been fulfilled, surrendered without firing a shot in return.

I took the liberty of writing in such detail about Ireland because I thought you might be interested in modern Ireland. They call it the "new Ireland" these days.

Hortense joins me in sending our warmest greetings to you and Natalia.

Yours,
Farrell

This summer I saw Alfred and Marguerite Rosmer a number of times,[33] and they were very well. Madame Rosmer talked very often of you and Mrs. Trotsky.

---

33. Farrell had met Alfred Rosmer in New York and had visited the Rosmers in Paris earlier in 1938.

Appendix: Farrell's Nonfiction Publications on Irish Subjects[*]

1929 "A Dostoievskian Story." *Saturday Review of Literature* 6 (30 November): 472. [Book review of Liam O'Flaherty, *The House of Gold*.]

1930 "Donn Byrne, Writer." *Saturday Review of Literature* 6 (8 February): 717. [Book review of Thurston Macauley, *Donn Byrne, Bard of Armagh*.]

"Irish Critics and Censors." *Chicago Sunday Tribune*, 17 August, p. 14.

1932 "The Rich and the Poor." *New York Sun*, 1 July, p. 21. [Book review of George Moore, *Esther Waters*.]

Untitled book review of Frank O'Connor, *The Saint and Mary Kate*. In *The New Republic* 72 (26 October): 301.

1933 Unsigned and untitled booknote on William Forbes Adams, *Ireland and Irish Emigration to the New World, from 1815 to the Famine*. In *The New Republic* 74 (1 March): 83.

"Neither to Advance." *The New Republic* 76 (16 August): 27. [Book review of Liam O'Flaherty, *The Martyr*.]

"An Irish Original." *Scribner's Magazine* 94 (September): 4, 13. [Book review of Maurice O'Sullivan, *Twenty Years A-Growing*.]

"Boyhood in the Slums." *The New Republic* 76 (13 September): 136. [Book review of Pat O'Mara, *The Autobiography of a Liverpool Irish Slummy*.]

"All in a Man's Reading." *Esquire* 1 (Autumn): 91. [Brief book reviews of O'Mara, *Autobiography*; O'Sullivan, *Twenty Years*; and O'Connor, *The Saint and Mary Kate*.]

1934 "Rescued at Last." *Scribner's Magazine* 95 (February): 16, 19. [Book review of James Joyce, *Ulysses*.]

---

*Extracted from Edgar M. Branch, *A Bibliography of James T. Farrell's Writings, 1921–1957* (Philadelphia: University of Pennsylvania Press, 1959); "A Supplement to the Bibliography of James T. Farrell's Writings," *American Book Collector* 11 (Summer 1961): 42–48; "Bibliography of James T. Farrell: A Supplement," *American Book Collector* 17 (May 1967): 9–19; and "Bibliography of James T. Farrell: January 1967–August 1970," *American Book Collector* 21 (March–April 1971): 13–18.

1935 "Books I Would Take to Sea." *American Traveler* 3 (February): 20. [Short appreciation of O'Connor, *The Saint and Mary Kate.*]

"A Spoonful of History." *New Masses* 17 (17 December): 44. [Review of Elsie Schnauffler's play *Parnell.*]

1936 Pages on Joyce and Marxist critics in *A Note on Literary Criticism.* New York: Vanguard Press. Pp. 82–85 and 97–106.

"Ireland in Its Novels." *The New Republic* 88 (14 October): 285–86. [Discussion of Brian O'Neill, *Easter Week;* Rearden Conner, *Shake Hands with the Devil* and *Time to Kill;* Sean O'Faolain, *Midsummer Night Madness, A Nest of Simple Folk,* and *Bird Alone;* and Frank O'Connor, *Guests of the Nation* and *The Saint and Mary Kate.*]

1939 "A Tribute to Kathleen Coyle." *News of Books and Authors* 1 (May–June): 1, 3–4. [Reminiscences of Kathleen Coyle in Paris.]

1944 "Joyce and His First Self-Portrait." *New York Times Book Review,* 31 December, pp. 6, 16.

1945 "Joyce and the Tradition of the European Novel." *New York Times Book Review,* 21 January, pp. 4, 18.

"Joyce's *A Portrait of the Artist as a Young Man.*" In *The League of Frightened Philistines and Other Papers.* New York: Vanguard Press. Pp. 45–59.

1946 "Revaluating James Joyce's *Exiles.*" *New York Times Book Review,* 21 July, p. 27.

1947 "Jim Larkin, Irish Revolutionist: Fighter for Freedom and Socialism." *New International* 13 (March): 86–89.

"The First Irish Marxist: A Portrait of James Connolly." *New International* 13 (December): 279–82.

1948 "Portrait of James Connolly—II: Connolly as Nationalist and Internationalist." *New International* 14 (January): 21–24.

"Portrait of James Connolly—III: Connolly's Democratic Views." *New International* 15 (February): 40–41.

"Novelist-Critic Praises Frank O'Connor for Accurate Portrait of Modern Irish Life." *Philadelphia Sunday Bulletin Book Review,* 29 February, p. 2. [Book review of O'Connor's *The Common Chord,* with comments on other works by O'Connor.]

"Portrait of James Connolly—IV: The Politics of Connolly's Catholicism." *New International* 14 (March): 78–80.

"The Irish Cultural Renaissance in Last Century: Serious, Talented and Versatile Writers Aided Inestimably in Progress from 1848 to 1948." *Philadelphia Sunday Bulletin Book Review,* 14 March, p. 1.

"Portrait of James Connolly—V: The Link Between Connolly's Catholicism and Marxism." *New International* 14 (April): 120–23.

"Exiles and Ibsen." In *James Joyce: Two Decades of Criticism*. Edited by Seon Givens. New York: Vanguard Press. Pp. 95–131.

"Joyce's *A Portrait of the Artist as a Young Man* with a Postscript on *Stephen Hero.*" In *James Joyce: Two Decades of Criticism*. Edited by Seon Givens. New York: Vanguard Press. Pp. 175–97.

1953 "The Irish Cultural Renaissance in the Last Century." *Irish Writing* 25 (December): 50–53.

1954 "Blanshard and the Catholics." *Commentary* 18 (October): 382–88. [Book review of Paul Blanshard, *The Irish and Catholic Power.*]

"Joyce and Ibsen." In *Reflections at Fifty and Other Essays*. New York: Vanguard Press. Pp. 66–96.

1955 "Moore: A Great Writer." *New York Post*, 25 December, p. 10M. [Book review of Malcolm Brown, *George Moore: A Reconsideration.*]

1956 "An Interview with James T. Farrell." *Thought* 8 (23 June): 13–14. [Farrell's reply to a question about Joyce.]

1957 "A Harvest of O'Faolain." *The New Republic* 136 (17 June): 19–20. [Book review of Sean O'Faolain, *The Finest Stories of Sean O'Faolain.*]

1958 "The Spur of Despair." *New York Times Book Review*, 13 April, p. 12. [Book review of Leonard Patrick O'Connor Wilberley, *The Coming of the Green.*]

1961 "Success of Irish." *Life* 50 (14 April): 19. [Letter to Editors on having been cited in a feature article in *Life*, 24 March.]

1964 "Lest We Forget: Jim Larkin, Irish Labour Leader." *Thought* 13 (27 May): 9–10, 18.

"Joyce and Ibsen." In *Selected Essays of James T. Farrell*. Edited by Luna Wolf. New York: McGraw-Hill. Pp. 119–49.

1966 ". . . To Bow One's Head." *Irish Echo Easter Week Special*, 9 April, p. 8. [On the Easter Day Rebellion of 1916.]

"The World Is Today." *Park East* 3 (28 April): 6–7. [Column on James Connolly and the Easter Rebellion.]

"The World Is Today." *Park East* 3 (19 May): 7. [Background of the Easter Day Rebellion.]

"Disappointment." *New Leader* 49 (6 June): 34. [Letter on anniversary of the Easter Day Rebellion.]

1967 *"Ulysses*—A Soporific Motion Picture." *Thought* 19 (10 June): 18.

1968 "The World Is Today." *Park East* 5 (14 March): 6, 9. [Column on Jim Larkin.]

"Joyce's *A Portrait of the Artist as a Young Man.*" In *A Portrait of the Artist as a Young Man*. Naples: Edizione Scientifice. Pp. i–xxiii. [Introduction to Russian-language edition.]

1976 "Finding My Irish Past Along Shannon's Shores." *Family Weekly*, 2 May, p. 11.

Index